The Language of Names

JUSTIN KAPLAN
AND ANNE BERNAYS

A Touchstone Book published by
SIMON & SCHUSTER

TOUCHSTONE
Rockefeller Center
1230 Avenue of the Americas
New York, NY 10020

First Touchstone Edition 1999

TOUCHSTONE and colophon are registered trademarks
of Simon & Schuster Inc.

Designed by Diane E. Dougal

Manufactured in the United States of America

10 9 8 7 6 5 4 3 2 1

Library of Congress Cataloging-in-Publication Data

Kaplan, Justin.
   The language of names / Justin Kaplan and Anne Bernays.
      p. cm.
   Includes bibliographical references (p.   ) and index.
   1. Names, Personal—Psychological aspects.   2. Identity
(Psychology).   3. Psycholinguistics.   I. Bernays, Anne.   II. Title.
CS2309.K37   1997
929.4'01'9—dc20   96-26439
                                                        CIP

ISBN 0-684-80741-6
     0-684-83867-2 (Pbk)

*The authors gratefully acknowledge permission to reprint excerpts from the
following:*

"Candle in the Wind" written by Elton John and Bernie Taupin. Copyright ©
1973 by Dick James Music, Ltd. Used by permission. All Rights Reserved.

"A Boy Named Sue," Words and music by Shel Silverstein. Copyright © 1969
by Evil Eye Music, Inc., Daytona Beach, Florida. Used by Permission.

From "Maiden Name" by Philip Larkin. Reprinted from *The Less Deceived* by
permission of The Marvell Press, England and Australia.

Tribute to Elizabeth Taylor by permission of Jack Cole.

To the memory of Billie Kotlowitz, 1927–1994

Contents

Preface

When I was a child, my mother insisted that I introduce her to my friends as Miss Fleischman. Each time I did this, my new friend would wait until we were alone and then ask, "Why isn't your mother married to your father?" I burned with embarrassment. Nowadays this sort of morally inflected discrepancy is common enough to go unnoted, but in the thirties and forties, to have your mother be "Miss" was daunting. I'm sure I was whispered about at school.

When I got married in 1954, I was thrilled to be a "Mrs." In those days marriage was not considered a beginning but a longed-for end: the conclusion of singleness, a shameful condition that was mere prelude to spinsterhood. It wasn't until I began to publish fiction that I reassumed my original last name. But still, the unresolved chord of this dissonance has remained with me. Sometimes I'm Ms. Bernays, sometimes Ms. Kaplan, sometimes Mrs. Kaplan. For anything that has to do with money, health, my children's schooling, or an official transaction, I'm Anne Kaplan or, even more hidden, Mrs. Justin Kaplan. Occasionally when I'm asked who I am, I say, "I don't know." This dilemma—not just about names but about identity—is part of the reason Justin

Kaplan and I decided to write this book. What is actually going on when a person is known by two different names? Is it psychically invigorating or does it make for energy-draining confusion?

Are we oversensitive if we bristle when someone gets our name wrong or spells it incorrectly or, even worse, forgets it entirely? Marian is Marion with one different letter, a letter that doesn't even figure in its pronunciation. Yet one is male and one female —a big difference—and Marian is distressed when she finds her name written as Marion. Likewise Anne as Ann, Hillary as Hilary, Alison as Allison—all familiar variants. Why should we feel we must correct someone who has misspelled or mispronounced our name? Isn't it because we feel diminished, less lovely, unimportant, not quite visible?

It seems obvious that name and self-identity are permanently wed. No one is more aware of this than a child. On his first day in school, a boy named Michael discovered that there were two other boys with the same name. (This is more or less predictable these days; in a recent coed class of nineteen, five were Michaels.) When his mother came to pick him up, he ran to her crying and demanding to know why she hadn't told him she had two other children. You can smile at this, but many adults have not outgrown such a primitive response to their own names. Why should we? Isn't a name not only an identifier but a metaphor for reliability and probity—"Sir, are you impugning my good name?"— and a guarantee that if we are who we say we are, we will do what we promise to do?

In writing fiction, I have to give my characters names that send the reader an assortment of manifest and subliminal messages. You know when you've got the name right and, conversely, when it's wrong. Can this process be analyzed? How have other writers come up with such singular fictional names as Sherlock Holmes, Lolita, Murdstone? How and why do we give our children the names we do? Is the trend toward informality of all kinds reflected in what we call one another? Does the black population have special problems with special solutions in the matter of names, both collective and individual?

Names are everywhere; they are preeminent in human discourse and social choreography. It's not simply that we all have a name, reproducing it thousands of times each year, in writing or orally, in countless transactions—signing receipts, getting online, making a dentist appointment, requesting a catalog, introducing ourselves to strangers, and on and on—weaving ourselves through an assortment of circumstances. Our name is our passport to wherever it is we need to go. Without one, we are paralyzed and naked. Separate a person from her name—as the Nazis did with their concentration camp victims—and you take away what makes her human rather than simply alive.

This is just some of the territory that Justin Kaplan and I decided to explore as we began our joint work on *The Language of Names*. To give the project a more abstract spin: since names have profound, almost magical, but often unacknowledged significance, and because the language of names is the lingua franca in so many areas of human activity, this language appeared to be an ideal way of examining American society at close range—its past and present; its literature, class systems, ethnic and religious practices and features; its manners and domestic life.

A.B.

On my birth certificate, I'm Justin, a name (rare in those days but rare no longer) my mother favored and my father barely tolerated. When she died (I was seven), he reimposed his own first choice, which had been Joseph, and when he died (I was twelve), I was left with a double first-name identity, as well as a confusion in school and medical records. By the time I went to college, I had begun to define the situation in this way. Joseph was the double orphan, alone, afraid, uncertain. Justin was an evolving, more confident, and more competent sort of person, who had begun to see the possibility of finding his way to definition through love and work. And by the time Justin arrived at this transitional stage in his evolution, he had started to resent and reject just about everything associated with Joseph. Even now—rather, especially now—when someone introduces me (Justin) as Joseph or Joe, my first response is one of outrage, and there's no canon of behavior I recognize that keeps me from correcting that person, sometimes rather abruptly. I've not only been mistaken for someone else, but everything about me in the way of personal and professional identity has been denied.

As biographer and critic I became a sort of aficionado of names and naming and began to view them in increasingly broad perspectives. What must it have been like, I wanted to know, for the first European settlers to arrive in a country where everything —mountains, rivers, wilderness trails—was new, strange, and nameless? (That they persisted in calling the natives Indians is one of the great naming blunders of history.) No wonder Adam, charged with naming all the creatures in the garden God planted eastward in Eden, has symbolized the experience of Americans from their beginnings as a new kind of society to the present day. Father of all namers, Adam was present in spirit when the colonies became the United States of America, when slaves stood on the auction block, when immigrants passed through Ellis Island, when moviemakers came to Hollywood. Like F. Scott Fitzgerald's Jay Gatsby, Americans claimed the right to name and rename themselves in order to become whoever they wished to be. Gatsby, as Fitzgerald wrote, "sprang from his Platonic conception of himself."

One day recently, turning the tables somewhat, I asked a doctor examining me how he felt about his name (let's call him Bernard Marsh). He said he didn't pay much attention to it—names are just names, after all, and what more is there to say? Then, casually, as if this were of no importance to him or had never occurred to him before, he mentioned another doctor at the same hospital, this one surnamed March, whose mail, telephone messages, patient records, and medical orders were often confused with his. This was bad enough, as a purely operational thing, so to speak, but also involved, Marsh went on to explain, was an unpleasant association. March's older brother, also a doctor, had once been involved in some sort of medical misadventure, and everybody on staff at the hospital knew about it. At stake, it now developed in our examining-room conversation, was not only Dr. Marsh's convenience, privacy, and confidentiality, but his very reputation, self-regard, self-definition, and identity. So names weren't *just* names, he finally conceded. In time he might have come around to believing, as I do, that names penetrate the core of our being and are a form of poetry, storytelling, magic, and compressed history. That's what this book is about.

J.K.

1.
Masters of the
Good Name

*A human being's name is a principal component in his
person, perhaps a piece of his soul.*
> Sigmund Freud, *Totem and Taboo*

Dan Jansen, the winner of a gold medal for one-thousand-meter
speed skating in the 1994 Olympics, drew from a well of primitive behavior patterns when he took a victory lap holding in his
arms the infant daughter he had named after his sister Jane, who
had died the morning of Jansen's crushing defeat six years earlier.
"The saga ended today," his wife told the press. "We wanted it
to end with the new Jane in our lives," she said, suggesting
that the dead sister would live again, a revenant, in her infant
namesake.

Psychiatrists might ask whether Jane, when she grows up, will
suffer from what they call replacement child syndrome, which is
typified in some namesakes by a sense that life is dangerous and
unpredictable, that their own identity is uncertain, and that they
will never live up to their parents' idealized image of the dead.
Vincent van Gogh was named for a brother stillborn a year to the
day before his own birth; probably every Sunday on his way to
and from his father's chapel, young Vincent passed the dead
Vincent's tombstone incised with the name they shared. Also
named for a dead brother, Salvador Dalí recalled that his teeth
chattered whenever he saw above the bed in his parents' room the

photo of the first Salvador, "a lovely child all decked out in lace" and often described to him as a "genius." "All the eccentricities which I commit, all the incoherent displays, are the tragic fixity of my life," he said. "I wish to prove to myself that I am not the dead brother, but the living one." *The Persistence of Memory* was the title of Dalí's most famous painting as well as a driving force in his life and art.

Names are what anthropologists call cultural universals. Apparently there has never been a society able to get along without them. They are among the first things we ask or learn when we meet someone new, and we use them to form immediate but often unreliable conclusions about personality and ethnicity. Names shape the language of the daily drama of gesture, avowal, and inference that is part of our social life. Full personal names, first and last taken together, stand at the intersection of opposing pulls: they set the bearer apart as an individual but also provide the bearer with family and extended kinship ties, and so focus both the present and the past. And beyond this, they have an occult associative and symbolic power. They are charms.

Muslims have ninety-nine names, or mantras, for God; Hindus, over a hundred for the holy river, Ganges. The Hebrew Bible condemns witches and sorcerers to death and forbids divination as well as swearing false oaths, but it also acknowledges the force of magic in names. When Moses asks for the name of God, the answer he receives from on high—"I Am That I Am"—is circular, arcane, even dismissive, with the idiomatic suggestion, as historian Karen Armstrong wrote, of "Never you mind who I am!" or "Mind your own business!" Transliterated in four Hebrew letters as YHWH (Yahweh) or JHVH (Jehovah)—the famous tetragrammaton—the name of God was so sacred that only the high priests of the temple were able and permitted to pronounce it.

On one level, this taboo meant that the nature of this Hebrew God was too great to be confined within a name that common people were permitted to invoke. They were to say Lord, Holy

One, Infinite One, Creator of the World, or some other euphemism or paraphrase. On a less theological, more primitive level, the taboo on knowing and speaking the secret name reflected a belief that if you know the name of your god you may be able to steal some of that god's power. Prometheus stole fire from Zeus. The Egyptian goddess Isis dethroned the sun god Ra when he divulged his name to her. "Just as the furtive savage conceals his real name because he fears that sorcerers might make an evil use of it," Sir James Frazer wrote in his classic study of magic and religion, *The Golden Bough,* "so he fancies that his gods must likewise keep their true name secret, lest other gods or even men should learn the mystic sounds and thus be able to conjure with them."

The founder of modern Hasidism, Israel ben Eliezer, was called Baal Shem Tov, Master of the Good Name, because, like the high priests of the temple, he knew the mystic sounds. This knowledge endowed him with miraculous powers: he walked over abysses, spoke in seventy tongues, turned icicles into candles, and at his death ascended to heaven as a blue flame. "Spirit-raising, exorcism, possession, sorcery, and oaths, in all their infinite variety, are based on this imperious handling of names," George Foucart, a student of primitive practices, wrote early in this century. "The chief operations of primitive magic-religion and black magic rest above all on the knowledge and pronunciation of the names which they claim to attract, subject, or obtain in an amicable or hostile manner." It's no wonder, then, that the appropriator of a name should be thought to have the power of life and death over its rightful owner, or that in some birth ceremonies the child receives an ordinary name for daily use but also a secret (or inner) name, whispered in its ear.

Naming touches psychic substrates associated with superstition, ritual, irrational belief, and primitive behavior patterns. Onomancy, the ancient practice of divining by names, could tell you, for example, that Achilles was destined to vanquish Hector because his name had a higher alphanumeric value, or that it was important for the Roman soldier first in the enlistment line to have a name that augured well for his cohort. Onomancy is still being practiced. "Names are magic in the Chinese-speaking world," Nicholas Kristof reported for *The New York Times:*

> Even amid the sophistication of Hong Kong, pinstriped businessmen with portable telephones bulging in their pockets sometimes scrutinize a visitor's card to see if the Chinese name has an auspicious meaning. A good name, people say, can bring wealth, a brilliant career, dazzling romance. And a bad name, according to a Chinese saying, "is worse than being born to a bad life."

Frazer cited many curious and (to the Western rationalist mind) inexplicable "primitive" taboos and magic practices governing personal names, the names of relations, dead people, kings, and gods. "Unable to distinguish clearly between words and things," he wrote,

> the savage commonly fancies that the link between a name and the person or thing denominated by it is . . . a real and substantial link which united the two in such a way that magic may be wrought upon a man just as easily through his name as through his hair, his nails, or any other material part of his person.

Knowing his name was like taking his picture—his soul and his shadow were at risk. But even looking down on the "primitive" world from the high peaks of Victorian intellectualism, Frazer acknowledged "our debt to the savage."

"The priest who christens the child 'in the name of the Father, Son, and Holy Ghost,' " the British folklorist and mythographer Edward Clodd wrote, "is the lineal descendant, the true apostolic successor, of the sorcerer or medicine man." Until recently, in the Roman Catholic ritual of baptism, the priest first asked the infant, through its sponsors, *"Quo nomine vocaris?"* (What is your name?) He then blew gently three times on the infant's face, made the sign of the cross on its forehead, placed consecrated salt in its mouth, with his own saliva touched the infant's ears and nostrils, asked the infant to renounce Satan, and anointed the child with "the oil of salvation," all of this preceding formal baptism at the font, with the water poured three times on the head of the infant.

Clodd, whose last name seems never to have been a handicap for him, belonged to a small group of late Victorians who, with conscious irony but at the same time a pronounced complacency regarding "lower" stages of civilization, cited "primitive" practices and superstitions as an underpinning of modern life.[1] "When all is said and done," Frazer wrote, "our resemblances to the savage are still far more numerous than our differences from him." These early anthropologists were mainly armchair collectors of curiosities gleaned from the work of others and then mounted like butterflies on the pages of their own books. ("Among the Amazulu the woman must not call her husband by name," Clodd wrote in his book *Magic in Names and in Other Things*. "In Ruthenia it is believed that if a wizard knows a man's name he can transform him by a mere effort of will.") Other magical practices, some current in advanced societies, involve the taboo on naming a child after a living person lest the angel of death pick the wrong victim; similarly, someone who is supposed to be dying might be able to foil the angel by taking a new name.

According to the contemporary public opinion scholar Andrew Greeley, writing in 1993, "Magic has not been exorcised from the human condition, not even in the enlightened North Atlantic world," where faith healers, witches, Tarot readers, numerologists, fortune-tellers, astrologers, and other contemporary counterparts of the ancient augur, auspex, and haruspex continue to thrive as both cult and business. In spectator sports, perhaps the only surviving communal rite, players turn for reassurance to rabbits' feet, chicken bones, lucky socks and shirts, magic numbers, spitting, and other fetishes and compulsive routines. Nancy Reagan regularly consulted a sidereal guru before approving President Ronald Reagan's travel plans and ceremonial appearances. Greeley reported that 73 percent of Americans surveyed believe in miracles and 40 percent report contact with the dead, while people in other Western industrialized countries score comparably high on the "magic" scale. Even in the postmodern, postindustrial world we have names to conjure with.

"What is your name?" the Roman mob asks an innocent bystander in Shakespeare's *Julius Caesar.* "I am Cinna the poet!" he answers, "not Cinna the conspirator." They kill him anyway —"It is no matter; his name's Cinna! Pluck but his name out of his heart, and turn him going." Melville's "Call me Ishmael" establishes one sort of understanding; W. S. Gilbert's

I'm called Little Buttercup—dear Little Buttercup,
Though I could never tell why

another. Think, too, of George M. Cohan's "H-A double R-I-G-A-N spells Harrigan," Leonard Bernstein's "Maria, I just met a girl named Maria!" and Giacomo Puccini's "They call me Mimi, but my name is Lucia" and "Miss Butterfly . . . A pretty name. That suits you perfectly!" Names mark every stage in more conventional encounters, all the way from full-dress ("How do you do?") introductions through first names, generics (Jack, Mac, Chief, Doc, Buddy, Bo, and Bub), nicknames (the Yankee Clipper, the Bronx Bomber, Old Blue Eyes, Lard Ass), and terms of endearment (hypocorisms like Honeybunch, Lambchop, Ducky, Chickadee, and Sugar Bun) to the terminal "My Ex."

Like personal names, collective (or nonpersonal) names have an instrumental role. They reflect and shape social values, group self-regard, and historical understandings. China means "central country"; Japan, "where the sun rises." For Jews (and for Mormons), outsiders are gentiles; for the ancient Greeks and Romans, barbarians. To distinguish themselves from blacks and "redskins," white Americans used to refer to themselves simply as people, citizens, or men. "Spanish-speaking," "Latino," "Hispanic," and the cumbersome "Ibero-American" denote people of Latin-American descent, although these broad terms identify European origins only and ignore the indigenous cultures of Mexico, Central America, and South America. In current usage, "Asian" (and "Asian-American") takes in Japanese, Chinese, Koreans, and other former "Orientals." [2] The evolution of such collective names as "Negro," "colored," "black," and "African-American" is a story in itself (see Chapter 4). Some name changes are self-contained historical narratives. Captured during the Peloponnesian War, the ancient Greek city of Thrace became Byzantium, capital of the Roman Empire, then Constantinople, and finally modern Istanbul ("If you've a date in Constantinople," an old popular song goes, "she'll be waiting in Istanbul"). In our time, Saigon fell and rose again as Ho Chi Minh City. St. Petersburg, renamed Petrograd and then Leningrad, reverted to St. Petersburg when the Soviet Union collapsed.

During the First World War, the British royal family, Wettin of Saxe-Coburg-Gotha, made an instrumental shift in the interests of patriotism, national unity, and just plain face. By decree of King George V, they renounced their German name, derived from Queen Victoria's prince consort, and anglicized themselves as Windsor, thereby invoking—instead of German bombers (incidentally called Gothas after the city in Thuringia where they were made) harrying the Home Counties, and subhuman Boches bayoneting Belgian babies—the heroic symbolism and sturdy grandeur of William I's thousand-year-old castle by the Thames. Two monarchs later, George V's granddaughter Elizabeth II resisted pressures from her consort, Prince Philip, another princeling of German descent (Hesse-Darmstadt), to take *his* family name, Mountbatten, which used to be Battenberg. Philip's paternal grandfather, a British admiral, had degermanized the family name at the same time the Wettins of Saxe-Coburg-Gotha were degermanizing theirs.

Politicians and auto salesmen know how essential it is to greet their constituencies by name. Conversely, there is no surer way to offend people than to mangle, forget, or, even more cruel, pretend to forget their names, in any case conveying a clear message that we not only don't find these people important but enjoy offending them. "The twisting round of a name when it is intentional," Freud noted, "amounts to an insult." Stephen Potter, British authority on the arcane arts of "one-upmanship," gives this example of games playing with names:

> For years Mr. Black has been calling Mr. White "White" —i.e., by his surname. Then one day he, Black, on some relaxed occasion, will call White "Arthur." This is a trap. White, encouraged by this, will call Black "Nevill" next time he meets him. This is what Black has been waiting for. He instantly calls White "White" like a sledge-hammer, repeating this with a strong suggestion of reproof, and more than a hint that he for one is not going to indulge in a forced matiness.

It's when anger, embarrassment, or a sense of helplessness and disadvantage well to the surface, as they did with Arthur White, that we realize that what others call us and what we call ourselves has a more than nominal importance and is not just a social convenience, like a stickum "Hello" badge. Names are profoundly linked to identity and to private as well as public declarations of self and purpose; they have considerable affective power and, however unacknowledged in daily usage, a magical role as well, the power to change people's lives.

The biblical Abram becomes Abraham, "father of many nations," when God makes his covenant with him, and his wife Sarai, Sarah; Jacob wrestles with the angel, demands a blessing, and is renamed Israel, "He strives with God"; on her deathbed Jacob's wife Rachel calls her newborn son Ben-oni (son of my sorrow), but her husband changes it to Benjamin (son of the right hand); the Jewish tentmaker Saul takes the Roman name Paul for his long apostolate.

In the modern world, Jean-Baptiste Poquelin became the famous Molière; François-Marie Arouet, Voltaire; Mary Ann Evans, George Eliot; Aleksey Maksimovich Peshkov, Maksim Gorky (the bitter one). At a crucial point in his life—his marriage to Constanze Weber, which was also an act of rebellion against his father—Mozart adopted Adam as one of his forenames in place of Gottlieb, Amadeo, Amade, Amadi, or Amadeus (all forms of his baptismal Theophilus, meaning "beloved by God"). Amandine-Lucile Dupin, baronne Dudevant, borrowed half of the surname of a fellow writer, Jules Sandeau, and then followed her own path as the novelist George Sand, who wore trousers along with her man's name.

Popes choose new names for themselves. They follow the example set by Mercury, a sixth-century priest, who upon his election as supreme pontiff decided that a pagan god's name didn't go with the highest Christian office and called himself John instead. In choosing the double name John Paul II, Karol Jozef Wojtyla asserted continuity with John Paul I, who in turn wished to honor two of *his* predecessors, John XXIII and Paul VI. Revolutionaries (Lenin, Trotsky, Stalin, Yasir Arafat) took new names. The twenty-five-year-old Cuban guerrilla leader Ernesto Guevara, earlier nicknamed El Chancho, "the Slob," became El Che, or "Buddy." "The most important and cherished part of my life," he said a few years before he was captured and executed in Bolivia, was the new name Che. "Everything that came before it, my surname and my Christian name, are minor, personal, and insignificant details."

Nuns, monks, and converts feel the same way about their earlier lives and names. Mother Teresa, for example, the founder of the four-thousand-member Missionaries of Charity, scarcely remembers her earlier life in Albania as Agnes Gonxha Bojaxhiu. And this is true also of black leaders (Sojourner Truth, Frederick Douglass, Booker T. Washington, Elijah Muhammad, Malcolm X), authors (O. Henry, Colette, Saki), immigrants, social climbers, and married women, at least until they realized what they may have surrendered by taking their husbands' names.

To call yourself by a single name requires confidence and a taste for glitter: Cher, Prince, Madonna, Houdini. Not incidentally are these men and women in show business. There's a paradox here. Those who go by a single name, whether a first name like

Cher or a surname like Houdini, are parading their success and popularity by dropping a name—"I'm so great that's all I need for instant recognition." On the other hand, no senator, college president, general, or any one of a number of other, less flashy though equally successful people would dream of going by a single name because, like wearing a sequin-covered dress to Sunday mass or running shoes to the governor's inaugural ball, it's considered vulgar, infra dig. One-nameism may challenge convention, but it does get you noticed.

"The average person is more interested in his or her name than in all the other names on earth put together," Dale Carnegie said in *How to Win Friends and Influence People,* one of the most popular (and apparently useful) self-help books ever written. "A person's name is to that person the sweetest and most important sound in any language. . . . From the waitress to the senior executive," Carnegie added, invoking the alpha and omega of his evolutionary scheme—names "work magic"—and if you can't remember a person's name, "you are headed for trouble." Other writers of practical advice have proposed ways of making sure you *do* remember. One is to focus on the face of someone you have just met, devise a mental caricature or mnemonic formula that fastens name to feature, and imprint it on your mind by reinforcement and repetition. "Upon meeting Dennis, you might associate his name with 'tennis.' You can then substitute a racquet for his long face," advised the author of "The Art of Remembering Names," Thomas Crook. "Don't be put off by bizarre concepts that come to mind; strange and ridiculous images are memorable ones." (For those who remember Watergate, the face of Richard "I am not a crook" Nixon might be a handy jog in case you have forgotten this memory expert's name.)

Mnemonic crutches like these carry the risk of overdetermination and inadvertent derision. The financier J. P. Morgan's grotesquely inflamed nose, which he once described as "part of the American business structure," is popularly supposed to have so preoccupied a nervous hostess that she asked him, "Do you take nose in your tea, Mr. Morgan?" (In another version: "Do you take sugar in your tea, Mr. Nose?") Like the Reverend William Archibald Spooner, eponym of the metathetic spoonerism ("shoving leopard," "half-warmed fish," "kinquering congs"), you may end up saying, "I remember your name perfectly, but I just can't think of your face."

That "sweetest and most important sound in any language," as Carnegie described a name, generates a significant degree of gratification. With either conscious or unconscious wit, a former defensive tackle for the Dallas Cowboys once remarked to a sportswriter, "If it weren't for a name like Jethro Pugh, I might be anonymous." This athlete loved his name; its oddness suited his personality; it pointed to his prowess on the football field and, like a pair of elevator shoes, gave him extra visibility and distinctiveness. The name can be a mantra, a readily available home remedy for psychic insecurity, as in the traditional grade-school doggerel:

George Brush is my name
America's my nation
Luddington's my dwelling place
And Heaven's my destination.

Celebrating his discovery of identity and vocation as a poet, Walt Whitman, known as Walter Whitman, Jr., for the first three decades of his life, wrote:

What am I after all but a child, pleas'd with the sound of
*   my own name? repeating it over and over;*
I stand apart to hear—it never tires me.
To you your name also;
Did you think there was nothing but two or three
*   pronunciations in the sound of your name?*

Alfred Tennyson, too, used his name as a mantra to induce "a kind of 'waking trance,' " he said. "This has often come upon me through repeating my own name to myself silently till, all at once, as it were, out of the intensity of the consciousness of the individuality, the individuality itself seemed to dissolve and fade away into boundless being . . . [for which] Death was an almost laughable impossibility." [3] The hero of Rudyard Kipling's novel *Kim,* an Irish orphan christened Kimball O'Hara, asks himself: "Who is Kim—Kim—Kim?" "A very few people, but many Asiatics," Kipling wrote, "can throw themselves into a maze-ment"—a trance—

> by repeating their own names over and over again to them-selves, letting the mind go free upon speculation as to what is called personal identity. When one grows older, the power, usually, departs, but while it lasts it may descend upon a man at any moment. . . . In a minute—in another half-second— he felt he would arrive at the solution of the tremendous puzzle.

Names are agents of personal perpetuity and give the dead a continuing social role and presence, and this is true of advanced as well as primitive societies. An earlier Carnegie, the steel master and philanthropist Andrew—like Benjamin Disraeli a self-made man who worshiped his creator—had his name installed over a great concert hall, the headquarters of several foundations, and the portals of nearly three thousand free libraries. As his friend Mark Twain said, Carnegie "bought immortality and paid cash for it." So did John Harvard, a thirty-one-year-old Puritan clergy-man of Charlestown, Massachusetts, who left 780 pounds and his library of four hundred volumes to a young college in nearby New Towne, later renamed Cambridge. Fund-raisers today rou-tinely offer prospective donors naming opportunities that range from the brass plaque on a hospital easy chair to buildings and entire institutions. In 1992 Glassboro State College in New Jersey renamed itself Rowan State College as a condition of accepting a gift of $100 million from Henry Rowan. Whether great or small, such self-commemorations are motivated by the same spirit that built the Great Pyramid of Cheops.[4]

In an age of numbers—telephone, Social Security, four-digit PINs, credit cards, ZIP + 4 mail codes, armed services serials, bank accounts, alarm codes, access codes, combination locks, and the like—one might expect that a language of names formed electronically by binary switching using only the digits 0 and 1 would be simpler, more practical and rational, less ambiguous, and in general more convenient than a language of letters and sounds, especially when one considers the peculiarities of English-language spelling and pronunciation.

In practice the opposite appears to be the case. Normal social traffic relies on a fair amount of latitude in the spelling, pronunciation, and variant forms of names, but this latitude is precisely what plagues designers of computerized indexes, databases, and alphanumeric codes. In conversation or writing, you can make mistakes in spelling and pronunciation and still come up with *something* that will serve its purpose for the moment. Phonemes are tolerant and malleable. The Boston telephone directory listing for Burk reads: "See also Berk, Berke, Bourke, Bourque, Burke." Coan, Coen, Cohan, Cohen, Cohn, Cone, Conn, Cowan, Coyne, Koen, Kohen, and Kohn (and the Zen Buddhist term "koan") are roughly interchangeable in speech. If it has the correct address, a letter with a garbled name will probably reach the person you have in mind, although he or she may not feel like answering if you've made a serious blunder, especially one that involves ethnicity: for example, confusing an Irish Cohan with a Jewish Cohen.

But traffic even in rest areas along the information superhighway is as unforgiving of even the tiniest swerve as a lap in the Indianapolis 500. There's no opportunity to guess or circle around the right answer when you call up a computer file or database or send a message by electronic mail. You won't get slapped on the wrist or laughed at if you make as little as a one-letter or one-punctuation-mark mistake, add an extra space, or use a virgule—/—instead of a backslash—\. You'll simply be ignored, booted (so to speak) into outer darkness. And with a few exceptions—for example, CATNYP, for the catalogue of the New York Public Library, or HOLLIS, also an acronym, this one standing for Harvard OnLine Library Information System (but also memorializing Thomas Hollis, an early Harvard Library benefactor)—computer names, codes, and addresses lack any kind of aural, visual, or mnemonic pattern to help you. If you have a query or comment about the subject of this book and wish to consult the electronic mail Onomastic Discussion Group in Binghamton, New York, you have got to remember the command LISTSERV-@BINGVMB (if you are on Bitnet) or LISTSERV@BINGVMB.-CC.BINGHAMTON.EDU (if you are on Internet).

Computer technology, however, can come to the rescue when too many people in the same national group have the same surname and thereby generate all sorts of Tower of Babel confusion, including wrongful arrest and medical malpractice, along with misdelivered mail, bills, and official notices. Researchers at the Chinese Academy of Social Sciences in Beijing report that almost one third of their country's huge population of over a billion people are surnamed Li, Wang, Zhang, Liu, or Chen, and this makes for even deeper confusion when they have the same first name as well: in Tianjin alone there are more than twenty-three hundred Zhang Lis. Forty-three percent of the 44 million South Koreans are Kim, Lee, or Park.

The problem occurs as well in the Scandinavian countries, with the patronymic suffixes "-son" and "-sen" (both meaning "son of") creating paradoxes like "Anna Andersson." The Oslo telephone directory lists four thousand Hansens, fifty of them called Hans. Seven out of ten Danish surnames end in "-sen," and Danes who share the same first as well as last names are sometimes distinguished one from the other on their tombstones as Mr. Managing Director Jensen and Mr. Unskilled Worker Jensen. "It is imperative that surname reform be carried out," the Beijing researchers say, "so as to avoid inconveniences brought about by ... confusion in identifying people in a society with a fast pace of life." Most large libraries in Sweden stock a reference book of newly generated surnames from which the Johonssons, Svenssons, Olssons, Peterssons, and Anderssons are invited to draw.

Everyone from hotel clerks to the evil geniuses of S.M.E.R.S.H. and S.P.E.C.T.R.E. knew that 007 was James Bond, had a license to kill, and took orders from "M." T. E. Lawrence tried to escape the celebrity he had won as Lawrence of Arabia (and at the same time confusion with D. H. Lawrence) by going under the names of John Hume Ross, T. E. Shaw, and E. Smith, together with accompanying sets of British army and R.A.F. serial numbers. "Dear 338171," Nöel Coward wrote to Lawrence in 1930, "or may I call you 338?"

The comedian Samuel Joel Mostel took the name Zero (his friends shortened it to Z) for his 1942 debut at Cafe Society in New York. A press agent remarked that the new name was the right one because Zero, an unknown stand-up who until then took his pay in pastrami sandwiches, was "starting from nothing." Mostel probably had in mind the pattern set by the Marx Brothers —Chico (born Leonard), Harpo (Adolph, but known as Arthur), Groucho (Julius Henry), and the expendable Gummo (Milton) and Zeppo (Herbert). Others have borne Latin number names: Una, Tertius, Quintus, Septimus, Octavius, Decimus, and Vicesimus; Cecil B. DeMille, who made movies with casts of thousands, and Eugene O'Neill's Marco Millions raised the ante even higher. At the lower ordinal end are five popes named Sixtus (a variant of Sextus, "sixth-born"), the next to last of whom, Sixtus IV, built the Sistine Chapel. The British Satanist Aleister Crowley (self-styled the Beast and the Wickedest Man in the World) signed himself "666," the number name of the great horned beast in the book of Revelation. Supposedly 666 is the alphanumeric equivalent of the Hebrew for Nero Caesar, who persecuted the Roman Christians.

T. E. Lawrence had the option of seeking anonymity through numbers; but others—prisoners and conscripts, for example— have no choice in the matter when they come under the control of a policy designed to strip away the identity and individuality personal names represent. Until 1967, when the demeaning practice was abolished, Canada's Inuits (commonly miscalled Eskimos) had no officially recognized surnames and wore numbered disks around their necks in order to collect benefits.[5] Products live happily with numbers—4711, Chanel No. 5 (so named because Coco Chanel believed five was her lucky number), 7UP (originally the name of a card game), WD-40 ("Stops Squeaks, Protects Metal"), Formula 409 ("Cuts Greasy Dirt *Fast!*"). Numbers, of course, have their own magic, symbolic, or semantic component: for example, 3, 7, 13, 18, 21, 30, 86, and 87. But when they are applied to persons, we think first of prisons, concentration camps, and military units and resist extending the practice on grounds that it is totalitarian, soulless, and dehumanizing, a sinister stage on the way to internal passports, tattooed IDs, and other forms of Orwellian regimentation. Even so, in the United States today you can't get a job (or pay your taxes) unless you have an identifying (generally Social Security) number.

When an ordinary taxpayer and working person who is neither a celebrity nor a prisoner decides for complex personal reasons that he or she wishes to be known *only* by a number, the resulting debate shows how volatile naming is as a social and legal issue. (See Chapter 11.) It also shows how fundamentally undecided we are, after almost twenty-five centuries of sophisticated and subtle debate, starting with Plato, about just what a name is in the first place: whether it acquires real meaning in and through the person who bears it, the way clothes take on the shape and scent of the wearer (and even "make the man"), or is just an arbitrary, intrinsically meaningless sign, like a chalk mark on a door, a tire, or a piece of luggage.

2.
American Adam

There is no part of the world where nomenclature is so rich, poetical, humorous, and picturesque as the United States. All times, races, and languages have brought their contribution.

Robert Louis Stevenson, *Across the Plains*

In the beginning no one except the natives knew for a certainty the name of anything in the Western Hemisphere. Christopher Columbus, Amerigo Vespucci, Giovanni da Verrazano, and Francis Drake were discoverers only in a parochial, Eurocentric meaning of the word (what they accomplished was more an encounter than a discovery). The gigantic landmass they called *Novus Mundus,* the New World, was, of course, as old as the old one, and had been settled since the Ice Ages. Some of its established cultures dated from around 10,000 B.C., which made them senior to the creation itself—that is, if one held with Archbishop James Ussher, the seventeenth-century Irish Bible scholar who calculated that God formed the heaven and the earth during a twenty-four-hour period on October 23, 4004 B.C.

Columbus made his first landfall in the Caribbean but thought he had reached the fabled Indies and the domain of Kublai Khan. Off by a distance equal to about half the earth's circumference, he had formed his expectations and conclusions on readings in the Hebrew Bible, the Greco-Egyptian geographer Ptolemy, and the Venetian traveler Marco Polo. He was "predisposed to be deceived," Washington Irving wrote in his account of Columbus's life and voyages. Never having believed that the earth was flat, Columbus decided it wasn't round either but rather breast shaped, as was only fitting for Mother Earth, with the New World, assumed to be the site of the Garden of Eden, as its nipple and aureola.

Columbus committed one of the great naming blunders of history by calling the inhabitants of the New World *los Indios,* "Indians." Recent attempts to rectify his error by substituting "Native American" have subsided even in tribal councils. The Sioux and other civil rights militants who made an armed stand against the federal government at Wounded Knee, South Dakota, in 1973 were members of an insurgent group that nevertheless called itself the American Indian Movement. "Indian" and "American Indian" are here to stay (along with the Cleveland Indians and Atlanta Braves), although some newspaper style-books reserve "Indian" for "people of India, the Asian country," and instead of "American Indian" recommend a specific tribal name, such as Seminole or Cherokee. The names of individual Indian nations, although value-neutral in general usage, convey powerful ethnocentric messages. Kiowa and Inuit mean "real or principal people," and Lenni Lenape, "original man" (just as the Hebrew *adam* is a generic term for "man"). Other names are "frozen curses." Iroquois means "real adders" or "killer people" (although their own word for themselves, Onkwehonweh, means "real people"); Mohawk, "cannibals or cowards"; Adirondack, "bark eaters"; Eskimo, "eaters of raw flesh"; and Pequot, "destroyers." Apache ("enemy") has a transatlantic history. By way of James Fenimore Cooper's *Leatherstocking Tales* it entered French slang, meaning a Parisian gangster, moved back to the States (any urban gangster), and survives in "apache dance," performed not in buckskins and feathers but berets, bandannas, and slit skirts.

Columbus also called natives of the the Caribbean basin Caniba, meaning "people of the Great Khan," the supposed ruler of the entire region. Caniba was also dialectally interchangeable with Carib, the name of a ferocious tribe of anthropophagi, or human flesh eaters; it spawned "cannibal" (and perhaps Shakespeare's Caliban as well). Referring either to Plato's sunken civilization of Atlantis or to the island reached just before—anterior to —Japan, Antilles is another durable term for islands in the Caribbean Sea. It's as mythopoetic as the name California, derived from a circa-1500 Spanish romantic poem describing a land rich in gold, precious stones, and lusty women.

Poor Columbus! He seems not to have got anything quite right, either during his lifetime or after. On the five-hundredth anniversary of his first landfall in the New World, war parties of multiculturalists and revisionist historians captured the Admiral of the Ocean Sea, stripped him of his honors, and put his feet to the fire for raping the New World. He is memorialized nevertheless. In one form or another, Columbus and Columbia (a name for the United States that was coined during the revolutionary period but never caught on except in song, as "the gem of the ocean") supply names for over seventy U.S. towns, cities (including two state capitals), and geographic features, as well as for parks and avenues, a university, a broadcasting system, a movie studio, and countless smaller ventures from delicatessens and day-care centers to chiropractic clinics and auto parts suppliers. But America, after Amerigo Vespucci, is the inclusive name of the gigantic landmass that stretches from Tierra del Fuego to the Arctic Ocean.

Vespucci, an upper-class Florentine related by marriage to the beautiful Simonetta Vespucci, Botticelli's model for Venus on the half shell, was a ship chandler, gentleman voyager, and travel publicist. He claimed to have been the first to recognize that the coast of present-day Brazil was not part of Asia but "what we may rightly call a New World . . . a continent more densely peopled and abounding in animals than our Europe or Asia or Africa" and blessed with "a climate milder and more delightful than in any other region known to us." As if this weren't reason enough for Europeans to take ship immediately, Vespucci also alleged that the women of this region were agreeably promiscuous, making no distinction, among the men they took for their sexual partners, between husbands, sons, brothers, fathers, and newcomers from across the ocean.

In 1507 Martin Waldseemüller, a German cosmographer, announced that a quarter of the earth's surface, "since Americus discovered it, may be called *Amerige* or *Land of Americus,* or *America.*" He favored the feminine form, America, because "both Europe and Asia have derived their names from women." But it is still not altogether a settled thing whether Vespucci was an accomplished navigator who went where he said he had or a self-serving fantasist and fake, a "pickle-dealer," as Ralph Waldo Emerson called him, who "managed in this lying world to supplant Columbus and baptize half the earth with his own dishonest name."

Nowadays America is shorthand for United States of America, but used in this sense it slights Canada, British Columbia, and the nations of Central and South America and the Caribbean basin. As for "American," it first referred to the so-called Indians and then to English colonists in the New World before arriving at its fixed, although arbitrary and exclusive, meaning: a citizen of the United States. Itself a collective noun and "barely a specific national name," Henry James complained, "United States" underwent a reverse-mitosis change after the Civil War from the plural form ("these United States" in Fourth of July orations) to a collective singular ("the United States is . . ."), personified by the figure of eagle-beaked Uncle Sam in his flag suit. "American," although unsatisfactory in many respects, has handily survived attempts to replace it with "Unisian," "Unitedstatesian," and "Columbard." By now it has acquired a freightage of historical, ideological, and emotional associations that makes it unique among nationality labels. Imagine the effect of substituting "Spanish" or "Chinese" in hallowed formulations like "American dream," "American way," "American standard of living," "American experience," and "House Un-American Activities Committee" (which, at the height of its inquisitorial powers in the 1940s and 1950s, demanded that the people it subpoenaed "name names").

• • •

The statistical tabulation and analysis of early American child-naming practices has generated dozens of serious comparative studies by social historians, sociologists, and students of family life. One such study focuses on the Massachusetts town of Hingham but derives patterns that apply to New England in general from the seventeenth to the nineteenth centuries. The Puritan settlers, many of whom bore traditional English names (William, Edward, and Richard, for example, and Elizabeth, Ann, and Alice), tended to choose names for their children drawn from a larger, Old Testament pool: Samuel, David, Joseph, Benjamim, Jonathan, and Joshua for Hingham boys, and for girls, Sarah, Deborah, Ruth, Rachel, Susanna, and Rebecca. Their parents believed such names had an inherent power, as well as the force of inspiring example, to shape the character and destiny of little Puritans.

"A good name," said one minister, "is a thread tied about the finger, to make us mindful of the errand we came into the world to do for our Master." This echoed the editors of the Geneva Bible, refugees from religious oppression in England, who warned that conventional children's names had become "signs and badges of idolatry and heathenish impiety," by which they had in mind Roman Catholic saints' names. They prescribed instead names that should be "memorials and marks of the children of God received into his household" and "bound by their names to serve God from their infancy." (Attribute names for girls— Charity, Comfort, Patience, Prudence, and even Silence—fell under this heading.) During the colonial period traditional non-scriptural names began to reappear, but the combined naming pool, even when gradually enriched from classical, literary, and historical sources, was never very large or inventive.

Many children bore the same first names as their parents, or a dead sibling, or an esteemed relative or friend. This thrifty recycling practice resulted in a proliferation of "juniors" and a great deal of name sharing among cousins, and sometimes even among brothers. Still, like their Puritan antecedents, colonial parents were aware of the occult as well as the practical and commemorative significance of the names they gave their children. These names strengthened kinship ties, brought the dead back to life, molded identities, established links within and between generations, and, by way of flattering namesakes and appealing to their generosity, even acquired a certain exchange value. American independence and the early decades of the republic provided a new naming pool. The revolutionary patriot Joseph Warren, shot dead by a British soldier at Bunker Hill on June 17, 1775, "was scarcely in his grave," Mencken wrote, "before babies were being named after him, and by the next year the custom was so firmly established that thousands were being baptized *Franklin, Jefferson, Otis,* and *Adams,*" not to mention the leading favorite, Washington.

Roman Catholics used to be bound by canon law to select a first or middle name for their children from the calendar of saints. Since there are hundreds of saint dollars in the name bank, this was not so much a hardship or restriction as it was a sign of obedience to authority, tradition, and community. Sephardic Jews, according to Leo Rosten, "often name a child after a living relative, but the Ashkenazim have a distinct and abiding dread of doing so" and tend instead to choose the name of a dead one, although Moshe may end up being commemorated as Mervyn and Nechama as Natalie (meaning a child born or baptized on Christmas Day). But with the exception of Catholics and Jews, Americans tend to follow naming fashions rather than naming systems. Triple-barreled names—Oliver Wendell Holmes, Franklin Delano Roosevelt, Alfred Gwynne Vanderbilt, Angier Biddle Duke—are still a marker of upper-class eminence. Nowadays they're heard less frequently, having yielded to folksy examples like Jimmy Carter, Bill Clinton, Newt (Newton Leroy) Gingrich, and Bob Dole. Social registers still abound in two-part names like Sheffield Boardman and Hobart Fullerton. F. Scott Fitzgerald, John Dos Passos's J. Ward Moorehouse, and T. S. Eliot's J. Alfred Prufrock are examples of another hoity-toity name style, this one apparently falling into disrepute by association with FBI director J. Edgar Hoover and convicted Watergate criminals E. Howard Hunt and G. Gordon Liddy. As John Wayne remarked in *The Searchers,* "Never trust anyone who parts his name in the middle." H. (for Henry) Ross Perot, the Mr. Fixit and Jiminy Cricket of American politics, has for years tried to shake off that first initial; at least subliminally it echoes the name of another counterpopulist Midas, J. Paul Getty, and distances Perot from the grass roots. As for what scholars call name suffixes—Jr., Sr., II, III, and so forth—these former upper-class status symbols, indicating continuity and pride in descent, have trickled down into working-class usage, although they still retain a certain measure of cachet and even authority.[1]

Ananias and Ellinor Dare, parents of the first English child born on the American continent, christened her Virginia in honor of Elizabeth, the Virgin Queen, patroness of Sir Walter Raleigh's ill-fated Roanoke Colony. Oceanus Hopkins was born aboard the *Mayflower* in mid-Atlantic. Peregrine White (younger brother of Resolved White) was born as the *Mayflower* rode at anchor in Provincetown Harbor in November 1620. Peregrine became a citizen of Marshfield, Massachusetts, and lived to the age of eighty-four. His name meant "stranger" or, more to the point, "pilgrim."[2]

"They knew they were pilgrims," wrote William Bradford, governor (and historian) of the Plymouth Colony, and in that one sentence gave the word its specific local and historical meaning. The Pilgrims used the word "ethnic" as an insult, meaning heathen or sinner. But at the same time they appropriated and turned to their own use "puritan," formerly an insulting term suggesting sanctimony, hypocrisy, and double dealing. (Tribulation Wholesome and Zeal-of-the-Land Busy, sanctimonious Puritan swindlers in Ben Jonson's comedies, had counterparts in real life: Fight-the-Good-Fight-of-Faith, Fly-Fornication, and Safe-Deliverance.) Cotton Mather, who viewed the settlement in New England as the fulfillment of God's plan to redeem "the depravations of Europe" and "irradiate an Indian wilderness," called the Pilgrims "Good People which had the Nick-name of *Puritans* put upon them" and carried it defiantly and triumphantly "into the Desarts of *America.*" They believed they had reenacted the exodus from Egypt and arrived in the promised land.

This new breed of humankind—"The peculiar, chosen people," Herman Melville declared in 1850, "the Israel of our times" —looked back to the earliest biblical precedent; Adam, namer of all the creatures in the Garden of Eden, symbolized their innocence, potentialities, and confidence of dominion over the land and all its creatures. Several centuries after Columbus, visitors to North America found that the natives—the misnamed Indians who were also called redskins, red men, and red devils—had been displaced and in many areas practically exterminated by a race of "palefaces" (a term apparently coined by James Fenimore Cooper). In one version of the landing at Plymouth Rock, the thankful Pilgrims first fell upon their own knees in prayer, and then they fell upon the Indians, described, a century and a half later, in the Declaration of Independence as "merciless," their rule of warfare being "an undistinguished destruction of all ages, sexes, and conditions."

Having thrown off the shackles of the king of Great Britain, the bearers of the ark of liberty called themselves the freest people on earth but owned and traded in slaves who were stripped of their African names and given new ones by their owners. As often reported, the nineteenth-century possessors of the land ("remarkable men," as they liked to say of themselves) were given to corn whiskey, chewing tobacco, dyspepsia, spitting, monkey-house eating habits, rocking chairs, personal violence, mob rule, lynching, jingoism, and sharp dealing. They spoke a language that was called English but was violently colored by peculiar and grating local usages, pronunciations, and vulgarisms. Their favorite word was "dollar" and their favorite interjection, "um-huh." These two syllables, the novelist Captain Frederick Marryat noted in 1837, "express dissent or assent, surprise, disdain" and are generally "used by the Americans as a sort of reply, intimating that they are attentive, and that the party may proceed with his narrative." Americans also commanded a considerable vocabulary of ethnic slurs for Indians, blacks, and new arrivals from Europe and Asia.

The Americans, for their part, were notoriously eager to be told who they were; where they were tending; whether they had a civilization and culture, or only a marketplace; and how their institutions compared with those of other countries. No people in history, it seemed, with the possible exception of the Jews, had ever been the subject of such unremitting scrutiny, by themselves as well as by outsiders, or so certain that they deserved this scrutiny because of their seemingly special consciousness and destiny. They showered gold, silver, and greenbacks on foreign writers, lecturers, social philosophers, adventurers, pundits, and literary lions, all of whom arrived and left with firm opinions.

The citizens did not always like what they heard or read about themselves. They howled with rage at Mrs. Frances Trollope's *Domestic Manners of the Americans* (a mischievous title, since the Americans appeared not to have any). They responded in the same way to Charles Dickens's *Martin Chuzzlewit,* a satiric novel detailing the near-fatal misadventures of an English architect who comes over to work for a fraudulent outfit called the Eden Land Corporation and meets up with repellent Adamites named Jefferson Brick, Elijah Pogram, Hannibal Chollop, and Colonel Diver, editor of the *New York Rowdy Journal.* Still, they rushed to dockside to welcome the next authority from abroad to tell them who and what they were. This might be Oscar Wilde, who declared Niagara Falls, rainbowed mecca of honeymooners, to be "one of the earliest, if not the keenest, disappointments in American married life." "Perhaps, after all, America has never been discovered," he wrote several years after his return to England. "I myself would say that it had merely been detected." The next authority might be the eminent biologist and champion of Darwinism Thomas Henry Huxley. "The great issue," he said in 1877, "is, what are you going to do with all these things? What is to be the end to which these are the means?" He was not "in the slightest degree impressed by your bigness, or your material resources, as such. Size is not grandeur, and territory does not make a nation." Many parts of this vast territory were still un-named in 1890, when the superintendent of the census declared that the frontier, the dividing line between settlement and wilder-ness, no longer existed.

According to guidelines of the United States Board on Geo-graphic Names, "A fundamental characteristic of elemental wil-derness is that features are nameless and the cultural overlay of civilization is absent." In order to preserve what little is left of the American wilderness and limit "human impact on the land," the board will not approve any new names "unless an overriding need exists" and "will not consider names that commemorate or may be construed to commemorate living persons." This last stipulation is designed to overturn the celebrated (and still vexed) example of the Alaskan prospector who in 1896 named the high-est mountain in North America for the Republican presidential candidate, William McKinley. (Alaskans are still campaigning to restore the Athabaskan Indian name Denali, meaning "the big one.") Today one must be dead for at least a year in order to have a geographic feature (a plateau or a creek, a gap or a geyser) named for him or her. "The person being honored by the naming should have had . . . some direct association with the feature," the guidelines stipulate, but "a person's death on or at a feature, such as in a mountaineering accident or plane crash, or the mere ownership of land or the feature, does not normally meet the 'direct association' criterion." [3]

The first Europeans in the New World had a contrary "overrid-ing need"—to name the rivers and mountains, the plains and passes, and other features of the wilderness they claimed as their own. All of these had to be marked in some agreed-upon way for settlers to have a sense of place, stability, and possession, estab-lish trade and travel routes, and find their way home. Place-names on the advancing frontiers of the New World were as urgently needed as personal names in any society, however unadvanced.

Never in history had there been such a concentrated demand for place-names. What had evolved in Europe over the course of millennia had to be done right away, and it was done with remarkable verve and originality.

"There is no part of the world," said a visitor from abroad, Robert Louis Stevenson, "where nomenclature is so rich, poetical, humorous, and picturesque as the United States." He was reflecting on the confluence of many different tributary cultures and languages, especially French, Spanish, and American Indian. He also recognized the inventiveness and exuberance, the play and sardonic humor on the part of surveyors and first settlers, that have gone into names like Go to Hell Gulch and Kiss Me Quick (both in South Dakota); Pee Pee Creek (Ohio); Maggie's Nipples (Wyoming); Cash (Texas), according to George Stewart "named in honor of J. A. Money, the first postmaster"; and Deathball Rock (Oregon), "a name given humorously to commemorate an unsuccessful attempt to make biscuits."

The poet-critic Matthew Arnold—in Walt Whitman's opinion "a total ignoramus" and "one of the dudes of literature"—took another view altogether, declaring that every force in the United States, naming included, was dead set against distinction and beauty. American names act "upon a cultivated person like the incessant pricking of pins," Arnold said. "What people in whom the sense for beauty and fitness was quick could have invented, or could tolerate, the hideous names ending in *ville,* the Briggsvilles, Higginsvilles, Jacksonvilles, rife from Maine to Florida; the jumble of unnatural and inappropriate names everywhere?"

Not that the Americans themselves were insensitive to the contrast with ancient, euphonious foreign names mossed over with romance. Some of the early place-names—Jamestown, Plymouth, Boston, Richmond, Providence—were backward looking, homely, and unlikely to stir anyone's imagination or rouse the national eagle to scream with pride. But Jacksonville, in particular, stuck like a fishbone even in American throats. Visiting Florida, Henry James remarked that "Jacksonville is not a name to conjure with." He compared American place-names in general to "the smudge of a great vulgar thumb," while the land itself, victim of "cruel" inflictions like Jacksonville, Jackson, Wildcat Creek, and Presidential Range, seemed to cast upward "the plaintive eye of a creature wounded with a poisoned arrow."

As further evidence of the alleged poverty of the American "artist-sense," Arnold cited the numbing succession of classical names that he saw from his train window while traveling through New York State on a leg of his moneymaking lecture tour. He had heard that this infliction of Greece and Rome on the upstate wilds had been the work of the state's surveyor general, Simeon DeWitt, "who, when the country was laid out, happened to possess a classical dictionary" and sprinkled Marcellus and Syracuse, Brutus, Cicero, and Pompey on bounty lands awarded veterans of the Revolutionary War. Maybe these names were no worse than the "congenital Briggsville," Arnold commented, but even so, "a people with any artist-sense would have put down that surveyor."

Another Englishman, the Reverend Isaac Taylor, had already voiced the same complaint about classical names. He fumed over "the intolerable impertinence" shown by Americans in wrenching grand historic names—Thebes, Troy, Rome, Corinth, Athens, Ithaca, Utica—from the Old World and applying them, with no sense of incongruity at all, to "collections of log huts in some Western forest" or "a wooden grog shop and three log shanties." But even these hypercritical foreign observers underestimated the extent of the epidemic that left nearly three thousand places in the United States pocked with classically derived names running from Alpha to Omega and Athens to Sparta and including several Olympias (one of them a state capital), a dozen and more Romes, and also, in tribute to Rome's legendary founders, a Romulus (New York) and a Remus (Michigan).

Arnold and Taylor also underestimated the extent to which Americans, especially during the revolutionary and federal eras, justified their national identity by drawing on Greece and Rome not just for place-names but for their architecture, commemorative statuary, speech making, official emblems, and concepts of public virtue. Commissioned by the federal government in 1832 for installation in the Capitol rotunda, Horatio Greenough's twenty-ton statue of George Washington emulated one of the Seven Wonders of the World, Phidias's *Zeus* at Olympia, but managed to provoke derision rather than awe: the Father of his Country, naked except for the towel covering his lap and legs, seemed to be getting ready for his bath.

If foreign critics had paused to consider just the name Minneapolis, a grotesque hammering together—a shotgun marriage— of the Sioux Indian word *minnehaha* ("laughing waters" in Longfellow's *Hiawatha*) and the Greek word *polis* (city), they might have noted the one tributary unique to the continent: the language and history of the American Indian, the richest naming source for states (twenty-six of them), cities, towns and counties, lakes, and rivers. Tallahassee, Susquehanna, Chicago, Kennebec, Potomac, Winnipesaukee, Council Bluffs, Wounded Knee—these "give a barbaric brilliancy to the American map," H. L. Mencken wrote. Kalamazoo (Michigan), celebrated manufactory of stoves and furnaces, derives from the Algonquian "It smokes, he is troubled with smoke." Canyon de Chelly (Arizona) comes not from an anomalous French source but from the Navajo *tseyi,* "among the cliffs." [4]

For Walt Whitman American names were "strong, copious, unruly," had "magic" force, were "the turning-point of who shall be master." "Mississippi!—the word winds with chutes—it rolls a stream three thousand miles long. . . . Monongahela—it rolls with venison richness upon the palate." (The forty-five letters of Chargoggagoggmanchauggagoggchaubunagungamaugg, a lake in Massachusetts, might have been too much for him.[5]) He also quoted someone less appreciative, a traveler returned from the Pacific Northwest in the early 1880s:

On your way to Olympia by rail, you cross a river called the Shookum-Chuck; your train stops at places named Newaukum, Tumwater, and Toutle; and if you seek further you will hear of whole counties labell'd Wahkiakum, or Snohomish, or Kitsar, or Klikatat; and Cowlitz, Hookium, and Nenole-

lops greet and offend you. . . . I suspect that the Northern
Pacific Railroad terminus has been fixed at Tacoma because
it is one of the few places on Puget Sound whose name does
not offend you.

"All the greatness of any land, at any time, lies folded in
names," Whitman concluded. "I say that nothing is more important than names. . . . All that immense volumes, and more than
volumes can tell, are conveyed in the right name. The right name
of a city, state, town, man, or woman, is a perpetual feast to the
esthetic and moral nature."

"I have fallen in love with American names," wrote a later
poet, Stephen Vincent Benét:

The sharp gaunt names that never get fat,
The snakeskin-titles of mining claims,
The plumed war-bonnet of Medicine Hat,
Tucson and Deadwood and Lost Mule Flat.
. . . .
I shall not rest quiet in Montparnasse.
I shall not lie easy in Winchelsea.
You may bury my body in Sussex grass,
You may bury my tongue at Champmédy.
I shall not be there. I shall rise and pass.
Bury my heart at Wounded Knee.

Joseph Smith, founder of the Church of Jesus Christ of Latter-Day
Saints, like Christian Science an indigenous American religion
with adherents worldwide, led his followers to a site in Illinois
that he called Nauvoo, "which means in Hebrew a beautiful plantation." (Smith claimed that Mormon, the name of the chief trans-
mitter of the new gospel, derived from an Egyptian word meaning
"more good" rather than from "mormo," an obsolete English
word of Greek derivation meaning "hobgoblin, bugbear, imaginary terror.") After Smith died in 1844 the Mormons moved
west to a region they called Deseret, "honeybee," symbolizing

sweetness and light, community and productiveness. Today, under seven hundred feet of solid stone in the Granite Mountain Records Vault twenty-two miles southeast of Salt Lake City, Mormon genealogists store microfilm records of about two billion names, estimated to be about a quarter of all the names generated since the beginnings of human society.

Realizing that for many outsiders—gentiles—the word Mormon has associations with polygamy and acts of violence, since 1894 the researchers have been doing their work under cover of a bland institutional pseudonym, as the Genealogical Society of Utah. "No genealogical archive or primary testament of human passage is remotely comparable," Alex Shoumatoff wrote in *The Mountain of Names.* "It is the closest there is, and the closest there will be, to a 'catalogue of catalogues' for the human race." The Mormon belief behind this, he explained, is that "the family is eternal and all-inclusive, and that each church member must seek out his ancestors and posthumously perform certain ceremonies for them so that they can all meet again in the Celestial Kingdom." Some overzealously benevolent Mormons, however, understood this obligation to extend to other people's ancestors too. In recent years the Mormon church has had to apologize for posthumously baptizing some 380,000 Jewish Holocaust victims and enrolling their names in the church's index. The one-hundred-thousand-member American Gathering of Jewish Holocaust Survivors construed this as an act of institutional busybodyism if not downright desecration. "I was incensed," said one of the protesters, "that my parents who were killed in Auschwitz were now listed as members of the Mormon faith." Names, it seems, are instrumental not only in this life but in what church authorities call the spirit world.

In the last chapter of her novel *In Country,* Bobbie Anne Mason described her young protagonist, Samantha, as feeling "sick with apprehension" as she approaches the Vietnam Veterans Memorial in Washington. "She has kept telling herself that the memorial is only a rock with names on it. It doesn't mean anything except they're dead. It's just names." At first sight the wall hits Sam like "a black gash in a hillside, like a vein of coal exposed and then polished with polyurethane." A little later she thinks of it as being "like a giant grave, fifty-eight thousand bodies rotting here behind those names. . . . The memorial cuts a V in the ground, like the wings of an abstract bird, huge and headless."

Sam, Mamaw (her paternal grandmother), and Emmett (her uncle, a Vietnam veteran badly damaged by the war) find who they are looking for, Sam's father: "There it is. . . . There's his name, Dwayne E. Hughes." Mamaw wants to touch her dead son's name chiseled into the black granite, but she's too short to reach it. Someone brings her a stepladder. "Mamaw reaches toward the name and slowly struggles up the next step, holding her dress tight against her. She touches the name, running her hand over it, stroking it tentatively, affectionately, like feeling a cat's back. Her chin wobbles, and after a moment she backs down the ladder silently." In Mason's closing paragraph, Emmett is "studying the names low on a panel. He is sitting there cross-legged in front of the wall, and slowly his face bursts into a smile like flames." What Sam, Mamaw, and Emmett experience is that in seeing and touching a name they are touching the person it belonged to, making palpable contact with the dead.

Jan Scruggs, who had served in Vietnam as an infantry corporal, conceived of the memorial not as a traditional or idealized structure—an obelisk, bronze soldier, eternal flame, Greek temple, fountain, or marble sarcophagus—but as something yet to be defined and realized. He organized a design competition that imposed two conditions: the monument was not to make any overt political statement and it was in some way to incorporate the name of every one of the approximately fifty-eight thousand Americans killed or listed missing in action between 1959 and 1975. The winning design, submitted in 1980 by Maya Lin, then a twenty-one-year-old Yale undergraduate, displays these names chronologically, by date of death, so that the memorial is an epic narrative in itself, a majestic recital like the great catalogue of warriors in Book Two of *The Iliad.*

Devoid of religious or patriotic symbols and inscriptions, Maya Lin's starkly elegant Vietnam Veterans Memorial has a transcendent power to arouse emotion and veneration, to console and conciliate, to heal the wounds of that war while making sure those who died in it will be remembered. Even visitors to the memorial who haven't lost anyone in the war, may have taken no part in protesting it, or were born years after it ended, feel this power. They say that as they walk the sloping path alongside black granite panels bearing the unadorned names of the American dead, their throats close up and they see a bruised look on one another's faces. According to scholars of religion and culture, the memorial has become a shrine, an altar, like Lourdes or the western wall of the second temple in Jerusalem: it's a place to which people make pilgrimages and bring candles, flowers, birthday cakes, wine, food, flags, letters, photographs, stuffed animals, uniform caps and insignia, baby booties. Some visitors make rubbings to take home with them. Others claim that if they stand long enough in one place they begin to see on the polished stone a reflection of the man or woman who bore that name.

Peter S. Hawkins, who teaches religion and philosophy at Yale, said, "The common impulse of grief is the reiteration of personal names and the titles of relationship; it is to cry out like King David, 'My son Absalom; O Absalom, my son, my son.' " "So that the voice may not fail, the names are written down," Hawkins wrote, citing two French World War I monuments: one a rank of huge arches bearing over seventy thousand names; the second, a gate with another fifty-four thousand. If the names of young men killed in a war are not recorded, they are essentially lost forever except to the members of the families they were snatched from. Each man's name is his immortality, as the biblical book Ecclesiasticus declares in a famous passage:

There be of them, that have left a name behind them,
That their praises might be reported.
And some there be, which have no memorial;
Who are perished, as though they had never been;

And are become as though they had never been born;
And their children after them.

"The memorial turned numbers into names," Hawkins wrote, "but it also helped transform the national response to Vietnam" from conflict to closure. "The dead would be honored and the living accorded some dignity." Hawkins linked the wall to the NAMES Project AIDS Memorial Quilt, finding it "impossible not to think of one memorial as successor to the other, impossible not to find the origin of the Quilt's panels in the intimate tableaux that mourners continue to create within the interstices of the VVM." The quilt's father, in the sense that Scruggs was the father of the wall, was Cleve Jones. Hawkins wrote that what motivated both Scruggs and Jones to "name names" was the "threat of oblivion to another . . . generation, a population America seemed eager to forget."

The quilt was first displayed, in Washington, not far from the wall, in 1987. Then it consisted of 1,920 three-by-six fabric panels, each containing the name of a person dead of AIDS, some formally, as on a document, and some informally, like Fuzzy, Clint, and Best Daddy in the World. Many panels incorporate odd relics like car keys, champagne glasses, wedding rings, credit cards, human hair, cowboy boots, jockstraps, tennis shoes. As of 1994, the quilt contained almost thirty thousand panels, representing only about 12 percent of all U.S. AIDS deaths, and if displayed in its entirety and without walkways, would cover eleven acres. The quilt travels about the country, where sections of it are shown in schools and other community buildings to raise money for AIDS research. The administrators of the NAMES Project, based in San Francisco, issue an information kit containing guidelines for "How to Make a Quilt Panel": use appliqué, paint, stencil, and so forth; cotton or poplin; hem it and back it; and "include the name of the friend or loved one you are remembering." They also publish a newsletter with articles like "Strengthening Communication with Panelmakers."

All this suggests that, like the wall, the quilt creates positive emotional waves, ever widening, that bring in more and more people in need. Hawkins called the quilt a "public metaphor," one that taps into our nostalgia for a genuine indigenous folk art even as it memorializes the victims of a contemporary plague. In addition, the quilt makes a political statement about a disease perceived by too many to be the result of aberrant, not to say antisocial, behavior and thus ignorable. The quilt, Hawkins wrote, "is most profoundly about the naming of names: the sight of them on the myriad panels, the sound of them read aloud. As with the Vietnam Memorial, the names themselves are the memorial."

3.
Names in the Melting Pot

We were the end of the line. We were the children of the immigrants who had camped at the city's back door.
Alfred Kazin, *A Walker in the City*

"All of our people, except the pure-blooded Indians," President Franklin Delano Roosevelt said in a 1944 campaign speech, "are immigrants or descendants of immigrants, including even those who came over on the *Mayflower.*" Echoed by countless other public figures, John F. Kennedy among them, declarations like this, once considered incendiary by the Daughters of the American Revolution, are now part of the conventional wisdom and as ritualized as Lincoln's Gettysburg Address. It's probable, however, that even "the pure-blooded Indians"—often called First Americans, Native Americans, or Amerinds—were immigrants themselves, having long ago migrated east to Alaska by way of the Bering Strait land bridge. Following "the hyphenate craze," the late William A. Henry III remarked, perhaps they should be called Siberian-Americans.

Roosevelt's paternal ancestor, Claes Martenzen van Rosenvelt (meaning, roughly, "open land overgrown with roses") was a Dutchman who arrived in New Amsterdam around 1644. The Delanos, on FDR's mother's side, descended from Philippe de la Noye, a Luxembourger who landed in Plymouth in 1621 with the Pilgrims. Apollos De Revoire, a silversmith of French Huguenot descent, came over from the Isle of Guernsey, set up shop in Boston, and to lubricate his business dealings with "the Bumpkins" there, anglicized Revoire to Revere. Apollos's son Paul learned the trade and in time gave his name to a classic design of silver bowls and a famous horseback ride to Lexington.

Voluntarily or not, the Roosevelts, the Delanos, the Reveres, and other by now unarguably American founding families had all been exposed to a common action, described by a student of surnames, Howard F. Barker, as "the abrasion" and "heavy grinding of common speech."[1] Syllables and letters disappear along with foreign identifying marks; names become shorter, and easier to spell and pronounce; and as Barker noted in 1932, "common names gain in usage because rarer ones are compared unfavorably with them."

Since then, administrative mechanisms such as the draft, automobile registration, Social Security, the Internal Revenue Service, credit card networks, and data processing in general have speeded up the standardizing of last names. Still, a 1984 tabulation ranks 8,414 surnames that appear five thousand or more times in the roughly 350 million individual records kept by the Social Security Administration since its inception in 1936. The top five are Smith (with 3,376,494 entries), Johnson, Williams, Brown, and Jones (with 1,930,318). Cohen, the commonest Jewish surname, ranks 243 (with 147,864 entries). Going alphabetically, Aaron (with 19,166 entries) ranks 2,367 in frequency; Zuniga (with 20,846 entries), 2,201. The 1984 tabulation yielded 1.7 million different names. Discounting the many minor variants in form and spelling, the gross figure suggests that there are roughly 25,000 unique surnames borne by a nation of immigrants who represent every language and ethnicity in the world. In contrast, China, with a population of more than a billion, four and a half times that of the United States, has a pool of only about 150 to 400 basic surnames (or about 3,000, including regional variants), even though the Chinese have had hereditary names a thousand years longer than any other culture.

Like stones at the seashore, foreign and difficult names yield their roughness and irregularity to the tidal wash of American convenience and usage: Pfoersching turns into Pershing; Huber,

Hoover; Roggenfelder, Rockefeller; Kouwenhoven, Conover; L'Archeveque, Larch; Bjorkegren, Burke. Smith is the ultimate catchall for linguistic naturalization: it takes in Schmidt, Schmitt, Schmitz, Smed, Szmyt, Schmieder, Smidnovic, Seppanen, Fevre, Kalvaitis, Kovars, Haddad, McGowan, and other variants that in their original language mean someone who works with metal. Comedian Ernie Kovacs, Simon Kuznets (winner of the Nobel Prize in Economics), and Stanley Kowalski of Tennessee Williams's *A Streetcar Named Desire* are all Smith brothers under the skin. Johnson is a similar linguistic melting pot, its original imported ingredients ranging from Johansson to McShane.

The inexorable Americanization of foreign names was "a mass movement as great in its way as the settlement of the West," Barker wrote—and, he might have added, the tide of immigration from southern and eastern Europe. Mounting in volume from the late 1840s, the influx from abroad reached a high point between 1903 and 1908, when a nation of about 80 million absorbed nearly 6 million foreigners. By 1910 the New York that expatriate novelist Henry James recalled from his childhood in Manhattan as a "small warm dusky homogeneous" island community had become the largest Italian city and the largest Jewish city in the world. Three quarters of its 6 million inhabitants were either foreign-born or first-generation Americans.

Visiting Ellis Island in 1904, James compared "this visible act of ingurgitation on the part of our body politic" to a circus performer eating fire or swallowing a sword. James was only a second-generation American (Scotch Irish on his father's side), but in a country as young as the United States, this gave him almost the status of an original settler. What he saw at Ellis Island left him with a "sense of dispossession." At the same time he acknowledged that alienness was a condition that all Americans shared, whatever their origin or date of arrival or degree of concern over "race-suicide" and "mongrelization" of the native blood stock. "Who and what is an alien," he asked, "in a country peopled from the first under the jealous eye of history?—peopled, that is, by migrations at once recent, perfectly traceable and urgently required."

A dialogue from a Jewish vaudeville skit a few decades earlier confronted the matter of alienness on a homelier level.

"Are you a foreigner?"

"No," says the greenhorn, "I'm an American from de oder side."

Over the three centuries since the Dutch settled in New York, Ellis Island was drastically enlarged, with landfill adding twenty-four acres to the original three. It changed in function, from oystering ground to gallows, fort, POW camp, convalescent hospital, and munitions depot. "No one wanted the island for anything," the novelist Mary Gordon wrote. "It was the perfect place to build an immigration center." After closing as a receiving station in 1954, Ellis Island became a Coast Guard training facility, a derelict property abandoned by the federal government, and finally a historic site that now draws a reverse traffic, this one of native tourists. It also went through the same naming and renaming cycle as many of the immigrants who passed through it. Ellis Island was Gull Island when the Dutch bought it from the Mohegan Indians; then Oyster Island, Dyre's Island, Bucking Island, and Anderson's (or Gibbet) Island, for a pirate who was hanged there in 1765; finally Samuel Ellis, a butcher, bought the place and left it to his heirs. Between 1892, when it opened for business and admitted Annie Moore, a fifteen-year-old from County Cork, and 1924, when Congress curtailed mass immigration, more than 12 million foreigners passed through Ellis Island—a record 12 thousand on one day alone in 1907—and saw their names placed in its registers. Today at Ellis Island a circular wall of names commemorates half a million immigrant families, with a new section scheduled to be added in 1998.

"The immigrant's arrival in his new home is like a second birth to him," journalist and novelist Abraham Cahan wrote. "Imagine a new-born babe in possession of a fully developed intellect. Would it ever forget its entry into the world?" The immigrant's first experience of officialdom on passing from the confinement of steerage reenacted a rite of birth: He was named, and the name that he took or was given often differed from the one he had carried in the old country, but this was not a time for sentiment and retrospection. In order to pass through the golden door, his first concern then was to be certified physically and mentally intact—free of loathsome, contagious, or incurable disease (trachoma in particular) and unlikely to be a public charge.

The recording of names at Ellis Island, at Castle Garden (its predecessor in New York harbor), and at about seventy other receiving stations in the United States generated colorful changes. Enhanced by anecdote, invention, and family transmission, they have become part of American folklore, along with the generally accepted belief, as the columnist Ellen Goodman wrote, that

> immigration officials at Ellis Island christened more Americans than any church in the Northern Hemisphere. One of my own grandfathers had a name twice as long as the one he was left by some efficient or harassed bureaucrat. Another relative nervously repeated the word spoken by the man in front of him in line. He assumed that "Goodman" was a password to get into the country.

Weary immigration offficers whose only language was English processed foreigners from a dozen and more language cultures as different as Arabic and Polish, Turkish and Italian, Finnish and Greek. Even with the help of interpreters, they could hardly help making goulash, baba ghanouj, or tzimmes of names they could neither pronounce nor spell. However, at least as much linguistic maceration and random christening had already taken place in passenger manifests drawn up on the other side of the ocean. According to the historian Robert M. Rennick,

> The belief that most "foreign" names were mutilated by ignorant or indifferent officials at the ports of debarkation in this country, at least after the Federal Government assumed

jurisdiction over immigration in 1882, seems to have little basis in fact. Under the provisions of the Act of 1891, whatever name was given on the immigrant's manifest, made out for him at the port of embarkation in Europe or on board the vessel taking him to America, was the name recorded at the place of entry. It was in the preparation of manifests and passenger lists that most of the name errors probably occurred until 1924, when immigrants were required to present visas for admission.

Yitzchak sailed from Bremen and landed on the American shore as Hitchcock; Yankele (little Jacob) as John Kelly, who went on to run a saloon; Harlampoulas as Harris; Rabinowitz as Robbins; Cheskel as Elwell; Ilyan as Williams; Levy as Lamar; Warschawsky as Ward; Katz as Feline and thence Filene, or so the story goes. According to another family tale, four Mikeloshansky brothers from the same Polish shtetl passed through separate immigration gates and emerged Finberg, Friedman, Reddinov, and Rubenstein. One Russian immigrant protested, *"Ne ponemya"* (I don't understand), and, according to legend, was admitted as Panama. In another familiar story the man who said *"Schon vergessen"* (I've already forgotten) in answer to a question he didn't understand became Shane Ferguson. A more likely explanation is that this Ferguson, if he ever existed, was originally a Feygelson. Often all that survived of a surname was its initial letter.

If first names whisper, surnames shout, and they often give misleading messages. "In daily life," Mary Waters, a sociologist, reported, "Americans routinely use surnames to guess one another's ethnic origins," but the conclusions they reach, based on folk knowledge of what is a typical Irish, Italian, or Dutch name, deal only with the father's ethnicity, ignore the mother's, and disregard mixed marriages, mixed ancestries, and earlier name changes. Even so, beginning with the first tidal waves of immigration, a surname could cut you off from employment and social acceptance as effectively as a criminal record. If it was O'Reilly or

Epstein or Bertucci, your destiny was shaped in the cradle. Some people with undesirable names went the pragmatic route and changed them. Others, who couldn't tolerate the psychic wrench of a name change, did not and often paid for their refusal in reduced earning power and career advancement, although they may have slept better at night than the name changers.

Of all the ethnic or national groups riding the tide of European immigration, it was the Jews who both underwent and initiated the most sweeping process of name changing. They were fleeing pogroms, conscription, and every variety of civil and commercial disability. They wanted to be Americanized and prosper in peace and freedom, and to this end were willing, if it seemed advisable, to shed conspicuous or difficult names. "Once they have lost the faith of their fathers," H. L. Mencken argued in his discussion of American proper names, "a phenomenon almost inevitable in the first native-born population, they shrink from all the disadvantages that go with their foreignness and their Jewishness, and seek to conceal their origin, or, at all events, to make it unnecessarily noticeable." Mencken was responding sympathetically to the fears that, during the three decades between world wars, drove many American Jews to attempt to hide their Jewishness. Their clumsier attempts at assimilation made rich material for jokes. In one story, four travelling salesmen sitting down to a game of cards introduce themselves: "Cole," "Kent," "Carleton," say the first three. "Also Cohen," says the fourth. Applying for membership at a WASP country club, Howard Frobisher, né Harry Abramovitz, lists his religious affiliation as "goy" and addresses the committee as "fellow goyim." *"Oy veh!"* exclaims a lunch guest at the same country club when she spills soup in her lap, but she quickly corrects herself—"Whatever that means!"

Like their forebears in the old country, most Jews coming to America had little reason—sentimental, symbolic, or historical—to feel attached to their family names. In England the practice of Christian hereditary surnaming went back to the Norman Conquest; and in Europe generally, to the thirteenth and fourteenth centuries, gradually filtering down from the nobility to the merchant, artisan, and peasant classes. But for the Ashkenazim—the often nomadic Yiddish-speaking Jews of central and northern Europe—conventional, fixed family naming was a relatively new thing. It dated from the late eighteenth and nineteenth centuries and had been forced on them by civil authorities. Up to then they had mostly used a patronymic system going back to biblical days: Isaac ben (son of) Abraham, Leah bas/bat (daughter of) Leban. Conforming in some respects to the inner, or sacred, name systems of primitive societies, this tribal practice survives today in Hebrew prayer, religious ceremony, and rites of passage—birth, confirmation, marriage, burial.

The system of permanent family names for Jews decreed by Austria, France, Prussia, Bavaria, and Russia made it easier for governments to levy and collect taxes, regulate business, conscript for military service, control movement, and, in general, impose their will. Either self-chosen or imposed from the outside, the family names Jews took—and were forbidden to change without official approval—had a considerable range and variety. Some were frozen patronyms, Europeanized biblical forms ending with "-sohn" (Mendelsohn) or other suffixes—the Latinized "-es" (Abeles), the Slavonic "-itz," "-ich," "-ski" (Lebowitz, Rabinovich, Lipski)—that also meant "son of." Many were derived from places of origin or residence: countries (Frankl, Schweitzer, Oesterreicher, Pollak), cities and towns (Cracauer, Frankfurter, Hamburger, Warschauer), neighborhoods (Altschul, meaning "near the old synagogue"; Teichmann, pond dweller), and picture signboards on stores and homes—Adler (eagle), Engel (angel), Gans (goose), Nussbaum (nut tree), Weintraub (bunch of grapes). Some were animal names, like Fuchs (fox), Ochs (ox), Hirsch (deer), Wolf. Others came from trades and occupations—Schechter (slaughterer), Schneider (tailor), Magid (preacher), Wechsler (money changer)—and from personal traits like big, small, old, clever, as in Grossman, Klein, Altman, Kluger. Names like Rosenblum, Greenblatt, Goldberg, and Blumenthal (flower valley, later anglicized to Bloomingdale) were ornamental, wishful, fanciful. Some local authorities recognized that the name decrees offered them an opportunity for extortion and bribery. They gave attractive names to those who could pay for them and withheld them from those who couldn't, giving instead comic and derisory names like Eselkopf (ass's head), Fischbaum (fish tree), Kussemich (kiss me), Raubvogel (bird of prey), Gimpel (dunce), and Karfunkel (carbuncle or boil).

On some level of awareness, even attractive or value-neutral Ashkenazi names still carried a stigma: they had been imposed from the outside, somewhat like slave names for black Americans, and for the specific purpose of setting their bearers apart from Christians. Jewish settlers and refugees in what was then Palestine and, later, citizens of the newly established state of Israel replaced their Ashkenazi names with Hebrew ones: David Ben-Gurion, Israel's first prime minister, was originally David Grun; Golda Meir, Golda Meyerson. The family name Goldberg was rendered as Harpaz, which also means "mountain of gold." Adolf became Abraham; Leopold, Bezalel; Leo, Yehuda; Felix, Uri; Veronica, Adina; Sylvia, Shifrah; Dora, Devorah. Other first names like Gideon, Joshua, and Samson invoked ancient pride, militancy, and heroism.

Jewish names in America often yielded to a contrary impulse, to deny or disguise rather than assert ethnic identity, and so were subject to pressures for change that went beyond the grinding of common speech and the normal immigrant drive to become Americanized. Since there were few historical or practical reasons to remain attached to them, Ashkenazi names were shed or changed "as easily as shirts," the ghetto saying went, and with little guilt or regret. "We honor our fathers just as much, even if we drop their names," said one "East Side patriarch" interviewed by a reporter for the *New York Tribune* in 1898. "Nothing good ever came to us while we bore them; possibly we'll have more luck with the new names." This had proved to be true in the case of August Schonberg (beautiful mountain), an earlier arrival from Germany who Frenchified his name to Belmont (same meaning), founded a banking house, fought a duel, married Caroline Slidell

Perry—the daughter of Commodore Matthew Calbraith Perry, the man who opened Japan to the West—raced thoroughbreds, and for fifty years called the tune for New York society, the so-called Four Hundred. August Belmont was the model for the arriviste financier Julius Beaufort in Edith Wharton's *The Age of Innocence.*

If the immigrant had not already been renamed on leaving for America or on arrival, he might soon after take the name of his sponsor, or the family he boarded with, or his employer. The hero of a Jewish joke called himself C. C. Rivington ostensibly to remind himself that he lived at the corner of Clinton and Rivington Streets. Some schoolteachers made calling the roll easier for themselves: they gave their pupils simplified or normalized names, and the parents followed suit. Charles E. Silberman, author of *A Certain People,* reported another process:

> After several years as a peddler in rural Iowa during the 1870s my paternal grandfather, whose name was Zarkey, settled in Des Moines. To make his way in America, friends told him, he would have to choose an American name. Still unfamiliar with American usage, he walked up and down the main shopping street looking for an American name. He saw the name Silberman on the window of a haberdashery shop. Liking its sound, and not having heard it in Kovno, his Lithuanian hometown, he chose it as his new name.

By the 1930s there were so many newly hatched Coopers and Gordons, Kings and Davises, Livingstons and Newmans, Gladstones and Harrises, Madisons and Taylors, to list some of the commoner examples, that these names had become recognizably Jewish, certainly to Jews. They were self-defeating, so far as their original purpose, to mask or assimilate Jewish identity, was concerned. One can imagine non-Jewish Coopers, Gordons, Kings, and so forth changing *their* names in order to protect themselves or, as actually happened, taking legal action to prevent their names from being appropriated. The Biddles of Philadelphia objected (to no avail) when a local bartender named Abraham Bitle, a Russian immigrant, made a common-law upgrade of his name; the Chicago meat-packing firm of Libby, McNeil, and Libby had no better luck in their suit against another Russian immigrant, Samuel Lipsky, a wholesale butcher in Boston, who said he had a right to an American last name that would carry weight in his business dealings.

The most celebrated of these rearguard actions pitted a Philadelphia man, Harry H. Kabotchnik, who in 1923 had petitioned the court for permission to shorten his name to Cabot, against an army of outraged bluebloods. In addition to the Pennsylvania branch of the Order of Founder and Patriots, the Historical Society of Pennsylvania, and the Genealogical Society of Pennsylvania, Kabotchnik's suit faced opposition from half a dozen genuine Cabots, representatives of what was universally, or at least New Englandly, acknowledged to be the first of Boston's first families, which made them so lofty, as a banquet toast of the time put it, that they talked "only to God." The founding Cabots—the name apparently comes from *chabot,* French for "catfish"—had made their money "in slaves, rum, and opium, in piracy, and by marriage," according to Leon Harris's biography of Godfrey Lowell Cabot. "There is even a story that one of the Cabots paid an impoverished historian to seek out his antecedents and that when the industrious historian traced the family . . . to some tenth-century Lombardy Jews, his employer paid him to forget his research."

Kabotchnik and his wife, Myrtle, argued that the name they wanted to change was "cumbersome, a hardship, and an inconvenience." In allowing their petition, Judge Charles Y. Audenreid of the Philadelphia Court of Common Pleas argued that the change was an acceptable example of normalization and that these new Cabots had no intention of wanting to pass themselves off as old ones. For his part, he added, he would have been flattered if the Kabotchniks had decided to call themselves Audenreid instead. The affair stirred up considerable attention and thoughtful comment. A *New York Times* editorial suggested that the Cabots might better have followed the example of certain medieval lords of the manor who permitted and even encouraged peasants to borrow their "lofty names." An editorial in *American Hebrew* deplored the loss of "Kabotchnik with its rich, sneezing tonal effects." The most enduring comment, however, parodied the familiar toast:

And this is good old Boston,
The home of the bean and the cod,
Where the Lowells have no one to talk to
Since the Cabots speak Yiddish, by God.[2]

The Kabotchnik process of preemption could be seen as well in first names, many of which became quintessentially Jewish. Parents preserved Hebrew name forms for ritual use and family record but gave their male children first names derived from Christian surnames, especially those of famous writers and aristocratic families. On the circumcision table the boy was Schmuel, but on his birth certificate Scott, Shelley, Sydney, Sheldon, or Sumner. Yitzchak was Irving, Irwin, Isadore; Benjamin was Barton; Avrum was Alan, Allen, Albert, Alvin, Arnold; Heschel, Herbert; Chaim was Hyman or Herman. Schlomo evolved into Sean or Shawn, while Moishe became Milton, Maxwell, or Morris, the last being the surname of the most Cabotlike and manorial of the old New York families, the only one not "in trade." In this patriarchal culture, dehebraized and deyiddishized girls' names —Florence (formerly Bluma), Harriet or Hope (Chaya), Shirley (Sarah), Phyllis (Freydel), Laura (Leah)—showed little of these high-class strivings, although they, too, became recognizable as Jewish. Like Philip Roth's Alex Portnoy, the wearers of these thin disguises, boys and girls alike—Digby Teitelbaum and Tiffany Finkelstein, Trevor Goldfarb and Heidi Istkovitz—seemed to be living "in the middle of a Jewish joke."
A generation and more of Ashkenazi Jews underwent a massive naming transformation. The immigrant Ehrich Weiss, born

in Budapest, the son of Rabbi Mayer Samuel Weiss, modeled himself on the celebrated nineteenth-century French conjurer and magician Jean-Eugène Robert-Houdin and became world famous as Harry Houdini, supposedly born in the heartland city of Appleton, Wisconsin. For this charismatic escape artist, origins and ethnicity were no more confining than his Chinese water torture cell or the manacles and leg weights he wore when he allowed himself to be dropped to the bottom of the Detroit River. With both Houdini and the Arthurian enchanter Merlin in mind, a fourteen-year-old Philadelphia boy, Meyer R. Schkolnick, fleetingly became Robert K. Merlin, and then Robert K. Merton, who did magic tricks at children's birthday parties and for a small traveling circus. He eventually settled into a distinguished career as a pioneer of modern sociology, university professor at Columbia, author of a classic work of humanistic scholarship, *On the Shoulders of Giants,* and formulator of the self-fulfilling prophecy and the law of unintended consequences. He recalled that when he was a high school student in the 1920s writing a paper about Houdini, he learned that "names in the performing arts were routinely Americanized; that is to say, they were transmuted into largely Anglo-American forms. For this, of course, was the era of hegemonic Americanization, generations before the emergence of anything resembling today's multiculturalism."

Among the vivid reminders of these transmutations is the list of Jewish entertainment stars, from the 1920s on, whose impeccably nonethnic names nevertheless declared to those in the know—and who enjoyed playing parlor games with their knowledge—a collective adaptation to American life, a victory over the odds:

Woody Allen (Allen Stewart Konigsberg)
Bea Arthur (Bernice Frankel)
Lauren Bacall (Betty Joan Perske)
Theda Bara (Theodosia Goodman)
Jack Benny (Benjamin Kubelsky)
Milton Berle (Milton Berlinger)
Fanny Brice (Fanny Borach)

George Burns (Nathan Birnbaum)
Dyan Cannon (Samille Diane Friesen)
Lee J. Cobb (Leo Jacoby)
Tony Curtis (Bernard Schwartz)
Rodney Dangerfield (Jacob Cohen)
Kirk Douglas (Issur Danielovitch)
Melvyn Douglas (Melvyn Hesselberg)
John Garfield (Julius Garfinkle)
Paulette Goddard (Marion Levy)
Joel Grey (Joe Katz—all cats are grey in the dark)
Lawrence Harvey (Larushka Mischa Skikne)
Judy Holliday (Judith Tuvim)
Danny Kaye (David Daniel Kaminsky)
Jerry Lewis (Joseph Levitch)
Peter Lorre (Laszlo Lowenstein)
Paul Muni (Muni Weisenfreund)
Larry Rivers (Irving Grossberg)
Tony Randall (Leonard Rosenberg)
Edward G. Robinson (Emmanuel Goldenberg)
Beverly Sills (Belle Silverman)
Mike Todd (Avrom Goldbogen)
Shelley Winters (Shirley Schrift)
Ed Wynn (Isaiah Leopold)

Name changing peaked in the late 1940s and early 1950s, Silberman wrote. He estimated that each year during that period about forty thousand Jews filed petitions with state courts for permission to change their family names, but this figure did not include citizens who exercised their right to change names without going through any legal process. The pressure to change abated dramatically during the 1960s. (The physical correlative of name changing, "the 'nose job,' " says Silberman, "did not begin to lose its popularity until Barbra Streisand's rise to fame.") Film stars like Streisand, Richard Benjamin, Richard Dreyfuss, Dustin Hoffman, Paul Newman, and George Segal kept the names they were born with. Meanwhile Caryn Johnson transmuted herself into the black superstar Whoopi Goldberg, a name singularly comic, multicultural, and self-assured. Israel's military victories and its continued survival bolstered group pride, cultural realism, and renewed respect for ethnic diversity. So did the consolidation of Jewish standing in cultural, academic, and business life. So did the parallel emergence of a unified ethnic consciousness—"Black is beautiful"—in another group of Americans for whom naming and renaming, the erosion and restoration of individual and group identity, also had a varied and painful history.

4.
Black Naming: "An Old and Controversial Issue"

black   Preferred usage for those of the Negro race. (Use Negro *only in names of organizations or in quotations.*) *Do not use* colored *as a synonym.*
                    The Associated Press Stylebook, 1994 edition

How to identify an American subgroup, comprising 13 percent of the population, that keeps changing its own name? The main alternatives: negro, Negro, black, Black, colored, people of color, African-American, African American (no hyphen), Afro-American. Each name implies something the others do not; each relies on a singular emotional idiom and set of associations. "Black"—sibling to "white"—trips off the tongue more easily, is not self-conscious, and unlike the next best—African-American—is a simple declarative tag with a minimum of subcutaneous fat, five characters instead of sixteen (including the hyphen).

That no blacks are truly black doesn't matter any more than the fact that no whites are truly white; both words are approximate. Here, the word "black" denotes American descendants of Africans; its use does not hide an awareness that it isn't as politically correct as "African-American," a designation preferred by many younger and/or militant segments of the black community. The stylebooks of *The New York Times,* the Associated Press, the *Hartford Courant,* and other news organizations use "black," the term favored by most Americans, regardless of color. The intensive, not to say inescapable media coverage of the O. J. Simpson murder trial appears to have standardized "black," at least for the present.

In December 1988 the leaders of seventy-five black organizations gathered in Chicago, determined to draw up a new agenda. During this conference, the Reverend Jesse Jackson announced that his people were no longer to be called "blacks." Henceforth they were "African-Americans." "To be called Black is baseless," he said. "To be called African-American has cultural integrity." Jackson's announcement sparked a debate as heated as if an un-elected white leader had proposed that the word "Columbian" replace "American."

Ebony, the voice of mainstream, middle-class blacks, entered the debate in July 1989, when an editorial introduced "an old and controversial issue. . . . What should we call ourselves, 'Blacks' or 'African-Americans'?" *Ebony* recruited ten high-profile men and women, among them California congressman Ronald Dellums, Benjamin Hooks (executive director of the NAACP), several church leaders, and fiction writer Gloria Naylor. They reacted to the call for cultural integrity as something they had been looking for all their lives. Most of those who liked what Jackson said vibrated to the notion that while "black" refers most immediately to a color (as well as invoking a host of negative asociations), "African-American," with its emphasis on the first word, embraces an entire culture.

Historically speaking, the campaign for "African-American" was hardly innovative, *Ebony* noted. Nearly a hundred years earlier, pan-Africanists W. E. B. Du Bois and Marcus Garvey had tried to coax the descendants of slaves in the United States into defining themselves as unlawfully displaced Africans who should seriously consider returning to their homeland. Garvey's followers anticipated the "Black is beautiful" movement of the 1960s and celebrated brown skin, kinky hair, and large, round buttocks —physical characteristics usually devalued by whites. The goal of Garvey's organization, the United Negro Improvement Association, was to raise his people's physical, spiritual, economic, and social self-image by emphasizing their African heritage.

One participant in the *Ebony* debate predicted that the new term "African-American" would contribute to a "healthy attitude toward our past." Several alluded to "homeland." Others mentioned "diaspora," a term generally reserved for the forced exile of Jews from the holy land after the destruction of the first temple in the sixth century B.C. When applied to black history, "diaspora" underscores a profound concern with ethnic as well as nationalist coherence, as does another borrowed term, "holocaust." Just as Jews are Jews no matter where they were born and where they live, many American blacks feel a connectedness with blacks in other countries.

The majority of the *Ebony* debaters applauded Jackson's proposal. Those who didn't were either leery of change per se or felt that neither term was "more appropriate than the other." Some, like the writer Carl Rowan, rejected the whole idea of this debate on the grounds that it was a diversion from more pressing problems. Rowan told Jackson, "To a black man who needs a job, it doesn't matter *what* they call him so long as they *call* him." Gloria Naylor, born in 1950, described herself as "old enough to have been [called] Colored, Negro, Black and Afro-American" and agreed with Rowan. She argued that the matter of "what you call me" was less important than the "economic and political power we have not used so far." In April 1995 the United Negro College Fund ran the following austerely dramatic advertisement:

1900   1,700 Negroes attend college.
1944   40,000 Colored People attend college.
1970   522,000 Blacks attend college.
1992   1,393,000 African Americans attend college.
                    Still I rise.

Black Americans are a people reshaping their own story so fast that their name is in continual motion, floating, looking for a place to land and remain permanently. This constant, deeply self-conscious name changing signifies a shift in self-definition; the way a minority group chooses to be known sends a politically magnified message to those outside this group.

The controversy over a collective name moved from a popular magazine into more scholarly precincts, where academics picked up on the complicated matter of self-definition. What seems to concern these writers most is *authenticity:* who and what are we, really? According to a 1995 *Newsweek* report, "Solidarity is hard to find. One third of African-Americans polled say that blacks should not be considered a single race." Many think of themselves as multiethnic or biracial, while race itself is no longer regarded as a material attribute like height or weight but instead as a social construct, an instrumental way of crystallizing prejudices and preconceptions. Does skin color mean more than geographical origins, or less? The most persuasive of these writers suggested that the story of groups with hyphenated labels is always one of conflict and struggle against formidable economic and social obstacles. It seems somewhat paradoxical, but a good many immigrants (with the possible exception of the Jews) who found America's arms to be less than embracing insisted upon defining themselves with a double name, hyphenated: Irish-American, Italian-American, Japanese-American, Chinese-American. Hyphenated Americans, then, are ambivalent—or perhaps defensive—about their nationality and heritage. The terms "Dutch-American" and "English-American" simply don't exist; the Dutch and the English not only got here first but never had any trouble figuring out who they were.

The forebears of Swedish-Americans lived in Sweden, spoke Swedish, embodied a discrete Swedish culture; there's only one kind of vegetable in this soup. But when you're trying to identify and name a people as various as the descendants of Africans, you're dealing with many elements: culture, geography, nationality, heritage, color. Since the African continent is home to peoples as disparate and dissimilar as Egyptians and Masai, Moroccans and Angolans, Bantus and Ibos, to call each of their great-great-

great-great-great-grandchildren African—both Anwar el-Sadat and Nelson Mandela, for example—is a distortion, since this is far too broad and loose a term to be meaningful as a cultural or ethnic, national, or even geographical definer. It becomes even more meaningless if one recognizes that the ancestors of the entire human species saw the light in Africa many millions of years ago and that in this drastically attenuated sense we're *all* Africans. Few present-day blacks know precisely where in Africa, the world's second-largest continent, their more immediate ancestors came from six or seven generations ago; the umbilical cord has been pretty much severed. Still, there is this large, intricate tapestry—Africa—and every black person who now lives in the United States is a descendant, frequently with other blood admixtures, white and American Indian among them, of a man or woman who once lived somewhere on the African continent.

The first shipload of blacks arrived in Virginia in 1619. What they and their children and grandchildren were called by the British settlers and later American colonists and what they called themselves has remained in flux ever since. Even in the sixteenth century, "Moor," "Negro," and "Ethiopian" were interchangeable; "Ethiopian," in that sense, survived through the nineteenth century (in minstrel groups, for example) and can still be found in church and organization names. "African" had been used in English to refer to dark-skinned people since the thirteenth century. It was the commonest term in eighteenth-century America, employed by both whites and blacks. This accounts for the ubiquitous "African," as with the African Meeting House on Boston's Beacon Hill and a host of black churches and institutional charters. Along with "African," the words "black" and "Negro" were also commonly used from the beginning of the slave trade until the Civil War. In 1819 a court ruling in South Carolina decreed that "Negro" and "slave" had identical meanings. As a remedy for the "vulgar" vibrations emitted by the word "Negro," the editor of the *New York World,* T. Thomas Fortune, proposed in 1880 that this population be referred to as "Afro-American." "Colored," the word favored during the decade after emancipation, became a portmanteau term that also took in Indians, Orientals, and Mexicans, who were classified thus by the U.S. Census Bureau until 1940, and is now described as derogatory in some stylebooks.

On his application to Yale in 1969, the scholar-critic Henry Louis Gates, Jr., wrote, "My grandfather was colored, my father was a negro, and I am black." The white people in the West Virginia hill town where Gates grew up were "only shadowy presences," he recalled in his memoir, *Colored People,*

> vague figures of power like remote bosses at the mill or tellers at the bank. There were exceptions, of course, the white people who would come into our world in ritualized, everyday ways we all understood. Mr. Mail Man, Mr. Insurance Man, Mr. White-and-Chocolate Milk Man, Mr. Landlord Man, Mr. Po-lice Man: we called white people by their trade, like allegorical characters in a mystery play,

the generic and collective white population being "the man." Gates suggested that in their lifetimes his children will probably

> go from being African Americans to "people of color," to being, once again, "colored people." (The linguistic trend toward condensation is strong.) I don't mind any of the names myself. But I have to confess that I like "colored" best, maybe because when I hear the word, I hear it in my mother's voice and in the sepia tones of my childhood.

"Maybe I over-stated my case," Gates recently said about his published preference for "colored" over other designations. Whenever he identifies another black by race he'll invariably use "colored," the first word that comes to his mind. The responses to "colored" by readers his age and older (he was born in 1950) were "cool" (in the admiring sense), while younger people wanted to know, "What the fuck is going on here?" He quoted his uncle Raymond as saying, "I'd rather white people call me *nigger* than call me black." The word "black" conveyed a challenge the old guard wasn't eager to meet. A good many whites didn't like what it implied either: an upheaval of the political and social terrain. "I was never a very threatening kind of black man," General Colin Powell said about his phenomenally successful adaptation to white military and political culture. "At different times, I was a good Negro to have around."

Still, "colored" seems an odd word for Gates to favor. It's literally pale compared to "black," says little or nothing about origin, heritage, or culture except "not white," and according to contemporary usage guides, is often considered derogatory and offensive. The term "colored" nonetheless possesses an unshakeable rhetorical and historical durability. "In all relations of life and death, we are met by the color line," Frederick Douglass declared at the Convention of Colored Men, held in Louisville, Kentucky, in 1883. Seventeen years later, W. E. B. Du Bois declared in an address to a London Pan-African conference that "the problem of the twentieth century is the color line," and this may hold true for the next century as well. The NAACP, founded in 1910 by seven whites and one black (W. E. B. Du Bois), is the National Association for the Advancement of Colored People; it has never changed its name, thereby holding on to the loyalty of an older, more moderate assimilationist group while losing that of the younger, the more militant, and those who want to reassert their ethnic and cultural heritage. After the older members of the NAACP die off, will this organization change its name to the National Association for the Advancement of African-Americans? And beyond that, should another name change occur, will it make yet another course correction?

"Colored" gradually gave way to "negro," then "Negro." But even this word was a reappearance, having been the way blacks in sixteenth-century England were known. It's interesting how much weight a large initial letter carries. A noun or adjective is a frog until you give it a capital first letter, at which point it becomes a prince, that is, a proper name. The word "jew," for instance, is often used as a verb, as in "I jewed him down." [1] *The*

New York Times did not feel obliged to capitalize the *N* in
"Negro" until 1930, and the U.S. government not until three
years later. The most visible institution employing the word
"Negro" is the United Negro College Fund, founded in 1944.
Like that of the National Association for the Advancement of
Colored People, its name sounds somewhat archaic; this works
both for and against it. You can easily catch retrograde echoes at
the same time you're picking up sounds of stability and tradition.

It was when the relatively uninflected word "Negro" was
deemed by its militant leaders to be hopelessly out of date, passé,
unacceptable, not forceful enough, that the black community was
again forced into self-examination. This gave rise to yet more
controversy. "Black" (without the capital *B*) was in use during
slavery and was, in fact, so associated with it that after emancipation it was discarded in favor of "colored." But the stark word
"black" resurfaced in 1966: Stokely Carmichael (now Kwame
Ture), cofounder of the Black Panther Party, delivered a call for
"Black power . . . for black people in this country to unite, to
recognize their heritage, to build a sense of community." It was
as if, in being so named, a large faction of the black population
realized for the first time the power they needed and had justifi-
able claims on. The name did it.

"Black is beautiful" wasn't just another slogan. A lot of blacks
quit trying to look like whites, gave up conking their hair, something they had been painfully doing for years. The James Brown
1968 song, "Say It Loud: 'I'm Black and I'm Proud,' " was a hit
on more than one level. Before the end of the sixties, black urban
youth had stopped calling themselves Negroes and had assumed
the new, openly antibourgeois label "black," a word that said,
"I'm not white," far more emphatically than it said, "I'm descended from Africans." Of all the words and phrases used to
designate this group, "black" is the most militant (yet the one
favored by the white community). The feisty spirit it represents
didn't sit too well with the older, more conservative leaders.
Roy Wilkins and Martin Luther King, Jr., for instance, found
themselves the object of open ridicule when, instead of "black,"

they used the word "Negro" in speeches before youthful audiences. The chasm was profound, a bonecrusher: Wilkins and King advocated accommodation with whites, while Carmichael denounced it.

By 1968, *Ebony* had replaced "Negro" with "black" in its editorial matter. Even so, the magazine's June 1968 poll disclosed that 69 percent of its readers still favored "Negro," while 15 percent went with "Afro-American" and only 6 percent liked "black." It wasn't until five years later that the word "black" was lodged firmly enough to win out over the others—Negro, colored, Afro-American. Many whites still use "black" rather than "African-American," and there are no doubt plenty of white people who also still use the words "colored" and "Negro," not to mention epithets like "nigger" and other vestiges of the Jim Crow era.

Just before Jesse Jackson's call for "African-American," there was a relatively short "Afro-American" phase. This term was also briefly popular right after the Civil War—another example of how these words and phrases come to the surface, dive, and then surface again, as if coming up for air. We tend to associate "Afro-American" with a style of dress and hair—the Afro, the term itself somewhat demeaning in its diminishment. "Afro-American" lacks bite, precision, and something that promises, in Jackson's phrase, cultural integrity.

Since every label contains its own code, the difficulties involved in persuading a group of people accustomed to calling itself one thing to change its own name are staggering; leadership has its work cut out for it, especially among Gloria Naylor's generation. Although many people insist that in print and in public discourse they be identified as African-Americans, they still say "black" when referring to themselves. "African-American" may sound altogether too politically correct for those who have a sense both of irony and of the capriciousness of history.

The problems connected with settling on a collective name for American blacks are, in a way, echoed in their individual choices of first names. The story of black American first names is likewise one of almost constant change, so much so that one man may go through several name changes in a lifetime, depending on where and when he was born.[2] It's as hard to imagine a contemporary black parent naming her child Franklin D. Roosevelt (as in Jones) or George Washington (as in Carver) as it is to imagine Charles Francis Adams or William Rhinelander Stewart changing his name because of a passing crimp in the political climate.

The first people brought to this country as slaves came from coastal west Africa—present-day Angola and Ghana, for example —and were rounded up by their own people, sold to Portuguese traders, herded onto sailing vessels, and transported under subhuman conditions to that part of the New World whose white population had few qualms about employing men and women to raise tobacco, sugar, rice, and cotton, sweep floors, pluck chickens, tend to their masters' children, and often bear them.

In transit from their homelands, these African captives, the majority of them Muslims, were viewed en masse as just so much transportable merchandise. The captain of one slave ship recalled, "I suppose they . . . all had names in their own dialect, but the effort required to pronounce them was too much for us, so we picked out our favorites and dubbed them 'Main-stay,' 'Cats Head,' 'Bull's Eye,' 'Rope Yarn,' and various other sea phrases." They remained nameless until they were delivered to their owners. At this point, before the year 1700, most were given English or Spanish names; a very small percentage managed to retain their original African names.

The first wave of slave owners knew in their bones what Friedrich Nietzsche was to write: "The master's right of giving names goes so far that it is permissible to look upon language itself as the expression of the power of the masters." In the case of the language of names, this meant that if you wanted to render a person or a people powerless and subservient you imposed a name of your own choosing. Robinson Crusoe made naming the crux of his defining transaction with the savage he rescued from the cannibals: "I made him know his name should be *Friday*, which was the day I saved his life; I called him so for the memory of the time: I likewise taught him to say *Master*, and then let him know that was to be my name."

Roots, by Alex Haley, is a work that spans two hundred years and chronicles seven generations of the author's family, tracing his destiny backward, like the explorer Sir Richard Burton retracing the White Nile, to its source in a village in Gambia.[3] There Haley learned the names of all the males in the Kinte clan from a griot, an old man who served as tribal archivist and genealogist. In this dramatized history, Haley described the naming ceremony of a remote forebear on the eighth day following his birth, after the father spends a solid week doing nothing but figuring out what to call his firstborn. "It would have to be a name rich with history and with promise, for the people of his tribe—the Mandinkas—believed that a child would develop seven of the characteristics of whomever or whatever he was named for." The infant is named Kunta, the middle name of his dead grandfather. Captured and brought to this country as a slave, Kunta learns the words "oberseer," "massa," and "nigger." "What, he wondered, was a 'Nigger?' "

Later, Haley "reconstructs" an exchange between Kunta and Fiddler, another slave. "Kunta's face flashed with anger. 'Kunta Kinte!' he blurted, astonished at himself. The brown one was equally amazed. 'Looka here, he can talk! But I'm tellin' you, boy, you got to forgit all dat African talk. Make white folks mad an' scare niggers. Yo name Toby.' " When Kunta's daughter, Kizzy, is sold, her last name is changed from that of her former owner, Waller, to that of her new one, Lea. In tears, she is soothed by a new friend: " 'You sho' know niggers takes whoever's dey massa's name. Nigger names don't make no difference nohow, jes' sump'n to call 'em.' "

As a child, Maya Angelou—then called Margaret—went to work for Viola Cullinan, a white woman who lived behind the post office in Stamps, the small southwestern Arkansas town where Angelou was born. Cullinan decided that the name Margaret was "too long. She's Mary from now on." Angelou was furious and made up her mind.

> That horrible woman would never have the chance to call me Mary because if I was starving I'd never work for her. I decided I wouldn't pee on her if her heart was on fire. . . . Every person I knew had a hellish horror of being "called out of his name." It was a dangerous practice to call a Negro anything that could be loosely construed as insulting because of the centuries of their having been called niggers, jigs, dinges, blackbirds, crows, boots, and spooks.

You don't have to have dark skin to have felt what Angelou termed the "horror" of being "called out" of your name; you can't help thinking that if you had made a better impression, been more commanding, charming, more memorable, they would have got your name right. Most of us have been bruised when called something other than our real name. But it's far worse when you recognize that arrogance and domination, not oversight, carelessness, or even indifference, are at work here. Angelou's employer knew what she was doing: by calling the child Mary rather than Margaret, her real name, she made the child her creature, her slave. Angelou took revenge. She waited a week, started leaving egg yolk on the dishes, and then deliberately dropped her employer's best casserole on the tile floor of the dining room. It was at this point that Viola Cullinan's genuine sentiments emerged like a snake from a hole: " 'That clumsy nigger. Clumsy little black nigger.' "

Growing up at the other extreme of the black social and professional scale, Bessie (Annie Elizabeth) and Sadie (Sarah) Delany, accomplished career women and daughters of the first black to be elected a bishop of the Episcopal church, also learned about being called out of one's name. Even at home with the children, their parents addressed each other as "Mr. Delany" and "Mrs. Delany." "In those days," Sadie wrote in their joint memoir, *Having*

Our Say (1993), "people used to call Negroes by their first names as a way of treating them like children. Our parents were blocking that. Very few people even knew Mama's and Papa's first names." First names have a reserved, even sacramental status and are not to be used unadvisedly or lightly. The Delany sisters referred to themselves as "Negro maiden ladies."

Black Names in America: Origins and Usage, by Newbell Niles Puckett, a sociologist, was published in 1975. Puckett's book is the most comprehensive and useful study of names and naming practices among blacks, the work most often cited by others in this field and the result of decades of painstaking research in original documents, lists and inventories, plantation and probate records, deed registers, church minute books, and official archives.

According to Puckett's findings, Jack, Will, Charles, Ben, Prince, Cato, and Daniel were among the names most frequently thrust on slaves by their owners during the eighteenth century. The most popular women's names included Bet, Hannah, Sarah, Dinah, Lucy, Susan, Grace, and Dine. That plantation owners frequently gave their mules and their slaves identical names— usually clipped monosyllables, more nickname than first name, like Jack, Kitt, Tom, Ned—should not give more than a moment's pause; the mule and the muscular field hand were considered to be comparable in convenience, resiliency, and foot-pound output. Toward the end of the slavery era, there was a slight but significant shift in men's names from the lightweight Dicks, Harrys, and Robins to those with a little more heft (John, Henry, and William, for example) and more apposite to people than to farm animals.

Before 1800 only about 6.5 percent of male slaves and about 1.5 percent of the females were given classical, chiefly Roman, names: Caesar, Cato, Pompey, and Jupiter; Diana, Dido, Phoebe, and Venus. Nevertheless, this tiny percentage swelled in the popular imagination and became a stereotype in historical novels and movies. What does a name like Jupiter do to and for a man born on the west African coast who still thinks of himself as Cuffee or Quashey? Does it elevate him, or does the tension between pretentious allusion and natural fact only demean him? It's likely that these Pompeys and Phoebes proliferated in the popular imagination because they so neatly matched the stereotypical style and demeanor of the antebellum plantation owner. He pillared, porticoed, and pedimented his house like a Greek or Roman temple, named any old water hole Athens, and preferred American heroes of the age of steam to be sculpted in marble togas and marble sandals.

The African practice of naming a child for the day of the week on which he or she was born—so-called day names—survived in the New World, especially Jamaica and the American South. The table below shows only eighteen names in all.

	Male	**Female**
Sunday	Quashee	Quasheba
Monday	Cudjo	Juba
Tuesday	Cubbenah	Beneba
Wednesday	Kwaco, Quaco	Cuba
Thursday	Quao	Abba
Friday	Cuffee, Cuffy	Pheba, Phibbi
Saturday	Quame, Kwame	Mimba

All but one of the female names end in the letter *a;* very few male names in any language end in this letter. Over the last thirty years or so, American social historians have been digging around in the records and discovering there that day-naming, once thought to be extremely rare in the United States, was a common practice. J. L. Dillard, a scholar who has written extensively on black names, put it this way: "Finding the day names, relatively unaltered, in the plantation records is an easy matter; those who haven't found them simply haven't looked." An interesting twist to this story is the disguise these names sometimes assumed, via translation, so that a slave originally known as Cudjo or Cuffy would be called Monday or Friday. Daniel Defoe didn't say outright, or even suggest, that Friday is the translation of a day name, although he surely must have known this.

There were few constants in black naming; names and their spelling tended to shift and slide around. Thus, it's not unreasonable to assume that a slave called Quack bore an altered version of Quaco, the African name for a male born on Wednesday. Taking this kind of naturalization one more step, slaves began to anglicize their children's names so that one generation's Cudjo would be Monday in the next and Joe in a third; similarly Quaco jumped to Wednesday and ended up Jack. The day names most of us would recognize today are Cudjo, Juba, Cuba, Kwame, and Cuffee, Cuff being the generic name for a black in Walt Whitman's time, the way Jerry and Fritz stood for any German soldier during the First World War. A society in which there are only eighteen options is both simple and complicated—simple because the parents have their minds made up for them even as the child emerges from the womb; complicated because you can't distinguish one Cudjo from another or one Cuba from her sister born on the same day of the week. Something has to be added or substituted to designate who is being called to supper.

During the period from 1800 until emancipation, in 1864, the spelling of slave names and the widening of the name pool went into a sort of baroque phase, partly because spelling was still ad hoc or roughly phonetic rather than normalized. For example, contemporary records show nine versions of the nickname for Eliza: Liz, Liza, Lizar, Lize, Lizee, Lizy, Lizza, Lizzie, and Lizzy. Social distinctions between slaves, based on the sort of work they did, house or field, skilled or unskilled, were dramatically confirmed when their owners allowed certain upper-level retainers to choose their own names. Some slaves took their masters' or mistresses' given names, hoping thereby to be rewarded for their loyalty. One mother who christened her daughter with the "gift names" Annie Virginia Cordelia Idella received a present from each of the white women who supplied a bead for this string. She then promptly turned around and called her daughter Tumps. Other names, some chosen by slave, some by owner, included months, religious holidays like Easter, and places like Aberdeen, Baltimore, Dublin, and Richmond.

As soon as slaves were permitted to name their children, they savored a morsel of what freeedom had to offer. But naming is one thing; getting a fair share of the pot involves far more than an awareness of what you've been missing. Blacks have had available to them only a limited number of gestures with which to emphasize both their independence and their particularity. The most obvious of these is immediately visible in clothes that are a distinct echo of native African flow and color. Less obvious and more complex is the search for roots. Running parallel to this is the search for one's "true" name. For the American black, name is a central fact of life, articulating and establishing connections to the immediate community, the largely white population beyond it, and the historically and geographically distant homeland.

Up to the First World War, Booker T. Washington (1856–1915) was known as the Moses of his race; forty years later he was being dismissed by civil rights activists as Uncle Tom. History had caught up with and outrun him. Washington was a complex man with a mixed background: his mother, Jane Ferguson, was a mulatto slave, his father a white slave owner. As a small child in Hale's Ford, Virginia, he was called Booker, and it wasn't until the day he started school that he realized most children had "at least two names and some of them indulged in what seemed to me the extravagance of having three." When the teacher got around to asking his name, "I calmly told him 'Booker Washington,' as if I had been called that all my life." Some time later he discovered that he once had a middle name, Taliaferro, that had been somehow misplaced or lost. "I revived it, and made my full name Booker Taliaferro Washington. I think there are not many men in our country who have had the privilege of naming themselves in the way that I have."

In his autobiography, *Up from Slavery,* he recalled that with the end of slavery "a feeling got among the colored people that it was far from proper for them to bear the surnames of their former owners, and a great many of them took other surnames. This was one of the first signs of freedom." A Hatcher slave who had been called John Hatcher, or Hatcher's John, believed this "was not the proper title by which to denote a freeman; and so in many cases 'John Hatcher' was changed to 'John S. Lincoln' or 'John S. Sherman,' the initial 'S' standing for no name, it being simply a part of what the colored man proudly called his 'entitles.' "

Ralph Ellison in a 1964 essay, "Hidden Name and Complex Fate," said the same thing in language tuned up many notches:

> We must first come into possession of our own names. For it is through our names that we first place ourselves in the world. Our names, being the gift of others, must be made our own. . . . When we are reminded so constantly that we bear, as Negroes, names originally possessed by those who owned our enslaved grandparents, we are apt, especially if we are potential writers, to be more than ordinarily concerned with the veiled and mysterious events, the fusions of blood, the furtive couplings, the business transactions, the violations of faith and loyalty, the assaults; yes, and the unrecognized and unrecognizable loves through which our names were handed down to us. So charged with emotion does this concern become for some of us, that we have, earlier, the example of the followers of Father Divine and, now, the Black Muslims, discarding their original names in rejection of the bloodstained, the brutal, the sinful images of the past. Thus they would declare new identities.

Washington's sense of impropriety becomes Ellison's outrage: to carry the name of the person who bought and held your grandparents in bondage is an intolerable violation of personal dignity, "verbal evidence of a willed and ritualized discontinuity of blood and human intercourse."

The "hidden name" Ellison referred to in his title was his own given name, Ralph Waldo, after the New England poet and essayist Ralph Waldo Emerson; the "complex fate," Ellison's destined vocation as a novelist. Why, Ellison asked, hadn't his father chosen some more predictable model for a black boy, the boxer Jack Johnson, for example, who was the first black heavyweight boxing champion, or Booker T. Washington, or Frederick Douglass? It was "too soon for me to have made the connection between my name and my father's love for reading. Much later, after I began to write and work with words, I came to suspect that he was aware of the suggestive power of names and of the magic involved in naming."

The linking of name and black identity is one of the dominant themes of Ellison's *Invisible Man,* characterized by the critic and biographer R. W. B. Lewis as "the finest and richest work of fiction by an American novelist since the end of the second war." Ellison's dissociated and disoriented protagonist—a young Southerner who, moving to New York, resolves to discover his true identity—is not only "invisible" but nameless as far as the reader is concerned (even Kafka's "K." is more informative). At one point, after electrical shock therapy, he finds that even he no longer knows his name: it has been wiped out of his memory along with all connections with his past. Recruited by "the Brotherhood" (the Communist Party), he accepts a slip of paper with a name written on it. "This is your new identity," they tell him. "Start thinking of yourself by that name from this moment. Get it down so that even if you are called in the middle of the night you will respond." He thinks of Frederick Douglass:

Douglass came north to escape and find work in the shipyards; a big fellow in a sailor's suit who, like me, had taken another name. What had his true name been? Whatever it was, it was as *Douglass* that he became himself, defined himself. And not as a boatwright as he'd expected, but as an orator. Perhaps the sense of magic lay in the unexpected transformations. "You start Saul, and you end up Paul," my grandfather had often said.

But at the end of the novel, Ellison's Invisible Man burns the slip of paper with his Brotherhood name written on it—he is overwhelmed by self-loathing for allowing others to "have named me and set me running with one and the same stroke of the pen. . . . Suddenly I began to scream."

Another major book dealing with the problematics of black identity is *Song of Solomon* (1977) by Toni Morrison (born Chloe Anthony Wofford). Lewis called this "a book of names, a novel about naming. . . . Names are what people think about and talk about in *Song of Solomon,* names and their relation to individual identity." The hero of Morrison's powerful, lyric, and mythmaking novel inherits the grotesque family name Macon Dead that a drunken Yankee soldier had imposed two generations back, and also bears the derisive nickname Milkman because his mother had nursed him even when he was "old enough to talk, stand up, and wear knickers." No one in the family remembers the grandfather's real name; the new one wiped out the past. He hates his name. "Let me tell you somethin, baby," his friend tells him. "Niggers get their names the way they get everything else—the best way they can." And later, "Slave names don't bother me; but slave status does." "When you know your name, you should hang on to it," Morrison wrote at the end of her hero's pursuit of the family mystery, "for unless it is noted down and remembered, it will die when you do." A children's rhyming game recapitulates a distant African past:

Solomon and Ryna Belali Shalut
Yaruba Medina Muhammet too.
Nestor Kalina Saraka cake.
Twenty-one children, the last one Jake!

The novel swells to its conclusion with a remarkable litany of sixty or so names, names that had come from

yearnings, gestures, flaws, events, mistakes, weaknesses. Names that bore witness. Macon Dead, Sing Byrd, Cowell Byrd, Pilate, Reba, Hagar, Magdalene, First Corinthians, Milkman, Guitar, Railroad Rommy, Hospital Tommy, Em-

pire State, Small Boy, Sweet, Circe . . . Tampa Red, Juke
Boy, Shine, Staggerlee, Jim the Devil, Fuck-Up, and *Dat
Nigger.*

When you find your true name—and for many blacks this is
the name of an ancestor—you find your true identity. A person
who digs for his or her roots is like an adoptee looking for a
biological mother, as if in finally discovering her in a real house
in a real town somewhere far away, he or she will at last achieve
both the self-definition he or she lacks and the freedom to move
on from that point. There is more than a little magic in such
quests, and who's to say the magic doesn't work? He or she might
think: I now know who I am and what I want to do with my life
because I have seen my mother up close, sat on her shabby couch,
eaten the brownies she baked for me, listened to her troubles,
watched her shoulders sag when I said good-bye. In the same
way I know who I am because I have heard the sound of my
great-great-grandfather's true name.

Most naming practices follow a more or less conventional pattern.
While the sounds of names vary somewhat over several generations, the size and constituency of the name pool remain fairly
constant, and names originate in similar places in the distant and
recent past of a particular family. You drop your line and come
up with a fish that looks like most of the other fish. Not so in
black naming; the pattern keeps unraveling even as a new one
forms. This has happened over and over again. We are now seeing
the latest form, in which a unique name, a neologism, often a
daring and imaginative coinage (especially in contrast to conventional white naming practices) is created for each baby that comes
along. Alexicor, Bogumila, Calendula, Damanl, Eddleavy, Fon-
tella, Gonorleathia, Hurie, Iniabase, Jivon, Kenee, Latif, Malakah,
Najja, Olithyn, Pelissar, Quadrinea, Rasheena, Salonla, Tajuan,
Unise, Vaneal, Wardsworth, Xtmeng, Yuriel, Zikkiyyia—these
twenty-six first names were culled from a printout roster of children enrolled in the public schools of Chicago, ZIP code 60609,

during 1990. Some are more euphonious than others, but each one is sui generis, which in turn suggests that the child who bears it is also one of a kind and that the parents who invented these names were prompted by their own unconscious cues. These names are about as removed from So-and-So Junior or Amelia named-in-honor-of-her-grandmother as it is possible to get. E. Ethelbert Miller, poet and black-studies scholar, saw names like Shaniqua, Starletta, LaToya, and LaDon as a distinctive "form of black style." Poet Sonia Sanchez saw them as expressions of creative force among people whose energy is often dissipated by social and economic problems. "These names may not be truly African, but they have the same polysyllabic flavor. LaTanya— you know that it is an African-American name right away. Listen to it. It tells you—I am."

So-called movement babies, born during the nineteen seventies and underscoring Black Pride, grew up with names like Kenyatta (after Jomo Kenyatta, first president of independent Kenya), Rhassam, and Rondia. According to Lisa Jones, writing in the *Village Voice* in 1992,

> Naming/renaming has been an issue for black folks . . . since the slave ships docked. . . . Sixties nationalism made an expressive but shrill link between "slave names," slave hair, and slave mentalities. It wasn't just Cassius Clay, Abbey Lincoln, and Stokely Carmichael who took African and Muslim names, but thousands of regular folk. (Even Clarence Thomas's son, born in '75, was christened Jamal.)

Cassius Marcellus Clay, Jr., became Muhammad Ali in 1964 after winning the world heavyweight championship from Sonny Liston and joining Malcolm X's Nation of Islam. Like other converts, he took the name as a sign of his allegiance and readiness to assume a new identity. The name he shed, however, was not a slave name but one given him in honor of a white Kentucky hero, the antislavery politician Cassius Marcellus Clay.

The man known as Frederick Douglass, born Frederick Augustus Washington Bailey in 1818, never knew who his father was, only that he was white and might have been a plantation overseer. His mother was a slave, Betsy Bailey (a surname probably derived from the Muslim *Belali* and common among Atlantic blacks). Farmed out as a field hand, at the age of twenty Frederick Bailey fled to Baltimore and became, first, Frederick Stanley, then Frederick Johnson. Soon after, having moved to the safer high ground of New Bedford, Massachusetts, where he was given shelter by an abolitionist named Nathan Johnson, he realized that the town was so full of other Johnsons that it was "quite difficult to distinguish between them." [4] With what his biographer William McFeely characterized as "astonishing casualness," he took the name Douglas, apparently after the hero of Sir Walter Scott's *Lady of the Lake,* adding a second *s* for good measure.

As for "Frederick": "I must hold on to that, to preserve a sense of my identity." Scott's long poem about medieval knights, Scottish clans at one another's throats, and ladies requiring rescue had about as much to do with the former slave's own life as ice fishing in Minnesota; his choice of name was prodded by unconscious purpose and, no doubt, the dream that he too would someday be a savior. Frederick was his core self, the name he was not to be called out of. Stanley and Johnson had been matters of simple expediency. But the change to Douglass was an act of self-determination and announced his mission as a leader in the antislavery movement and its most effective orator. "You have seen how a man was made a slave," Douglass wrote in his 1845 autobiography; "you shall see how a slave was made a man." The name he finally chose for himself stood for the final stage in this self-transformation.

New name equals new identity equals newfound power. Pay attention: I'm not Mary; I'm Margaret. You'd better get it right. Listen again: I'm no longer Margaret, I'm Maya. Listen yet again. Margaret is an ordinary sight, a rock in the forest clearing; behold Maya, a *presence,* a fountain.

Hundreds of well-known blacks have shed the old, taken on the new: plain Robert Poole became Elijah Muhammad—literally "the messenger of Allah"—who went on to found the Nation of Islam. Basketball player Lew Alcindor—a beautiful sound—turned into Kareem Abdul Jabbar, an equally beautiful sound. Playwright LeRoi Jones transformed himself into Imamu Amiri Baraka. Would more than a handful of people know that the man baptized Louis Eugene Walcott is Louis Haleem Abdul Farrakhan? Enrolling as a Muslim in 1955, Walcott wrote to Elijah Muhammad, "I desire to reclaim my Own. Please give me my Original name. My slave name is as follows . . ."

Martin Luther King, Jr., stuck with his name; Malcolm Little changed his. It wasn't simply that King, his surname connoting power to begin with, wore two overlapping names associated with power (Martin Luther, the founder of Protestantism; Martin Luther King, Sr., a prominent preacher) or that "Little" is a diminisher. That King kept his name and Little changed his was largely a consequence of their characters, personalities, and political strategies. Malcolm Little was impatient with caution and determined to do nothing less than "build an organization that could help cure the black man in North America of the sickness which has kept him under the white man's heel." His diagnosis of a condition that has all the earmarks of masochism must have been a stunning corrective for blacks who realized that caution gets you exactly nowhere.

In Boston, where he had moved from Lansing, Michigan, Malcolm wore the nickname Homeboy. Later, partly because of his reddish hair, he was known as Detroit Red. After his conviction for drug dealing and theft, his cell-block mates called him Satan because of his outspoken antireligious views. In jail he was introduced to the Nation of Islam by his brother Philbert, who saw this movement as "the natural religion for the black man." Little found reading, he found history, he made himself over from thief and addict to orator and leader. When he joined the Nation of Islam he substituted, as did all the devout followers of Elijah Muhammad, the letter *X* for his surname. When you take a single letter for a last name you are removing all but one association from your name. You are obliterating family, friends, culture,

lineage, even ethnicity. To be X is to be Muslim and nothing more
—nothing more need be understood. Every orthodox Muslim
feels that he or she must make a pilgrimage, the hajj, to Mecca,
in order to fulfill a religious obligation. This Malcolm X did in
the middle 1960s, and it was there that he assumed his final name:
El-Hajj Malik El-Shabazz. The journey from Homeboy to this
elaborate title was long and meandering; each leg of this trip was
profoundly transformative.

Change inevitably leaves scars: within the black community, the
matter of name choice is far from resolved. For instance, according to Lisa Jones, names like Sheniqua, Twanda, Laskesia,
"sound African, to some ears, but they're made in chocolate cities
like Detroit." These so-called Watts names are considered infra
dig by members of the black intelligentsia, one of whom commented that at least she hadn't named her baby Toyota Corolla.
Jones is sorry that "some folks" can't distinguish between authentic African names, now popular, and those—like Toyota Corolla—not the real thing: glass diamonds, soybean burgers, plastic
tableware. Is Jones implying that people in chocolate cities don't
know the difference between ersatz and genuine either? Perhaps
they don't. What they do know is that white names are not the
names they want their children to carry around. Anything is preferable to Cynthia and Oliver.

In 1989 a journalist, born Jill Lord, having changed her name
legally to Itabari Njeri, suggested that most blacks have no idea
what their original family names were. She told her own story in
a *Los Angeles Times* feature, a story made especially poignant by
her examination of the uneasiness this kind of name change raises
among blacks reluctant to assume their original African family
name.

"You're one of those black people who changed their name,
huh," they are likely to begin. "Well, I still got the old slave
master's Irish name," said one man named O'Hare at a party.
This man's defensive tone was a reaction to what I call the

"blacker than thou" syndrome perpetuated by many black nationalists in the sixties and seventies. Those who reclaimed their African names made blacks who didn't do the same thing feel like Uncle Toms.

It seems to be something of a no-win situation: those who take back their African names are apt to be regarded as blacker than thou by those who don't, while those who don't are apt to be dismissed as Uncle Toms by those who do. Others suspect that those who *do* shed their slave names in favor of African names are motivated as much by the theater of it as by an authentic and profound desire to touch and cling to their once lost heritage.

5.
City of Names

Now, why did you name your baby "John"? Every Tom, Dick, and Harry is named "John."
Samuel Goldwyn (attributed)

In 1887 Harvey Henderson Wilcox, a man from Ohio who had made a pile in Kansas real estate, laid out a town site on a 120-acre tract he owned in the Cahuenga Valley just north of Los Angeles. Like Brigham Young, who led the Mormon migration to the valley of the Great Salt Lake and announced, "This is the place," Henderson envisioned a sort of New Jerusalem, a city of the righteous, springing up amid citrus groves, pepper trees, and barley fields. He offered free land to any church willing to build there, named streets in honor of purchasers, and in other ways tried to attract wealthy family people who respected the sabbath and abhorred drinking, gambling, and low company. Recalling a country estate in the East she had heard about from a fellow train passenger, his wife, Daeida, gave their development the rustic and alluring name of Hollywood, even though holly was no more native to California than the Wilcoxes themselves or the Hawaiian palm trees and Australian eucalyptuses that soon adorned Sunset Boulevard and Wilcox Avenue.

In 1911 a vanguard with a radically different drive and temper arrived in Hollywood and nearby Edendale: movie industry pioneers drawn to southern California by low nonunion labor costs, open spaces, the temperate climate of the Frostless Belt, and abundant natural light (the Los Angeles Chamber of Commerce promised 350 sunny days a year) for indoor as well as outdoor shooting. The Horsely brothers, William and David, owners of the Centaur Company (a reference to their surname), opened the first Hollywood motion picture studio. They specialized in Westerns, which, like centaurs, were part man and part horse. Soon after, *The Squaw Man,* a Western directed by Cecil B. DeMille, marked the birth of the feature-length film. In 1923 a group of real estate promoters put up a gigantic sign along the summit of Mount Lee that spelled out HOLLYWOODLAND in sheet-metal letters almost fifty feet high. Later trimmed to HOLLYWOOD, the sign itself, even for people unfamiliar with the Roman alphabet, is as emblematic and universally recognizable as the Rock of Gibraltar and the Statue of Liberty. When Peg Entwhistle, an aspiring actress, ran out of hope in 1932, she jumped to her death from the top of the *H.* "Other disillusioned starlets followed her lead," according to Kenneth Anger's classic *Hollywood Babylon,* "and the Hollywood Sign became a notorious signing-off place." The Wilcoxes' virtuous oasis had become the core, symbol, and generic name of an industry that created a new art form, dominated the world market for its product, and shaped the culture of the twentieth century. Few other names carry as large a cargo of association and meaning as Hollywood, boomtown and dream factory: glamor, imagination, extravagance and extravaganza, celebrity, venality, deals, ostentation, hype, and sex.

The moviemakers had to invent a new vocabulary for almost every function and functionary of their young industry. Hollywood was a name factory before it was a dream factory. At different points in its development, the product itself, projected on a screen in a darkened hall, was called a motion picture, film, moving picture, picture show, photoplay, biograph, cinematograph, photodrama, flicker, feature, silent drama, silver screen, and movie. Silent pictures—with quotable subtitles like "Comes the dawn," "Wedding bells," "Meanwhile, back at the ranch," and "Kiss me, my fool" and popular ensembles like Mack Sennett's Keystone Kops and Bathing Beauties—gave way to the talkies; black-and-white gave way to Technicolor and advanced

filming and projection methods with names like Cinerama, Pana-
vision, Todd-AO, 3-D. The nickelodeon, as polyglot a coinage as
"Minneapolis," gave way to the generic Odeon, picture theater,
movie palace, music hall, cinema, Alhambra, Orpheum, Palla-
dium, Savoy, art theater, nabes, bijou, and drive-in (or passion
pit).

Every aspect of the making of movies, from financing,
scripting, casting, direction, makeup, set decoration, and filming
to editing, printing, distribution, and promotion, created new
words, new usages, new names. Some, like "studio," "set," and
"extra," were borrowings from older arts. Others—"close-
up," "pan," "dub," "dissolve," "fade," "flashback," "klieg
light," and "long shot"—were nonce terms that proved their
usefulness and passed into common usage, together with
"animation," "blowup," "double feature," "documentary,"
"newsreel," "coming attractions," and more recent terms—"au-
teur theory," "new wave," "film noir," "cinema verité," "snuff
movie." [1] The same lexical process applies, of course, to other
decisive innovations—the automobile, for example, and the computer, which has generated entire new languages of its own
(COBOL, FORTRAN, Pascal, BASIC) in addition to vocabula-
ries (byte, RAM, ROM, icon, macro) that were mystifying at first
but are now familiar to every schoolchild.

In one crucial respect, however, Hollywood differed from other
innovations. More than product or process, it was the men and
women involved—actors and actresses—who had to emerge
from namelessness so that the movies could grow to full stature
as a cultural force and entertainment commodity. Since early
movie companies "never divulged their actors' given names,"
David Nasaw wrote in *Going Out: The Rise and Fall of Public
Amusements,* "the fans had to refer to them by their brand names
—the Vitagraph Girl, or the Biograph Girl." The Kalem Company (an acronym formed from the surname initials of its princi-
pals, George Kleine, Samuel Long, and Frank Marion) "was the
first to identify its actors and actresses by name in a group photo-
graph published as an advertisement in the January 15, 1910,

Moving Picture World." Two months later Carl Laemmle, founder of the Independent Motion Picture Company of America, known more familiarly as IMP and Imp (symbolized by the figure of a horned devil armed with a pitchfork), scored a spectacular publicity coup by floating a story that a popular actress hitherto known only as the Biograph Girl had been run over and killed by a streetcar. His story identified the victim as Florence Lawrence (her authentic name, as echoic as Fay Wray's, the queen of screamers). Laemmle followed this up with newspaper advertisements denouncing the reports of her death as "a black lie" put out by the Biograph people, whose payroll she had just left: Florence Lawrence was not only alive and unscathed, he trumpeted, but available for personal appearances and working for him instead of Biograph. "On the day Miss Lawrence moved her make-up kit from Biograph to Imp," movie historians Richard Griffith and Arthur Mayer wrote, "the star's salary became the most important single item in the budgets of most pictures."

Her successor as the anonymous Biograph Girl was known as Little Mary or the Girl with the Golden Hair. This was a seventeen-year-old Canadian christened Gladys Smith who had made her child-actress debut billed as Baby Gladys. Laemmle's next coup was to lure Little Mary away from Biograph and unveil this newest and most important Imp of all to the public as Mary Pickford, a name suggested to her by the famous actor-manager-playwright David Belasco. In 1909 Biograph had paid Little Mary $40 a week. Six years later Pickford signed with Adolf Zukor's Famous Players Company for $10,000 a week, a $300,000 bonus, and a profit-sharing arrangement with an affiliate, the Mary Pickford Company, which made only Mary Pickford movies. Soon after, she entered into a business partnership, United Artists, with three other superstars—her husband, Douglas Fairbanks (born Ulman), Charlie Chaplin, and D. W. Griffith—whose names by then were known to practically everyone in the world. "The lunatics have taken charge of the asylum," a publicist said about the formation of United Artists, recognizing a seismic and prophetic shift in the way movies were going to be financed and made by "bankable" actors. "For twenty-three years, Mary Pickford was the undisputed queen of the screen," according to Griffith and Mayer. "For fourteen of these years she was the most popular woman in the world. She was literally what she was billed: America's Sweetheart." The dazzling emergence of the adult butterfly Mary Pickford from the larval Gladys Smith and the pupal Little Mary marked the full beginning of Hollywood's star system with all its attendant glamor, celebrity, unprecedented salaries, remoteness from the lives of ordinary people, and power to make or break a movie at every point from seed financing to promotion, reviews, and ticket window.

In the aftermath of this decisive rejection of anonymity, finding memorable names—exotic or English sounding but definitely not Jewish—for their clients became an essential part of the job for actors' agents and studio executives. Renaming was as important a leg on the trip from obscurity to stardom as the screen test and casting couch. After making an unremarkable debut on the Broadway stage as Theodosia de Coppet, Theodosia Goodman of Cincinnati, Ohio, daughter of a Jewish tailor and a former hair products saleswoman, was transformed by a touch of the publicist's wand into Theda (pronounced *Thay*-da) Bara, archetypal film vamp. Judging from publicity handouts and the roles she played on the screen, this latter-day serpent of the Nile, conceived and born in the shadow of the pyramids, had been endowed with appetites that, once indulged, left her male lovers little more than corpses. Her fans understood "Theda Bara" to be an anagram for "arab death."

Another Hollywood femme fatale, Pola Negri, started out in Janowa, Poland, as Barbara Apollonia Chalupiec, became a star of the silent screen, and enjoyed a widely publicized romance with the prince of screen lovers, Rudolph Valentino, the son of an Italian horse doctor who christened him Rodolfo Alfonzo Raffaelo Pierre Filibert Guglielmi. Introduced to American audiences as the Swedish Sphinx, Greta Louisa Gustafsson made Greta Garbo a household word for reclusiveness and enigmatic femininity, although she hated her first name, referred to herself as GG, and dressed like a man. Anna Sten, whom Goldwyn imported from Europe in the belief she was another Garbo, was the onetime waitress Annel Steskaja Sudakevich. Lucille Vasconcellos Langhanke of Quincy, Illinois, emerged as the silent era star Mary Astor, a name that conveyed both simplicity and grandeur. At one time the mistress of John Barrymore, she achieved national notoriety when her husband's divorce lawyers cited diary entries in which she recounted moments of her adulterous affair with the playwright George S. Kaufman: "Ah, desert night—with George's body plunging into mine, naked under the stars," and, not quite so lyrical, "He fucked the living daylights out of me."

"The big-eyed girl we saw in the office who had two children . . . I certainly think she is worth testing," producer David O. Selznick wrote in a July 1941 memo. Phyllis Walker, the twenty-two-year-old actress who caught his attention, was Phyllis Isley of Tulsa, Oklahoma, when she married the actor Robert Walker. Recognizing in her the makings of what he called "an electric screen personality," Selznick told his advertising and publicity director,

> I would like to get a new name for Phyllis Walker. I had a talk with her and she is not averse to a change. Normally I don't think names very important, but I do think Phyllis Walker a particularly undistinguished name, and it has the additional drawback of being awfully similar to Phyllis Thaxter. . . . I don't want anything too fancy, and I would like to get at least a first name that isn't also carried by a dozen other girls in Hollywood.

Soon out of patience with his staff ("Where the hell is that new name for Phyllis Walker?"), Selznick decided on Jennifer (a variant of Guinevere, King Arthur's faithless wife), then a fairly uncommon girl's name in the United States. (By the 1970s, especially after millions of people wept over the death of Jennifer Cavalieri in Erich Segal's *Love Story*, the name rose to the top of the popularity lists and became virtually inescapable, even generic). Next, Selznick needed "a one-syllable last name that has some rhythm to it and that is easy to remember. I think the best synthetic name in pictures that has been recently created is Veronica Lake" (née Constance Frances Marie Ockleman). The final result was Jennifer Jones; the Jones, though lacking in "rhythm," certainly was not "too fancy." Jennifer Jones starred in *Song of Bernadette* (1943), for which she won an Oscar for best actress. "That name satisfied David," the writer S. N. Behrman recalled; "it was democratic and yet it had piquancy." Selznick named Jennifer Jones, shaped her career, supervised her scripts, dress, hairstyle, and lighting, and having played Pygmalion to this extent, went a step further and married her.

Those old enough remember that Anne Shirley is the name of the movie actor who played Anne Shirley, the heroine, in Hollywood's first (1935) version of L. M. Montgomery's gooey children's classic, *Anne of Green Gables.* But how could this be? The person we know as Anne Shirley was born Dawn Paris, a name more theatrical than the one that, perhaps superstitiously, perhaps in gratitude, she assumed *after* playing the role that made her a star; up until then, she had appeared in movies under the name of Dawn O'Day. As for Montgomery's fictional Anne, she didn't much care for her real name either: "Please do call me Cordelia," she begs her foster mother. "Anne is such an unromantic name. . . . But if you call me Anne please call me Anne spelled with an *e*. . . . If you'll only call me Anne spelled with an *e* I shall reconcile myself to not being called Cordelia."

The list of invented names, which includes Joan Crawford as well as the delectable Helen Twelvetrees, reaches a climax of sorts with a twenty-year-old divorcee, Norma Jean Dougherty, née Mortenson (although she never knew who her father was), who at the suggestion of Ben Lyon, executive talent director at 20th Century–Fox, took the name Marilyn Monroe: Marilyn, because she reminded Lyon of the actress Marilyn Miller, and Monroe, her mother's maiden name. Norman Mailer called her "every man's love affair with America," "our angel, the sweet angel of sex." Heroine of a wild ride to fame, waif as well as goddess, psychically frail and tragically vulnerable, she was an apparent suicide at thirty-six. "Goodbye, Norma Jean," Elton John and Bernie Taupin wrote in their 1973 song "Candle in the Wind":

They set you on a treadmill
And they made you change your name.[2]

When the name Sony replaced Loews on movie theater marquees in 1994, the parent company announced, "Like so many other movie stars, we've changed our name. Most stars change their names before they become stars. We're changing ours after." For the most part, however, the movie moguls themselves—including Marcus Loew, who rose from the peep-show business to ownership of a chain of theaters and a producing company, Metro-Goldwyn-Mayer—did not follow the example of the stars. The Jewish actors and actresses who worked for them were WASPs in their public identities and the roles they played, but the moguls kept the names they began with: Balaban, Cohn, Laemmle, Lasky, Loew, Mayer, Schenck, Selznick, Schulberg, Zanuck, Zukor. Samuel Goldwyn was a celebrated exception, but the name he arrived at was not so much a change as the end result of an evolutionary and consolidating process.

Born Schmuel Gelbfisz in Warsaw, Poland, in 1879, the future prince of independent film producers worked as blacksmith's apprentice and sponge peddler, crossed the Atlantic in steerage, entered the United States illegally from Canada (he was Sam Goldberg on the passenger manifest), and swept floors in a glove factory in upstate New York. He was Samuel Goldfish, naturalized citizen, when he went into the movie business with his brother-in-law Jesse Lasky and Cecil B. DeMille and made *The Squaw Man* in Hollywood. Something of a show business celebrity by 1916, he minded being teased about his name, especially when a Broadway gossip column circulated the quip, "Behind glass is the place for a Goldfish." When he went into partnership that year with the Selwyn brothers, they melded first and last syllables into Goldwyn, a company name that preserved the identities of the participants and at the same time connoted wealth and success for their venture. Neat as it was, it nevertheless invited joke-work speculation that Goldfish and the Selwyns could just as well have taken the other two syllables and gone into business as Selfish or Sell-Fish Pictures.

Sam Goldfish, however, liked the name Goldwyn so much that in 1918 he successfully petitioned the court for permission to take it. The Selwyns, for their part, were angry with him for "stealing half our name," as they said, and threatened to sue him. Five years later they did. Sam had left the partnership and resumed business on his own (this chronic loner once chose "Include me out" as his epitaph), only to find himself temporarily enjoined by the Selwyns from calling his company Samuel Goldwyn, Incorporated, and using the legend "Samuel Goldwyn presents" on his releases. In the brief they filed with the United States District Court in New York, the Selwyns argued that they had been using the name Goldwyn for their company "before Samuel Goldfish became Samuel Goldwyn." "Years later," Goldwyn's biographer, A. Scott Berg, wrote, "tears would literally roll down [his] face whenever he thought of what he called that 'black period' of his life, that time when 'they wouldn't let me have my name!' "

Judge Learned Hand, himself burdened by his parents with a problematic handle, heard the case.[3] His ruling probably incorporated some of his own perturbations:

> A new name, when honestly assumed and worn, may well be of as much or nearly as much consequence to its bearer as though it were familial. Our names are useful or dangerous to us according to the associations they carry among those who hear them. If we have by our past conduct established a good name, that is an interest, pecuniary or honorific, of which we may well object to being deprived, and which may exceed in value that which we inherited. A self-made man may prefer a self-made name.

It wasn't just vanity that motivated this self-made man to claim and keep his self-made name, Berg suggested, but the survival instinct. "Goldwyn" had become the created identity through which Schmuel Gelbfisz could face the world and prevail, even against a rival studio called Metro-Goldwyn-Mayer. "For the rest of his life, whenever fear or anger or grief threatened to pull him under, he would indulge in a short crying jag, then pull through by saying to himself, 'I've still got Goldwyn.' "

Among male superstars, Robert Taylor, introduced to the public as the Man with the Perfect Profile, was born Spangler Arlington Brugh. The spectacularly handsome Roy Scherer, Jr., took the name Roy Fitzgerald when his mother remarried and Rock Hudson when he had his teeth capped. Rip Torn, who specialized in violent and unbalanced roles, came with the mild-mannered first name of Elmore. Probably the most dramatic evolution of them all was that of Marion Michael Morrison into the superstar and American institution John "Duke" Wayne.

Even when he was a gangling teenager in Glendale, California, Marion didn't fit him. The local firemen called him Duke, because he was always seen with Duke, his Airedale, and the nickname stuck. ("I wasn't named for royalty," Wayne was to say, "I was named for a dog.") Six feet four inches tall, Duke Morrison got his start in the movies as a propman and bit player. Director Raoul Walsh, who gave him the lead in a Western, *The Big Trail* (1930), said, "To be a cowboy star, you've got to be six-foot-three or over, have no hips, and a face that looks right under a sombrero." Marion Michael Morrison had all of these qualifications but needed a manly name to go with them. The production head at Fox, Winfield Sheehan, came up with John Wayne.

In *Stagecoach* nine years later, Wayne achieved full-fledged stardom and was well on his way to an enduring Mount Rushmore eminence as archetypal patriot and fighting man, who embodied the frontier spirit and defended American values in *The Alamo* (1960) and *The Green Berets* (1968). According to Richard Slotnick's study *Gunfighter Nation: The Myth of the Frontier in Twentieth-Century America,* the John Wayne Syndrome, reported by veterans of the Vietnam War, combined "internalization of an ideal of superhuman military bravery, skill, and invulnerability to guilt and grief" with opposing "feelings of guilt or grief . . . for responding to battlefield stress with a normal human mix of fear and bravery." In this and in other contexts "John Wayne," like "Gary Cooper" and "James Stewart," had become a figure of speech, a symbol, a personality type, a way of life. A 1987 Primerica newspaper advertisement showed "John Wayne . . . born Marion Morrison" in a Western outfit complete with gun belt. The headline copy ran: "Sometimes the name you grow up with doesn't fit you any more. That's why *American Can* has changed its name to Primerica. . . . After all, it doesn't make much sense to go on calling yourself American Can when you no longer make cans." A 1994 advertisement for "the First Officially Authorized John Wayne Collector Plate" read: "He began as a movie star and became a legend. Loved and respected around the world as the symbol of America at its very best." According to a 1995 Harris Poll, sixteen years after his death John Wayne was still America's favorite movie star.

What conflicts, if any, Wayne may have felt about his rebirth under a new name, he apparently never talked about, nor did he seem to regret that Marion Morrison had been forced to take early retirement. But it was a different story for others who underwent a similar transformation and enjoyed at least vaguely comparable success. For them, taking or being given a new name involved a loss of identity as well as a forward career step. They felt twinges of phantom pain from an amputated limb, heard the voice of the other person they once were or might have become.

"The longer you wear pearls, the realer they become," the novelist Colette wrote in *Cheri.* In her autobiography, *Shelley: Also Known As Shirley,* the actress Shelley Winters, born Shirley Schrift, applied this maxim to her memories, but not to her stage name. She said it did not become any "realer" to her in time, even though it had taken her on a long journey "out of the Brooklyn ghetto" to two Oscars, three marriages, four hit plays, five Impressionist paintings, and "ninety-nine films." She recalled that when she was about fifteen and trying out for an understudy part in a play by Irwin Shaw she was told that "Shirley Schrift isn't a very good name for an actress." She chose Winter, her mother's maiden name, and instead of Shirley— "There's millions of Shirleys all over Brooklyn, all named after Shirley Temple"—a name that sounded similar enough not to be jarring, Shelley, "my favorite poet." "Years later," she added, "Universal Studios added an S to 'Winter' and made me plural." And plural she remained, in her late sixties still trying to reclaim a buried identity and achieve the sense of "a complete self." "Who is Shirley Schrift?" she asked. "What happened to her?" She recalled that in Venice once she ran into a young woman who looked "exactly like the adolescent Shirley Schrift. . . . I took her hand and as I did, I experienced, in some deep mysterious way, a merging of that long buried part of myself with the rest of me."

"Deep down in my deepest heart," Edward G. Robinson wrote in his autobiography, *All My Yesterdays,* "I am, and have always been, Emanuel Goldenberg." Born in Bucharest, he studied at the American Academy of Dramatic Arts in New York, where he was told that his was "not a name for an actor"—too long and too foreign, which meant, it was clear to him, too Jewish. He tried out some translated equivalents: Goldenhill didn't work; Goldenmount sounded pretentious; the French Dormont and the Italian Montedore, contrived. He says that a line he heard in a play, a butler announcing, "A gentleman to see you—a Mr. Robinson," solved the last-name problem. Robinson not only sounded right but was loyal to his origins, he claimed, since it had become virtually a Jewish name as a common substitute for Rabinowitz, Rosenberg, Roth, and so on. As for Emanuel, he settled on Edward, although he, like his friends, continued to think of himself as Manny (which was the title of a 1979 play about his life). The middle initial, *G,* a vestigial form of Goldenberg, represented "my private treaty with the past." Despite Robinson's long and rewarding screen career, *All My Yesterdays* told a sad story with undertones of regret and self-reproach.

Nonforeign names were no longer so important and obligatory for movie actors and actresses, Robinson said in 1973, the year he died. "In my day it was inconceivable for an actor to be named George Segal, Barbra Streisand, or Steve McQueen. I think today Tony Curtis might still be Bernie Schwartz." Had Robinson lived longer he might have cited as well the examples of Sylvester Stallone, Arnold Schwarzenegger, John Travolta, Robert DeNiro, Richard Dreyfuss, and Al Pacino. According to a January 1996 news story out of Hollywood, a previously unknown actress named Renee Zellwegger, known to her friends back in Texas as Renee Z., had just been chosen for the female lead opposite Tom Cruise in a big-budget movie titled *Jerry Maguire*. "If Arnold Schwarzenegger can keep his name," she said, "I can darn well keep mine."

6.
"A Strange Kind of Magick Bias"

No good can come of association with anything labelled Gwladys or Ysobel or Ethyl or Mabelle or Kathryn. But particularly Gwladys.

P. G. Wodehouse, *Very Good, Jeeves*

Much like Freud's "Anatomy is destiny," the shape and substance of a life, its varied activities and vicissitudes, are often seen as affected, if not predetermined, by a name. Carried to an extreme, those who believe that names are destiny—*"Nomen est omen"*—and interpret coincidence as magic find it unremarkable that someone named Scratch should be a dermatologist; Sleis, a butcher; Peake, a roofer; Sipper, a soft-drink magnate; Charles Hartwell Bonesteel, a military commander; Sir Ronald Brain, a neurophysiologist. Umberto Eco, eminent student of signs and symbols and author of *The Name of the Rose* and other international best-sellers, says that his surname is an acrostic derived from *"Ex caelis oblatus,"* Latin for "offered by the heavens." Like Eco, the others are all real people, not invented, but, of course, the argument doesn't account for all the similarly named people who ended up doing something quite different, and this, in turn, suggests an opposite conclusion. Names carry no more weight in governing an extended personal history than any other trait, physical or emotional, and perhaps less, although it would be gratifying to have one as apt as those just cited. It seems that, finally, so long as namers—mother, father, or both parents—remain within certain boundaries of taste, convention, common sense, and creativity, the names we end up with are what we make of them and not the other way around.

The names-are-destiny argument figures notably in Laurence Sterne's eighteenth-century novel *Tristram Shandy.* Tristram's father, Walter Shandy ("shandy," by the way, carries the meaning of "half-crazy") believed that "there was a strange kind of magick bias, which good or bad names, as he called them, irresistibly impressed upon our characters and conduct." "How many Caesars and Pompeys," he would say, "by mere inspiration of the names, have been rendered worthy of them? And how many . . . are there, who might have done exceedingly well in the world, had not their characters and spirits been totally depressed and *Nicodemus'd* into nothing?" A child called something "neutral," like Jack, Dick, Tom, or Bob, could turn out to be either a fool or a sage, a knave or a good man. William stood "pretty high"; Andrew was "like a negative quality in Algebra"; while "of all the names in the universe, he had the most unconquerable aversion for Tristram . . . unison to *Nincompoop.*" If you named the child Judas (or Iago or Adolf), in all probability "the sordid and treacherous idea, so inseparable from the name, would have accompanied him through life like his shadow, and, in the end, made a miser and a rascal of him."

Father Shandy's argument holds a certain amount of water, especially for parents looking beyond the cradle into the future of their offspring. Your name is not necessarily your fate, but it's something you've got to live with all the same, just as Shandy's son, Tristram, had to live with a name the father loathed but for some "malignant" and perverse reason foisted on the infant.

In line with these general principles about "magick bias," a group of British psychologists asked their subjects to rank a list of first names by positive and negative traits. The consensus was: John is trustworthy and kind; Robin, young (as in A. A. Milne's Christopher Robin, "forever young"); Tony, sociable; Ann, non-aggressive; Agnes, old (as in David Copperfield's prudent, grave, and sisterly second wife, Agnes Wickfield); Matilda, definitely unattractive. Other studies put Michael, James, and Wendy in the active category; Afreda, Percival, and Isadore in the passive category.

Without thinking about it, many people are convinced that first names send out fervid, compressed messages: "Watch out for me," "Come closer," "Vote for me," "Buy my product," "Marry me," "Call the cops." Daily soap operas on television in particular rely on this primitive antenna system. The systematic study of names used in television dramas is relatively new; its results reinforce this unnuanced reading of the language of names. Until very recently soap operas rigidly upheld the prevailing social order and gender roles. For instance, a "bad" woman's true character is signaled by the fact that her name has been masculinized, so that thoroughly rotten Phyllis becomes Phil; Jacqueline, Jackie; and Martha, Marty. The reasoning goes that these women, having challenged society's basic and enduring values by parading around in men's (nick)names, are more likely to turn to crime and misdemeanor than those content with their pretty girls' names.

One 1992 study of names in television administered a questionnaire to about two hundred undergraduates at SUNY–Stony Brook. They were asked to match character traits with names of characters in soap operas that had been aired some years earlier (in order to reduce the possibility that memory would influence the answers). Here are two of the questions:

1. Which of the following is the most educated?
   a. Andrea Wolcot
   b. Kathy Brannon
   c. Ruby Daniel
   d. Elisa Asler

2. If you wanted to have a character who was a preppie, young, blond high school girl who was the only daughter of well-to-do parents and who was slightly spoiled, which

of the following would you name her?
a. Lillian McNeal
b. Marina Sheldon
c. Kimberly Channing
d. Karen Coleman

The answers. To the first question: Andrea Wolcot, doctor and radical feminist, was the most educated; Kathy and Elisa were waitresses; Ruby, a black jazz singer. To the second question: Kimberly Channing was the correct choice; Lillian was married to a New York cop; Marina was a gypsy con woman; while Karen was the widow of a rich pharmaceutical manufacturer. Among other television characters, those who have achieved financial success had fancy names like Avery, Bret, and Andrea. Bumblers and stumblers along life's pathways were apt to have cropped names like Ken, John, and Joe. Israel Sanchez (what do you get when you marry a Jew and a Latino?) turned up murdered. Stanley Nitski was a criminal, as was Clyde Regan. Jewish-sounding names were often given to people who commit crimes or are, at the very least, sleazy. Writers for television count on a basic transaction in which viewers pick up on such subliminal clues as the connection between "inappropriate" names and unacceptable behavior.

In 1965 an enterprising sorehead named Harvey Edwards somehow managed to organize 150 other Harveys to protest a series of television commercials featuring a klutz named Harvey who was always ankle deep in soapy water, having failed to operate the washing machine properly. These 150 Harveys hassled sponsors and advertising agencies into bagging the offensive commercials. The people who had given top billing to a loser named Harvey were at the very least subliminally aware that certain names give off a disagreeable odor, as if a cat had peed in the hallway. Harvey not only isn't as robust as, say, Robert, Sebastian, or William but brings to mind the mild-mannered rabbit —imaginary playmate to a hopeless drunk—in Mary C. Chase's 1944 play. It would probably take a famous Harvey with the personality of General George S. Patton, Jr., to alter the psychic image most of us form when we hear the name Harvey.

Some years ago researchers in Chicago discovered that about half the men in prison referred by the courts for psychiatric evaluation had peculiar names like Oder and Lethal. (Add to this list Sid Vicious of the Sex Pistols, the rocker who stabbed his female companion to death in Room 100 of New York's Chelsea Hotel.) Comparably, it's been argued that children with unpopular names turn out to be unpopular in school. It's reasonable to question, however, which first gave rise to the unpopularity—Bertha's name or her habit of wiping her runny nose on her sleeve, Homer's name or his tendency to snitch on his classmates. A group of grade school teachers, asked to grade essays turned out by students identified only by a first name, gave high marks to Karen, Lisa, David, and Michael (for almost the last fifty years the most popular boy's name in the United States, perhaps because "it goes with everything") and low marks to Elmer, Adele, Bertha, and Hubert, all of the latter deemed to be losers' names. But what about the children with rare, strange, or funny names who were popular with their schoolmates, favored by their teachers, and went on to notable careers? What about Senator, Vice President, and presidential candidate Hubert Horatio Humphrey (whom Jimmy Carter once introduced as Hubert Horatio Hornblower, confusing him with C. S. Forester's fictional hero)? What about the Pulitzer Prize–winning playwright Elmer Rice (né Reizenstein) and other men and women with "funny" first names who became eminent citizens or at least made a pile of money?

If it were possible to leach all meaning from a name, you would be left with pure sound—the smile of the Cheshire Cat. Sounds can be soft or sharp, protracted or brusque. They can be equally or unequally stressed. They can roll along merrily or wobble like a flat tire. All of this feeds into the ear's reaction to a name, some of it conscious, the rest under water. Although the heroine of one of his major poems is "the lovely lady Christabel," Samuel Taylor Coleridge thought girls ought to be given two-syllable trochaic names, that is, accented on the first syllable, as in Laura, Doris,

Emma (he named his only daughter Sara). Other name fanciers prefer the iamb, accented on the second syllable: Annette, Maureen. Then there are the advocates of the trisyllabic, with the accent on the first syllable, as in Abigail and Eleanor. Each kind of sound has its supporters, but it's silly to worry about a first name without considering what comes after it. Ideally, first and last names should meet and marry to create a strong, supple, melodic line. If your last name is a monosyllable like Jones and you can't do anything about it short of changing it, you probably ought to give your child a longer, more fluid first name, like Jeremy for a boy, Margaret or Elizabeth for a girl.

Fashions differ from region to region in the United States, but if one were to arrive at a national consensus (based on 1994–1995 figures) of the most popular boys' and girls' names for whites, blacks, Hispanics, and Asians together, it would read roughly like this, with the rankings varying somewhat by region:

Boys
Michael (number one since about 1960): Hebrew, "Who is like God?"
Kevin: Gaelic, diminutive of "comely, beloved." In 1994–1995 the most popular name for Hispanic boys in New York City and for Asian boys there and in San Francisco and Florida.
Christopher: Greek, "bearing Christ."
Joshua: Hebrew, "God is salvation."
Matthew: Hebrew, "gift of God."
Brandon: Old English, "gorse hill."
Andrew: Greek, after one of the twelve apostles.
Girls
Ashley: Old English, "ash" plus "wood." In 1994–1995 the most popular name for all girls in New York City, Texas, and Florida.
Stephanie: French, feminine form of Stephen.
Brittany: Latin, "Britain."
Jessica: Hebrew, "Iscah" (Abraham's niece).

Amanda: Latin, "worthy of being loved."
Sarah: Hebrew, "princess."
Emily: Latin, probably from *aemulus,* "rival."

Over the past twenty-five years, Jeffrey and Jennifer have suffered the steepest declines in popularity.

A patient of Dr. Oliver Sacks, Carl Bennett, suffered from Tourette's syndrome, a condition in which the victim is compelled, through some neurological anomaly, to repeat words (often obscene or offensive) over and over again, to his or her public embarrassment. Bennett craved new sounds to sing out, especially names, the way a child craves sweets, and he called his list of more than two hundred real names of real people "candy for the mind." Among the earliest entries were Oginga Odinga and Slavek J. Hurka. He insisted that the names he repeated in his fits of echolalia were meaningless; he was attracted to them only for their sound: Boris Blank, Floyd Flake, Morris Gook, Lubor J. Zink were among his short, staccato favorites. Yelberton A. Tittle and Babaloo Mandel were more complicated and, Sacks wrote, marked by "euphonious polysyllabic alliterations." Echolaling might not be a bad idea for parents trying out names for their offspring.

The comical name of Ima Hogg (1882–1975), philanthropist and community leader, has generated two virtually unkillable stories: one, that she had a sister, Ura (not true—she had no sister, and her brothers had ordinary names: William, Michael, Thomas); and, two, that her father, Texas governor James Stephen Hogg, named her Ima Hogg so she wouldn't be vain about her looks (also not true: Ima was the heroine of an epic poem written by one of her uncles). Ima and Ura Hogg, meanwhile, continue to keep company with Ophelia Butt, I. Seymour Hare, I. P. Daly, Claude Balls, and such jokey phantoms.

Some parents, like Ima Hogg's father, are oblivious to secondary meanings or simply have tin ears and can't tell the difference between sounds that sing and those that squeak like chalk on a blackboard or thud like a ripe tomato landing on the kitchen floor: Stanley Conley and Martin Hensen, for example, are like dissonances in music or bad off-rhymes. The ear tends to be vexed but also captivated by names composed of two monosyllables. Sean Penn, James Joyce, Hale Boggs, James Bond, John Wayne—these work quite well, but possibly the best-worst name ever in this category is Shane Stant; he was the youth hired by the husband of skater Tanya Harding to break the kneecap of her rival on ice, Nancy Kerrigan.

Before you name your child, it's a good idea to view your options from implausible as well as expected angles. Will his or her initals create a funny acronym, like Francis Albert Gilman's? As soon as his classmates learn to read, they'll figure it out and know what to call him. Or Barbara Upshaw Grasso? Once there was a young American boy whose first two names were John Thomas. When his family moved briefly to Australia, he came home from school every day in tears. What his parents didn't know was that John Thomas is British and Australian slang for penis. Someone should have told them to read *Lady Chatterley's Lover* before they took off for down under.

A new firm, Whatchamacallit, working out of Boston and San Francisco, is in the business of naming other firms and products. "The whole point of the Rumpelstiltskin story is that when you have the right name for a thing, you have control over it," said Sam Birger, one of the partners. "Starting with Adam, there's a long history of people doing my job." Whatchamacallit's founders, Birger and Danny Altman, are psycholinguists who understand that "a name should be recognizable and intelligible, but sometimes being memorable has nothing to do with sense." One such name, coined by the inventor George Eastman in 1888, is Kodak, a neologism that works extremely well without meaning anything at all, while associations of vigor, directness, and reliability spin off it like energy from the sun. Eastman favored the letter *K,* he said, while Birger liked *X* because it's underused. This is why, he claimed, the names Exxon, NYNEX, and Xerox (not to mention Malcolm X) stick in the memory.

Similar in function to Whatchamacallit, Namelab, a San Francisco–based company specializing in constructional linguistics since 1981, carefully lays out the theoretical and procedural principles they follow in developing new company, product, and service names like Acura, Compaq, Lumina, and Zapmail. They begin with an input statement, the message the client wants to convey, and break it down into morphemes, indivisible, irreducible linguistic units—"semantic kernels"—of which American English has nearly sixty-two hundred, by Namelab's count. (The "van" in the word "advantage," for example, is a morpheme that means "front of," "top of," or "leading edge of.") Namelab combines morphemes into candidate names, genuine neologisms that are then evaluated for "speechstream visibility" (how they will be recognized in normal speech), "notational visibility" (how they will read in print), "phonetic transparency" (how easily they are pronounced), and "multilingual function" (how well they travel across language borders).[1] It would be interesting to know what sort of advice Whatchamacallit and Namelab would be able to give new or prospective parents and what these parents would write in their input statements.

Herbert Barry III, a University of Pittsburgh psychologist, has studied what he called, in a 1964 paper, "Phonetic Differentiation of Popular First Names of Boys and Girls." He reported:

> The 100 most frequent first names of boys and girls born in Pennslyvania in 1960 and 1990 were each given a quantitative phonetic score, which is the sum of several phonetic attributes. Criteria for a high score, which is associated with names of girls rather than boys, are three or more syllables, accent after the first syllable, and the last phoneme being a vowel, especially the *schwa* sound, such as Melissa. Mean phonetic scores of names of both sexes were higher for the

most popular names in 1990 than in 1960. This difference is consistent with a recent increase in acceptance of feminine attributes.

Barry has been working on names for many years. His scoring system is elaborate and somewhat daunting. Example: a rating of minus one means a name must have an obstruent consonant, subcategorized into fricative (*f, v, th, s, z,* or *sh* sounds—as in Joseph, Kenneth, James), affricative (*ch* or *j* sounds—as in George), and plosive (*p, b, t, d, k,* or *g* sounds—as in Philip, Caleb, Craig). The obstruent consonant is only one of four components of Barry's scoring system. His work involves analyzing the sounds inside names to pick up characteristics associated with gender. He concluded, on the basis of this well-tempered analysis, that names have softened, becoming more feminine over the long haul. That is, there are fewer on the minus side and more on the plus—the plus side being more female than male. There isn't a single boy's name on either the 1960 or the 1990 list that rates higher than a three, the score for Joshua, which ends in what Barry would deem a feminine schwa, or schwalike exhalation: "ah." Almost no boys' names end with an "ah" sound, while this is a common feature in girls' names—for example, Rebecca, Cynthia, Lisa, Maria.

Barry is on the right track: for almost one hundred years names have been moving toward the middle, that is, the androgynous. Traditionally masculine names like Shawn (and its cousin Sean), Robin, Chris, Toby, Tracy, Lee, Leslie, Billie, Bobbie, Jaime, Carey, and the unavoidable Michael are far more common for girls nowadays than, say, one hundred years ago, when women didn't wear trousers either, or swear, smoke, or spend the night in a man's abode. Among traditionally feminine names for boys are Carol, Evelyn, Jocelyn, Vivian, Joyce, Kelly, Kerry, and Lynn. Shannon, Courtney, Jody, Terry, and Dana are genderless or sexually ambiguous.

Philosophically, unisex or crossover names suggest equality,

but in practice they enhance confusion and make life more difficult for people who feel the need to identify gender. How do we
know whether to address Lee Snyder as Ms. or Mr. when writing
to him/her or asking for him/her over the telephone? Some feminists would no doubt counter with, "What difference does it
make? When we approach true equality between the sexes, we'll
dress alike, work at identical jobs, and have names mercifully
free of sexist data." And yet these same people would be the first
to protest when both Lee and Shawn turn out to be males and the
program, class, or other kind of group ends up with more guys
than girls. Androgynous names look good on paper, but when you
try to work with them without matching them up with the people
they belong to, you may run into trouble.

In 1900 those masters of the rational and orderly, the Germans,
compiled a manual called *The Law of Names* and made it part of
the civil code. Almost a century later, Hans Peter Hainen, who
works in the registry department of the Bonn city administration,
published a short monograph, also called *The Law of Names,*
designed to serve as a guide to past and present regulations.
Among other features of the German code under Hitler was a list
of first names to be used exclusively for Jewish newborns. Adults
who were readily identifiable as Jews by their last names were
forbidden by law to change them; those who weren't readily
identifiable had to take Israel or Sarah as a middle name.[2] (Present-day French practice calls for Jewish children to have either a
first or middle name from the Old Testament, and for Christian
children, a first or middle name from the Calendar of Saints).
There are still many ways that Germans must bend to the will of
the state when naming their children, legitimate and otherwise, or
themselves when they marry or have a sex-change operation.
"In Germany," said Hainen, "the gender of the child must be
recognizable from the first name." Junior, Jr., and Jun. are verbo-
ten, as are Hemingway, Jesus, and Woodstock as first names,
according to recent legal rulings. The most popular current names
for boys, in what used to be West Germany, are Alexander, Dan-

iel, and Maximilian; for girls, Julia, Katharina, and Maria. Their counterparts in former East Germany are Philipp, Maximilian, and Paul; Lisa, Maria, and Julia.

Official imperatives and proscriptions strike the American psyche as odd and unnerving. But we do the same thing, within a slightly different context. The following names were some of thirty-nine permanently retired by the National Hurricane Center because they had once belonged to the worst, most havoc-wreaking hurricanes: Agnes (1972), Bob (1991), Camille (1969), Gilbert (1988). According to *The New York Times,* they were retired in order to "avoid confusion in legal actions, insurance claims, studies, and other documents that arise in the storm's aftermath." Lurking beneath this reasonable explanation may be the idea that Agnes, Camille, and the rest now have bad karma. "Batten down the hatches, head for high ground, here comes Agnes again!"

The word "nickname" compresses the Middle English "an eke-name," meaning "an additional (or supplementary) name" ("eke" as in "eke out a living"). Nicknames have a much longer history than surnames, which in many cases themselves derive from nicknames (Piers the baker and Jankyn the miller, for example, practiced their trades in the age of Chaucer and sired a long line of modern men and women surnamed Baker and Miller). We tend to think of nicknames as being slightly frivolous, even though they carry more freight than birth names; they describe, record, imply, deride, or deplore something specific about the person to whom they are attached. Birth names, on the other hand, mainly say something about the people who attach them.

Some nicknames are tokens of genuine trust and familiarity, inner (or secret) names offered only to a few close friends. So-called pet names, or hypocorisms, a kitchen variety of nicknames, are often related to food or eating: Lambchop, Sweetie Pie, Honeybunch, Sweetpea, Cupcake, Dumpling. While these names imply intimacy and can be uttered in the dark, for one pair of ears only, they are actually impersonal and generic, as there's nothing about them that distinguishes one Sweetie Pie (or Pussycat) from another. There are also nursery mispronunciations that carry over into adulthood, like Decca for the Honorable Jessica Mitford. Girls in private schools acquire cute nicknames like Muffy, Bibsy, Cissy, Moo-face, and Tigger, evidence of a kind of upper-class Peter Panism a few are lucky enough to outgrow. Some—Lard Ass, Stinky, Four Eyes, Shorty, Red—are closer to epithets, but not so allusive as Cal (for Caligula, itself a nickname, meaning "Little Boot"), the poet Robert Lowell's unshakable nickname. Others are public nicknames that are used for reference rather than address. You might say, "Hello, Yogi," to Lawrence Berra, but you would be an idiot to say, "Hello, Yankee Clipper," to Joe DiMaggio. Whether or not Grimm's originally unnamed seven dwarfs, as they appear in Walt Disney's 1938 movie, bear true first names or more sobriquets, it's hard to imagine this septet, who often turn up as the answer to a trivia quiz, as being, for example, Larry, Bill, Kenneth, Charlie, Frank, Marvin, Tom. It just wouldn't work. Edging close to the unbearably cute, these walking positives and negatives manage to dominate Disney's full-length cartoon feature by behaving exactly as their names suggest—until the moment when Grumpy smiles at Snow White, breaking the rules and humanizing all seven at once.

Aristocles, an Athenian aristocrat born in the fifth century B.C. and endowed with pronounced philosophic and discursive inclinations, has been known ever since as Plato, a reference to his broad forehead and shoulders (from the Greek *platys,* meaning flat). The roster of Renaissance artists might puzzle anyone unable to recognize Alessandro di Mariano Filipepi as Botticelli (little barrel), Paolo Caliari as Veronese (Verona was his hometown), Jacopo Robusti as Tintoretto (little dyer, from his father's trade), or Domenikos Theotokopoulos as El Greco (the Greek, even though he was a Cretan who lived in Spain). The nicknames of early rulers of England and Great Britain are a series of capsule histories: Alfred the Great, Edward the Martyr, Aethelred the Unready, Harold Harefoot, Edward the Confessor, William the Conqueror, Richard the Lion-hearted.

Nineteenth-century Americans sent Old Hickory, Old Rough and Ready, and Honest Abe to the White House, their nicknames suggesting an imagined democratic familiarity of the sort enjoyed by people who never met Ernest Hemingway but still refer to him as Papa. The golden age of nicknames came during the first half of the present century, with celebrity criminals and their henchmen making up a rich array of colorfully named antiheroes: Pretty Boy Floyd, Baby Face Nelson, Machine Gun Kelly, Dutch Schultz (born Arthur Flegenheimer), Ma Barker, Lucky Luciano, Bugsy Siegal, Alphonse "Scarface" Capone, his brother Ralph (known as Bottles), and an array of professional killers that included Seymour "Blue Jaw" Magoon, Jacob "Greasy Thumb" Guzik, Martin "Muggsy" Goldstein, and Max "the Jerk" Colob. Any ballplayer named Webb or Rhodes is bound to be nicknamed Spider or Dusty. Some nicknames lead to comical confusions. This was the case with Mrs. Henry Parish 2d (born Dorothy May Kinnicutt), the society interior decorator known in her family, and later in the trade, as Sister Parish; she once figured in a page-one newspaper story headlined: "Kennedys Pick Nun to Decorate White House."

Knowing the derivation of a nickname is like getting an allusion in a poem, song, movie, painting, and so forth. You're the richer for it, as when you're clued into the fact that Leroy "Satchel" Paige earned his nickname because he had once landed in jail for stealing a bag in a railroad station; or that pop singer Gordon Sumner got his professional name, Sting, when he showed up at rehearsal wearing a black and yellow striped sweater that made him look like a wasp; or that British master spy Harold Adrian Russell Philby was given the nickname Kim by his father because the old man admired the hero of Rudyard Kipling's *Kim,* a boy who played his part as a spy in the "Great Game" of British struggle with Russia for control of India and central Asia. Young Philby grew up to be a spy who played a game so complex we don't know for sure whether he was a double or a triple agent.

Nicknames, as H. L. Mencken demonstrated in his classic

study, *The American Language,* are a defining feature of the nation's vernacular culture. "All the States have nicknames, and some have more than one," he wrote, citing familiar examples such as Old Dominion (Virginia), Empire State (New York), and Nutmeg State (Connecticut). As for cities and inhabitants, "rough popular humor" yields Chicagorillas, Baltimorons, Omahogs, and Louisvillains. These supplement Whitman's catalogue of Civil War usages, at least half a dozen of them still current:

Those from Maine were call'd Foxes; New Hampshire, Granite Boys; Massachusetts, Bay Staters; Vermont, Green Mountain Boys; Rhode Island, Gun Flints; Connecticut, Wooden Nutmegs; New York, Knickerbockers; New Jersey, Clam Catchers; Pennsylvania, Logher Heads; Delaware, Muskrats; Maryland, Claw Thumpers; Virginia, Beagles; North Carolina, Tar Boilers; South Carolina, Weasels; Georgia, Buzzards; Louisiana, Creoles; Alabama, Lizards; Kentucky, Corn Crackers; Ohio, Buckeyes; Michigan, Wolverines; Indiana, Hoosiers; Illinois, Suckers; Missouri, Pukes; Mississippi, Tad Poles; Florida, Fly up the Creeks; Wisconsin, Badgers; Iowa, Hawkeyes; Oregon, Hard Cases.

Paul Leslie and James K. Skipper, Jr., academic investigators in a field they call socio-onomastics, maintain that many nicknames have an "internal rationality" that can be understood only if you're aware of "situational and contextual exigencies," or, in other words, how they came to be. Leslie and Skipper cited the example of a professional athlete, Joan Emerson, a shortstop in the All-American Girls' Professional League, who became known during her playing career as Venus. With a runner on first, a batted ball took an erratic bounce off Joan's head into the glove of the second basewoman, who made the out and threw to first base to complete a textbook 6-4-3 double play. "For her part in this play," Leslie and Skipper reported, "and because of the unique circumstances under which it occurred, her teammates dubbed her *Venus* after Venus de Milo, the famous statue that has no arms." They vouch for this as they do for a story about another professional shortstop, a rookie named John Barney Miller. He was known as Dots because a teammate who had a thick German accent, when asked who the new kid was, answered "Dot's Miller." Drawing on his own experience, Skipper gave this example of the "social robustness of names and the naming process" as they played themselves out in a faculty meeting:

> A colleague went into the meeting expecting Skipper to be supportive of a particular proposal. At the beginning of the meeting, the colleague addressed him as *Skip* (his public nickname), conveying to those who were present friendship, familiarity, and perhaps even expected support. But as the meeting developed, it became clear that Skipper was unwilling to support the position of his colleague. It was not long before the colleague was addressing him as *Jim*. By the end of the meeting the nickname and first name form of address had totally disappeared and his colleague now referred to him openly as *Professor Skipper.*

According to Skipper and Leslie, over the past hundred years there has been a decline in the use of public nicknames like Stonewall Jackson, the Swedish Nightingale, Vinegar Joe Stilwell, and Ike Eisenhower. They attribute this in part to "the decline of the folk hero in popular American culture," which may be true, but only to the extent that folk heroes, with the exception of an occasional Mafia godfather, don, or capo thrown in for variety, now tend to be mainly sports figures. They have nicknames like O.J. (also known as Juice) and Refrigerator; Dizzy, Daffy, and Ducky; Catfish, Mudcat, and Oil Can; Schoolboy, Preacher, and Big Train; the Rocket and Charlie Hustle; Peewee and Duke; and, of course, Babe.

7.
A Boy Named Sue
and Others

*I was Timmy then; now I'm Tim. But the essence remains
the same. . . . Inside the body, or beyond the body, there is
something absolute and unchanging.*

Tim O'Brien, *The Things They Carried*

In 1918 a bigwig in the Freudian establishment, Dr. Clarence
P. Oberndorf, published an article titled "Reactions to Personal
Names" in *Psychoanalytical Review.* Dr. Oberndorf used his initials, C.P., rather than his full name, when he signed this remarkable contribution to knowledge. He probably figured that C.P.
sounded more muscular and authoritative than Clarence, which
may suggest someone who mends gloves or winds clocks. C.P.
started out by declaring that

> the name a person bears is often a determining factor in
> influencing definite psychic reactions, such as scorn, pride
> or shame, upon the person himself. Such a tendency is exem-
> plified by the remark of one of my youthful patients, in a
> profound depression, "My name is Chrystal and I should be
> pure"—a comment which, by the way, revealed the gist of
> his depression.

C.P. presented several cases to illustrate how name and identity
are as one. A nineteen-year-old patient so detested his name,

Leroy, for being sissy that he "blushed whenever he mentioned it." Leroy had remained a "spoilt baby," a stage he was unable to outgrow because he was protesting "against a quality which he felt to be very strong in himself and revealed by his name." Next we encounter a young man named Aristarchos Panthos, answering to Harry, the name his boss had given him because his real name was too foreign sounding. The patient hated his last name, loved his first, an emotion that "began early—probably when his rivalry and hatred of his father, now undisguised, was still in its most rudimentary stages. He recalls the flush of pride which he experienced even as a little boy, when in calling him to return home from his play, his father would sing out, 'Oh, Aristarchos.' " Common sense would dictate that this would make the little tyke love his dad. But no, there were other, sinister forces at work:

> The patient's fondness for Aristarchos in antithesis to his dislike for Panthos is a reflection of the typical father rival complex. As the patient's love for his youthful mother (35 years younger than his father) has assumed a frank conscious sexual aspect, it is quite natural that he should hate the man who possesses her and the name which he (and she) bears (Panthos).

(Poor Aristarchos apparently couldn't figure out who in the family should wear the Panthos.)

Dr. Oberndorf saved the best for last: a stunning case in which "the repugnance [to a name] reverts to infantile echolalia which represents one of the earliest forms of rhythmic muscle and mucous membrane eroticism." "Robert 'Braun,' a [German-American] patient under analysis for a psycho-neurosis, could 'never stand' his Christian name. It appears," wrote C.P., "that the origin of his antagonism may be traced to the period when he acquired the first rudiments of sound expression." A chilling narrative then unfolded: It was seven years before the next child in the family was born—Robert was the baby for a long time, and he identified himself as "bay-bee." So far so good. "Inasmuch as 'Bob-bee' and 'bay-bee' were one and the same," the child probably used the two words interchangeably. "Before long," commented C.P. vaguely, Robert picked up yet another name: B.B., his initials. "Thus presently the echolalia incorporated these three pet names, now assuming the serial form: Bob-bee, bay-bee, bee-bee (B.B., *i.e.,* Bobbie Braun)."

Although they lived in the United States, Robert's family still used German expressions, one of which was *bo-bo,* a variant of *po-po,* for posterior parts, or buttocks. "Accordingly, with this amplification of his echolalia, the sounds produced by the little boy, then about four years old, assumed this form: Bob-bee (Bobbie), Bay-bee (Baby), Bee-bee (B.B.), Bo-bo (Behind)."

And what happened to Robert, by this time thoroughly confused, all those sounds mixed up together and forming a disgusting hodgepodge in his infantile brain? Why, he turned to anal-erotic ("Bo-bo") activities and became addicted to little sneaky acts. "Robert's sexual life (bo-bo activities) until manhood consisted of constant clandestine indulgences, while to his family he maintained the semblance of chastity. In other words," Dr. Oberndorf concluded on a note of triumph, "he persisted in being Bobbitzky (stealthy) with his bo-bo." Psychoanalysis hasn't made much progress with such matters. Forty years after Oberndorf's pioneering report, an article in the professional journal *American Imago* argued that the very act of naming expresses a basic hostility, which may explain why the elder Mr. Shandy named his infant son Tristram.

When you name the baby, you're imposing what you believe you see in her, project for her, wish her to become—or him. Because infants have so few characteristics that set them apart from other newborns, naming them is, in one sense, as meaningless as giving a name to a puddle on the sidewalk; naming a suckling is an exercise in either wishful or dutiful thinking. Not many mothers are so anxious about naming the baby as the writer Megan Marshall, who in a 1984 issue of *New Age Journal* worried that she had misnamed her firstborn, a girl. "Is this child . . . really a Sara?" It doesn't occur to most mothers to fret over whether the child and its name are an appropriate match. For one thing, new mothers are too busy and too tired. And for another, they're probably pleased with the name they have given their baby; it's self-reflexive and satisfies a natural narcissism.

When the authors of this book, both born and raised in New York City, decided to move to New England, they named their second daughter Hester, an act of self-indulgence that ignored the likelihood she might not appreciate either its singularity or its association with the adulterous heroine of Nathaniel Hawthorne's *The Scarlet Letter.* Hester, now in her thirties, admitted for the first time recently that throughout her childhood she hated her first name, not for its sound or associations but because most people, having (unaccountably) never heard it before, called her Esther or Heather. "It wasn't my name; it was as if they didn't know who I was." In her view, "Hester" deserved not an A but a C minus. Most of us, in the first flush and excitement of parenthood, don't consider the possible side effects of the names we thrust so enthusiastically on adorable babies.

Bernays and Kaplan had been slightly more deliberative when naming their first child Susanna; in fact, five discrete elements were compressed into this one name. The first element was Bernays's grandmother's name, Anna, for whom Bernays herself was named. The second was her parents' admiration for Mozart's opera *The Marriage of Figaro,* whose main female character is Susanna. The third was Bernays's curtsy to Suzanne, the mother of a school friend at whose house she had spent a great deal of time as a child. Element number four was their decision to give their child a biblical name. This is the famous Susanna, spied on while bathing by some prurient elders who had nothing better to do. The final element involved sound: it should have three syllables and should complement Kaplan (insofar as this is possible) by having the stress on the second syllable and ending in a schwa.

Megan Marshall said, "I hated having the kind of name you

had to spell out for strangers." At first, this seems a point well taken, until you realize that most of us have to spell out our names for strangers: "Anne—with an *e* at the end, please." "Justin— that's Jay You Ess Tee Eye En." Susanna? Could be Susannah, Suzanna, Susana, Suzannah. We know a Polly once rendered on a Boston hospital admission record as Paulie. But it wasn't just the spelling of her name that troubled Marshall. She learned, she said, to avoid toy store displays of "bicycle license plates and lunchboxes stenciled with BETTY's, CAROL's, and DIANE's." Being different—and that includes bearing an unusual name— makes children uneasy. "Inwardly," Marshall said, reaching to touch the heart of the matter of name and identity, "I feared I was as weird as my name." What she didn't say is that having an unfamiliar name does not automatically make you a victim. Megan and Hester are beautiful names, suggesting substance and delicacy at the same time. But tell that to a little girl who goes to school with Jennifers, Debbies, and Dianes. "Despite our best intentions, choosing a name is probably the time when most modern parents give in to sexism," Marshall said. "We draw the line at giving our sons fanciful names that might brand them as sissies"—like Dr. Oberndorf's patient Leroy. Marshall wound up by admitting that she gave her baby an "ordinary" name so that she wouldn't feel more self-conscious than any other child.

Parents who give their children peculiar names fall into one of several categories. Some are nonconformists and want their offspring to follow their example. However unconsciously, others may be voicing a slightly sadistic sense of humor or just plain hostility, like the father in Shel Silverstein's ballad "A Boy Named Sue":

Well, my daddy left home when I was three,
And didn't leave much to Ma and me,
Just this old guitar and an empty bottle of booze.
Now I don't blame him because he run and hid,
But the meanest thing he ever did was
Before he left, he went and named me Sue.[1]

Sue vows to "kill that man that gave me that awful name." On the other hand, the late Carter Burden, christened Shirley Carter Burden, Jr., simply dropped the Shirley (and the Jr.) when he ran for office in New York City.

What do we think of parents who give all their children names starting with the same letter? Is this solipsistic, as some psychologists insist, or does the initial letter act as a kind of familial glue? Now consider the extreme case of prizefighter George Foreman, who named every one of his four sons George. We tend to laugh when we hear this, neglecting to ponder the hideous effect it must have had on the boys. Naming them One, Two, Three, and Four would have been preferable, because at least they are different words. Most people wouldn't dream of giving an entire litter of pups the same name, yet here was this man so in love with himself that he did his best to erase the first thing after gender that sets one child in a family apart from his siblings: his name. It puts one in mind of pictures that used to run in the Sunday edition of your local paper, eleven girls in a row, holding their stiff little handbags, wearing identical starchy outfits stitched together by Mom. Unfortunately, names are not clothes; they cannot be easily removed and dropped on the floor. The four junior Georges are burdened—for life?—by a father who obviously mistook his children for his clones.

You can read behavior like the senior George Foreman's as just this side of cruelty. Another example involves a University of Arizona microbiologist, Charles (Chuck) Gerba, whose field is domestic germs. Germs on the dish sponge and the refrigerator door handle. Germs in the bathroom (when you flush the toilet, Gerba advises you to jump to one side if you don't want zillions of germs to fly up your nose), germs on the pillow. Germs crawling all over the telephone receiver. Germs ubiquitous. If you took Dr. Gerba literally, you would go around spraying disinfectant before you touched anything in your house. The germ specialist named his son Peter Escherichia Gerba. The middle name is arcane enough so that most people who see and hear it will probably think it's a family name, perhaps Spanish. But scientists

will immediately recognize that Escherichia is the *E.* in *E. coli,*
an occasionally fatal stomach germ that gives its victim terrible
cramps and diarrhea. Why would a man name his son after a
lethal bacterium? Could this be a joke? Maybe Peter is so in tune
with his father's sense of humor that he not only does not mind
but positively enjoys his middle name. (Coincidentally, the author
of an article about the Gerbas, "How to Win at Germ Warfare,"
is named Mary Roach.)

A single college faculty roster contained the following odd
names: Sherlock Bronson Gass, Enger Kathryn Lenore Robert-
son, Rodney Waldo Bliss, Prosser Hall Frye, Melanchthon B.
Posson, Berthus Boston McInteer, Rizpah Anna Douglas. In spite
of one's initial shock, there's a temptation to say, "So what?"
because these names don't seem to have caused the people who
bear them any permanent damage. They must have ignored snig-
gers and smiles as they went about achieving what they had to in
order to qualify as scholars and teachers.

Child development expert Lee Salk was convinced that "parents who give their kids weird names are weird themselves." The
mother who named her daughter Stonewall Jackson, the father
who blessed his four sons by giving them the same name, the
deadbeat dad in "A Boy Named Sue": by Salk's standards they're
all more than a little mental. Even so, are grievously misnamed
children necessarily destined to trip and fall as they grow up?
There's more than enough evidence to demonstrate a causal connection between an odd name and emotional instability. But wait
—a name isn't something you can remove and isolate from all
the other influences that propel a person toward a good or a rotten
life. It's not the name so much as the atmosphere you grow up
breathing and absorbing in a million different ways every day.
Dad's romance with booze, Mom's screaming fits, big brother's
drug habit, auntie's bipolar disorder. Even the dog in such a
family pees on the dining room rug.

You can't read Lethal's psychopathic behavior backward and
blame it solely on his name, even taking into account the mockery
he must have suffered at the hands of his mates. But is there a

single boy or girl who hasn't had to prevail over a manifest or imagined handicap? The child with kinky hair called Brillo by her straight-haired classmates, the boy with a lisp or jug ears, the girl with a limp, the twins whose mother sends them to school identically overdressed, the boy so shy he can barely say hello, the adolescent with zits (Pizza-face), and so on—was there ever a child who didn't feel that one or more of her features was deformed, gross, totally unacceptable? Names simply get thrown atop the pile of things to focus on when you're feeling unlovely. I hate my hair, I hate my fat neck, I hate my name.

Apparently convinced from his study of faculty and armed service rolls that names shape destiny, a University of Nebraska professor, Wilbur Gaffney, has suggested

> two tentative rules for parents: 1. If you want your child to have the best chance of becoming an athletic coach, or an Army officer (especially if he is drafted), give him an extroverted name, such as Harry, Jack, Joe, or Tom. (On the other hand, if you want to help him reach staff level, by way of West Point, give him a professorial-type name; consider Dwight David Eisenhower and Lucius Dubignon Clay.) 2. If you want him to become a professor (or a writer, or an editor), give him one of the less usual names—for example, Wilfred, Eustace, or Kenneth. (For whatever reason, a surprising number of professors seem to be named Kenneth.) . . . If you want him (or, more likely, her) to be an artist, or to teach fine arts, provide an artistic-type name such as Ariadne Diana or Minella Clairene.

Professor Gaffney's rules hold about as much water as a colander. Following his logic, you might conclude that because most nuns wear glasses, it's a good idea to have bad eyesight if you want to enter the convent.

Investigators like Gaffney have gone to astonishing lengths in attempting to gauge the importance of a name on its bearer's life.

The literature includes studies in which, for example, names were rated on fifteen bipolar-adjective scales, like good-bad, overconfident-uncertain, and creative-uncreative. What's amazing is that there was 80 percent agreement on everything except masculine-feminine. Which serves to underscore the point that a name pulses with all sorts of overtones and undertones, shimmers with lights and darks, shadows, speaks with flickers of meaning and half meaning. But this is not to imply that if you name a child Winston, say, he's going to lead his country or that Wystan will be a poet. Still, there are questions to be asked about the role of names. Why, for example, is there such a large proportion of uncommonly named people in *Who's Who?* Perhaps it's because men and women of accomplishment have parents who are not much concerned with the latest fashion, the sort of nonconformists who name their baby Lincoln rather than Michael, Bernadette rather than Jennifer. This refusal to go along with the crowd is also reflected in the nature of the intellectual push and emotional support they give their children. It's all of a piece.

Very few people name their babies carelessly but are guided, consciously or unconsciously, by a variety of imperatives. They may like the sound or associations of a name, wish to please a relative or to commemorate someone living or dead. They may choose a name as a prophetic spur, hoping the child will emulate an example. Still other names are selected for the sake of family tradition and continuity, to make a political or ideological statement, or, as is the case with many American blacks, to invent something completely new and original. Finally, there are unformed, half-fetal and wholly unconscious or adventitous factors that determine the choice of one name over another.

The woman who in the 1960s named her child Tiffany—thinking, she said, of a "rare, precious jewel"—was upset when Tiffany became one of the most popular, even inescapable girls' names of the 1980s. The mother also complained that her child had "grown into" her name and had developed extremely expensive tastes. It's reasonable to ask whether the mother, having given her daughter the name of a jewelry store, wasn't passing her a message any moron could understand and should not have been surprised at her hunger for baubles.

An astonishing number of people require outside help when naming their infants. It's hard to imagine asking a stranger to suggest something as idiosyncratic and intimate as a name, but then a lot of people invite—and pay—decorators to furnish their houses, head to toe, not realizing that sofas and chairs, pictures, tables, and bric-a-brac are personal props and only they themselves can faithfully furnish their own rooms. Books on how to name the baby, some of them hardly more than page after page of names, their origin and meaning, sell the way self-help and New Age scripture do—by the millions. One of these is *The Best Baby Book in the Whole Wide World,* published in 1991, which lists that year's fifteen most popular names, starting with Michael, Matthew, Joshua, Ryan, and Nathan for boys and Jessica, Ashley, Amanda, Sarah, and Megan for the girls. These are an interesting mix of the Bible, pop culture (Ryan, for *Ryan's Hope;* Ashley, for Ashley Wilkes), and a whiff of nostalgia for the nineteenth century. In the thirties and forties the leaders were blander, less resonant names like Anne, Jane, Patricia, Barbara, George, Howard, Philip, and Robert. During the 1990s Justin was among the top eleven on the boys' list, a complete turnaround for a name that was virtually unheard of during the preceding five or six decades.

Christopher P. Andersen's *The Baby Boomer's Name Game,* published in 1987, divides names into categories that pick up on subliminal messages and associations: fat (Olga, for example) and thin (Sally), active (Jody) and passive (Boyd), winners (Janet) and losers (Elroy). This kind of game can get pretty silly. It's only when you're asked by a psychologist how you feel and what you think about a particular name that you're likely to articulate a response. But it's absurd to believe that on meeting an Elroy for the first time, you're going to say to yourself, "Boy, is this guy a loser!" Still, there are some piquant nuggets in Andersen's book. For instance, you'll learn that the ancient Egyptians believed a name had an existence of its own, separate from the person it belonged to. Suppose one day your name got fed up with your attitude and walked off the set? What would that leave you with?

By far the most engaging of the what-to-name-the-baby books is *Beyond Jennifer and Jason* by Linda Rosenkrantz and Pamela Redmond Satran. They have also turned out similar books specifically for Irish parents (*Beyond Shannon and Sean*), Jewish parents (*Beyond Sarah and Sam*), and Anglophile parents (*Beyond Charles and Diana*) seeking guidance. In what they subtitle "An Enlightened Guide," Rosenkrantz and Satran have fractured the usual categories and lists and reassessed the name pool in terms of what they call the "real world." Thus, they have divided the reservoir into four main categories—Style, Image, Sex, and Tradition—and within these are smaller subcategories such as "Volvo," "Creative Power," and "Wimpy" names; "The Hillary Era," "The Hundred Year Cycle," and "Into the Pool" (inspired by "foreign-born celebs" of the Elke Sommer and Nadia Comenici stripe). In each case the authors supply credible commentary, pros and cons, and fresh-eyed analysis. "Volvo names," for example, "are solid, dependable, trend-resistant, classy but not flashy, chic of the reverse kind." These names—Susannah, Isabel, George, and Henry, for instance—are like the skirts, sweaters, and low-heeled pumps purveyed by the Talbot's chain. They probably will never go out of fashion but could hardly be labeled trendy, like Maya and Zack.

The authors suggest choosing a name through the same sort of semiconscious process you embark on when furnishing a house or buying clothes, that is, remaining faithful to your own style. This seems so obvious you wonder why it needs articulating. Is this book written for people who may be unaware they possess a particular style, those who wouldn't know the difference between the feel of Tobias and that of Sven? And if they can't recognize their own style, what is *Beyond Jennifer and Jason* going to do for them except possibly throw them into more confusion than they're already in? This book sells like Pampers.

The easiest name to choose is the one bristling with imperatives. We must call him Paul because that's his father's name. She's Catholic and must be named after a saint. Here is Roger Welsch, a folklorist, writing in the magazine *Natural History:* "My children's names are heavy with family and cultural history. My youngest daughter is Antonia (after two ancestors and [Willa] Cather's fictional heroine) Emily (after two ancestors) Celestine (after a grandmother)." The Welsches, then, were limited in their choice of names by deference to several forebears, a common practice. Welsch warned that "one can go too far, loading a kid down with a meaning-drenched name." How far is too far? Celestine seems quite far if you measure by scarcity—she may never, in her entire life, run into another Celestine. But luckily Celestine has an amiable sound, reminding you of musical instruments and angels (cello, celesta, celestial). If Grandma's name had been Bertha, would Welsch's desire to honor her memory have been quite so urgent?

The pool of American given names has swollen like the Mississippi at flood time, suggesting that fewer people nowadays feel bound to honor a dead relative. During the late 1960s, when the counterculture was in full and fragrant bloom, hippie parents gave their children names that unmistakably identified them as their offspring. These tie-dye names complemented clothes that were vaguely Gypsy in feeling. Moondog went to school dressed in rainbow-hued gauze, carrying a lunch box packed by her mother, Sunflower, with homemade almond butter and honey on eight-grain bread, organically grown carrot strips, an apple, and a carob candy bar. Moondog's name transmitted a message as clear and strong as that of the little guy who sat next to her in class, Brinley Hall IV. In fact, their two names are cousins because both are on inference overload. "I'm Moondog—my parents question authority, do drugs, eschew underwear, and believe in flower power and pyramid power." "I'm the fourth—my family is American aristocracy. We believe in continuity and tradition." Since most people, at some point in their lives, do the opposite of what their parents expect them to do, one wonders what the Moondogs and all the others with hippie names did when they reached the age of rebellion. Did Seashell rename herself Amelia? Did Sunflower become Frances?

Given the opportunity, a lot of us would have chosen a name different from the one our parents gave us. Moreover, conventional wisdom says the less you like yourself, the less you like your name. It doesn't always work that way, but it does seem to be true that if you're unsure of or unhappy about your identity and your place in the world, you and your name feel like a bad match.

In Herb Gardner's 1962 play *A Thousand Clowns*, Murray, uncle of Nick, a young boy who has been left with him by a neglectful mother, tells a social worker,

> Not having given him a last name, [Nick's mother] felt reticent about assigning him a first one. When Nick first came here this presented a real difficulty. Nick answered to nothing whatsoever. Even the parakeet recognized its own name.

Murray goes on to explain that he had told Nick, "known rather casually as Chubby," that he could try on as many names as he wanted, until he was thirteen, at which time he would have to make a decision.

> He went through a long period of dog's names when he was still little, Rover and King having a real vogue there for a while. For three months he referred to himself as Big Sam, then there was Little Max, Snoopy, Chip, Rock, Rex, Mike, Marty, Lamont, Chevrolet, Wyatt, Yancy, Fred, Phil, Woodrow, Lefty, The Phantom. . . . He received a library card last year in the name of Raphael Sabatini, his Cub Scout membership lists him as Barry Fitzgerald, and only last week a friend of his called asking if Toulouse could come over to his house for dinner.

A funny bit of dialogue conveys the poignancy of an abandoned love child trying his best to read his own face, his own palm. One day he's a sheriff, another a painter, another an automobile, an actor, a dog, and so on. A lot of children go through what the fictional Nick does, their sense of themselves as separate, distinct characters in their own life narratives flawed and anxious. It's hardly surprising that children fool around with their given names. In *Memories of a Catholic Girlhood,* Mary McCarthy wrote,

> Names had a great importance for us in the convent and foreign names, French, German, or plain English (which, to us, were foreign, because of their Protestant sound) bloomed like prize roses among a collection of spuds. Irish names were too common in the school to have any prestige either as surnames (Gallagher, Sheehan, Finn, Sullivan, McCarthy) or as Christian names (Kathleen, Eileen).

How to resolve a contradiction that, on the one hand, asserts that names play a role no more crucial to the story of a life than any other physical trait or emotional characteristic and, on the other, provides fairly persuasive evidence that your name determines or, at the very least, affects your future?

About Catholics, McCarthy wrote, "The saint a child is named for is supposed to serve, literally, as a model or pattern to imitate; your name is your fortune and it tells you what you are or must be." Looked at this way, a Catholic child's name is similar to Junior tacked on to the end of a name; both incorporate a heavy set of expectations. McCarthy continued:

> Catholic children ponder their names for a mystic meaning, like birthstones; my own, I learned, besides belonging to the Virgin and Saint Mary of Egypt, originally meant "bitter" or "star of the sea." My second name, Therese, could dedicate me either to Saint Theresa or to the saint called the Little Flower, Soeur Therese of Lisieux, on whom God was supposed to have descended in the form of a shower of roses. At Confirmation, I had added a third name . . . "Clem-

entina," after Saint Clement, an early pope—a step I soon regretted on account of "My Darling Clementine" and her number nine shoes. By the time I was in the convent, I would no longer tell anyone what my Confirmation name was.

The unsettling thing about this is that after she became prominent as a writer, McCarthy also spoke her mind often and sharply, and rather than "star of the sea" was considered "caustic," a near synonym of "bitter." Having deciphered the code, did she feel trapped inside her name? "Names have a queer kind of sorcery for me," she said when she was in her sixties, "like guarantees of reality."

The article most often referred to by students of American naming practices was written in 1965 by sociologist Alice Rossi and published in the *American Sociological Review.* Many still rely on her study "Naming Children in Middle-Class Families" because it's so thorough and also because it was the first to investigate the subject in a systematic and statistical way. But with hindsight enhanced by Rossi's work, one can read in American naming patterns and practices the same strains of restlessness, envy, striving, confidence, and overconfidence to be found in other indices of middle-class behavior: the accrual of possessions, for example, or clothing, leisure activities, political groupings. If the brand of beer you guzzle and the way you spend your Sunday afternoons say something piquant about you, so does your name.

The problem is that the codes that govern naming are subtle and tacit rather than spelled out and easily followed. Through interview and questionnaire, Rossi queried 347 urban middle-class mothers about their children's names—where they came from, why they chose them. Among her conclusions: "Kin are the major source of the personal names chosen for children. . . . Boys are more apt to be named after kin than girls, and first-born children more than later-born children." It's worth noting that Rossi had two assumptions already in place when she began her study. One was that white parents do not pick a name out of thin air for their children or invent a new sound, as many blacks do. The second was that the mother is the principal namer, taking over in this department as she might (traditionally, at any rate) with folding the laundry or driving the kids to soccer practice or picking the color of the family car.

Rossi discovered that naming a child for a parent or parent-in-law or other relative may be a "painless way to ease stressful relations," a "balm to ruffled feelings." She wrote: "A few [women] reported that they purposely avoided naming a child after a particular relative because they disliked that relative, but no respondent mentioned any dislike or ambivalence toward a relative a child *was* named after." We apparently assume, at some unverbalized level, that a name incorporates the soul or spirit or personality of the person who bears it. If your Grandma Bessie is a virago, you wouldn't dream of naming your baby girl Bessie, not because you don't like its sound or because it's an old-fashioned name or even because it reminds you of a cow, but because you're afraid that if you do, she'll turn into someone like her great-grandmother. This is a code of naming behavior as rigid as any in so-called primitive cultures, although it's not often openly acknowledged. One of Rossi's respondents, however, had no hesitation in articulating her belief in the magic of names; she admitted naming her son for a "dear friend of ours who died just before my son was born. He was a brilliant, admirable person, and we hoped our son, *by having the same name,* would be the same."

"The prevalence of naming children after kin," Rossi reported, "has not changed during the past 40 years: children born in the fifties are just as likely to be named for kin as children born in the 1920s. What has changed, however," Rossi went on to explain, is which side of the family children were apt to be named for. In the fifties, more boys were named after relatives of their mothers than in the twenties. The opposite held true for girls, more of whom were named after relatives of their fathers than thirty years earlier. What does Rossi make of this pattern? It "may be part of a trend toward diminishing barriers among adult age groups and between the sexes." It may be comparable to the trend toward unisex or androgynous names Herbert Barry noted in his study. But how, one wonders, do these shifts come about? When pregnant women get together, do they ask one another whether they're going to name the baby after someone on their side of the family rather than the husband's? Not likely. While you can understand how trends and fads spread (the "in" vehicle, the "in" running shoe, the "in" name), this shift—from father's side to mother's—remains as baffling as how and why the general pool of names changes as time goes by and why certain names, like Delphine and Ambrose, drop out altogether, while others, like Sarah and Michael, keep on reappearing.

8.
Maiden Names

*Nancy kept her own name for all purposes, refusing to be
called "Mrs. Graves" in any circumstances. She explained
that, as "Mrs. Graves," she had no personal validity.*
                    Robert Graves, *Good-bye to All That*

In 1881, Judge Robert A. Earl, finding for the plaintiff in *Chapman v. Phoenix National Bank,* issued a declaration that would
hearten the most mean-spirited misogynist. "For several centuries," he wrote,

> by the common law among all English-speaking people, a
> woman, upon her marriage, takes her husband's surname.
> That becomes her legal name, and she ceases to be known
> by her maiden name. By that name she must sue and be
> sued, make and take grants and execute all legal documents.
> Her maiden name is absolutely lost, and she ceases to be
> known thereby.

(A century earlier, in his *Commentaries on the Laws of England,*
William Blackstone said that when a man and woman exchange
marriage vows, they become one person, and "the husband is that
person.") Whenever there was a legal tangle over names, Judge
Earl's opinion was trotted out in support of the status quo. Although widely subscribed to and largely unchallenged until the
1940s, Judge Earl's ruling was based on nothing more than wishful thinking. In fact, the opposite is true: anyone, male or female,

single or married, has a common-law right to take any name he or she wants (as long as it's considered a name).

That Judge Earl's pronouncement prevailed for so many years, in spite of its being about as reliable as a formula for turning base metals into gold, attests to both the pervasive power of resistance to change and an atavistic terror of women. But as far as they have given it any thought at all, most men believe it seemly for a woman to give up her name when she marries. Most women agree with them—yet another reason not to put all one's trust in democracy's basket.

"Light of my life, dearest girl, you have the power to make me the happiest man in the world. Oh, island of loveliness, my heart's serenity, passionate tigress, darling Jennifer, say that you will marry me."

"I thought you'd never ask, Harvey. There's just one little thing."

"And what's that, sweetest pea?"

"I think I'd like to keep my name after we're married."

"Do *what?*"

"Keep my birth name. You know: Jennifer Pickens."

"Why would you want to do a selfish thing like that, Jen? What's wrong with my name? What's wrong with Masters?"

Harvey, threatened to his very marrow, backs off. They consult a premarriage counselor. Harvey complains, "If I go along with this whacko plan, what do I do when we go out together? Do I say, 'This is my wife, Jennifer Pickens'? It sounds stupid. I can't say that. People will think, Who the hell does this dame think she is . . ."

"I'm not a dame, Harvey."

"Girl. Woman. Whatever."

The counselor gives them equal time and eventually comes down on Jennifer's side. At this, Harvey accuses his heart's serenity of being in cahoots with the therapist, and they split for good. Jennifer's well out of it, and Harvey, no doubt, will find a woman more to his taste, a girl who doesn't have an attitude problem. A

freethinking woman like Jennifer doesn't belong with a man who
believes that sharing a name means he shares his name while hers
falls into desuetude. Poet Philip Larkin wrote:

> *Marrying left your maiden name disused.*
> *Its five light sounds no longer mean your face,*
> *Your voice, and all your vanities of grace . . .*
> *Now it's a phrase applicable to no one.*[1]

Men like Harvey, and there are probably many more like him
than not, see a she-devil rather than the love of their life as soon
as they discover how reluctant she is to give up her name. These
men are baffled and hurt: "If you really loved me, you'd be
overjoyed to take my name." The question the woman ought to
ask—but not many do—is, "Let's turn this thing around. How
about giving up *your* name and taking *mine?*" Sam Howe of *The
New York Times* split the difference, you might say, when he
married Lisa Verhovek, the bearer of a unique surname that, since
she had no male siblings, was in danger of fading out in another
generation. His marriage license and all subsequent records, including his byline, transformed him into Sam Howe Verhovek.
"Names mean a lot," he reflected in an "About Men" essay:

> And what to do with them—keeping, changing, hyphenating
> them—is a problem for a lot of couples as their wedding
> day approaches. I feel in no way diminished by taking my
> wife's name, and I don't think a woman should feel dimin-
> ished by taking her husband's name. Personally, I think it's
> a privilege to have all those names, and it's not confusing at
> all. Howe is my maiden name, and Verhovek is my maiden's
> name.

The woman who refuses to submit to the conventional practice
of taking her husband's name risks having her loyalties ques-
tioned and, except in relatively sophisticated communities, being
viewed as a subversive. This isn't so far off the mark, for she's

tossing a custard pie in custom's face at close range. What has always been done is what's generally deemed the correct thing, whether or not it defies reason. And so, since men long ago owned their women the way they owned cows and outhouses, why not keep on doing it that way? Why change?

During the late eighties and early nineties, there was a trend, on the East and West Coasts, at any rate, identified in newspaper wedding stories by the words "The bride is keeping her name." [2] It is probably a mistake, however, to assume this to be true of the population in general, since brides whose weddings are reported in *The New York Times,* for example, tend to be achievers and individualists who have already established their names professionally, or wish to, and see no reason to surrender them. The higher their educational level, the less likely they are to follow conventional practice. According to a 1994 survey conducted for *American Demographics,* "Fewer than 5 percent of wives who do not have a college education use something other than their husband's name, compared with 15 percent of those with bachelor's degrees and more than 20 percent of those with postgraduate degrees."

But now comes the backlash: the aggressively traditional woman who says, explaining why she took her husband's name, "I wanted to buck that feminist viewpoint that in order to be a real woman you have to have your identity, and it's defined by what you're called. I know who I am and I'm going to follow the tradition that I choose." The woman being quoted, Crystal Dozier, a black twenty-nine-year-old middle manager, went even further: "You have to look at it from the man's point of view. I think it's an ego-booster for a man to have his wife take her husband's name, especially for a professional black woman. It makes a statement to the world that even though I'm professional, I still stand by my man," the last an argument used by some black women to justify their support of O. J. Simpson regardless of his record of spousal abuse and guilt or innocence in the murders of his wife and Ronald Goldman. Dozier's statement raises the question of whether she would be so committed to standing by her man, with all that that self-effacing posture implies, if she weren't black. It also makes you wonder why Ms. Dozier thinks that it's necessary to boost her husband's ego to keep her marriage intact.

Harvey's "dame" probably has a better idea of who she is than the woman—let's call her Emily Fisher—whose embossed stationery identifies her as Mrs. Paul Johnson. Mrs. Johnson is probably not aware that Mr. Johnson has swallowed her whole, leaving no trace, not even a few bones or feathers to mark the person who was once Emily Fisher. What sort of person is Emily that she doesn't mind being invisible?

Those who embrace the traditional will haul out an argument that goes something like this: "If a woman loves a man deeply and truly, she will take his name when she marries him because a name is merely nominal. That is, it has no more significance than a label, like 'pickled beets' or 'Chanel No. 5.' [3] What you're called matters not half as much as the quality of the relationship between this man and this woman; how they absorb life's pleasures and disappointments; how they raise their children; their respect for one another. If she's profoundly aware of both who she is and what her roles require of her, it doesn't matter what she's called, so why not stick with ways tried and true? Keeping her own name confuses rather than clarifies; the children's school doesn't know who their parents are; assuming her husband's name ensures the maintenance of a tradition that goes back centuries and unambiguously reinforces the formal structure of the nuclear family."

To continue this argument is to venture into parody. The first part of it is nonsense, ignoring as it does the profound significance a name has for the person who bears it, and the last is mischief. To blame maiden-namism for the breakdown of the family is to disregard the fact that the mom-and-pop-and-the-kids type of American family is, statistically speaking, a thing of the past since almost half of today's mothers have no husbands. If a family collapses it's because one of its members is absent, not because one of them refused to change her last name.

The idea of women's independence arouses panic in otherwise reasonable men. Cultural observer Susan J. Douglas, in her 1994 book *Where the Girls Are,* found evidence of this in old television programs like *Bewitched, I Dream of Jeannie,* and *The Flying Nun.* These long-run sitcoms featured females with supernatural powers their guys viewed as suspiciously as a pair of strange trousers hanging in the closet. "If women did use them their powers had to be confined to the private sphere," Douglas wrote. "Whenever women used these powers outside the home, in the public sphere, the male world was turned completely upside down." She blamed the news media for popularizing two feminist archetypes: the "female grotesque" and the "femme fatale."

World folklore is replete with warnings against the female, especially while she's menstruating but also, it would seem, just for the hell of it. Some African tribes believe a barren woman can blight the crops. The Bible minces no words when it comes to female toxicity:

> If a woman have conceived seed, and borne a man child, then she shall be unclean seven days. . . . And she shall then continue in the blood of her purifying three and thirty days; she shall touch no hallowed thing, nor come into the sanctuary, until the days of her purifying be fulfilled. But if she bear a maid child, then she shall be unclean two weeks, as in her separation: and she shall continue in the blood of her purifying threescore and six days.

James Frazer theorized that the human race is slowly crawling out of the magic mode up to and through the religious and will finally emerge in the sunlight of science and rationality. Yet Frazer's demonstration of the measureless dread of women among cultures just a little less civilized than ours gives one pause; how far, in fact, have most men come from believing that "if any one drank out of the same cup [as a menstruating female] he would surely die"? Today, an Orthodox Jewish boy still recites a morning prayer thanking God for not having made him a girl. The great white father of psychoanalysis, Sigmund Freud, alleged that a woman's conscience is to a man's as a clitoris is to a penis: in other words, underdeveloped and not especially useful. What with primitive man investing his mate with magic sufficient to kill off the corn and dry up the milch herd and civilized man questioning her ability to tell right from wrong, it's not surprising so many men are more frightened of an independent woman than they are of contracting a sexually transmitted disease.

New Woman, a magazine with a surprisingly large circulation, published an article by Anne Bernays in the summer of 1993 (the editors titled it, inevitably, "What's in a Name?"). Bernays took the position that a name is too important to give up as blithely and mindlessly as most women do when they marry. "Whenever a woman marries, sheds her name, and substitutes her husband's," Bernays wrote, "she's also shedding part of herself, part of who she's been since birth. Whether she's conscious of it or not, if she changes her name her marriage will be lopsided, like a scale with five pounds of nuts on one side and two on the other." If anything, she added, a woman needs to be more herself after she marries than before, "because there's nothing that tests so often and so profoundly who you are as living with someone else in close quarters."

The piece generated a record share of reader responses, including some from an unexpectedly large number of men. Here's a sampling.

Men:

If she hadn't taken my name I would have seen it as a definite negative statement that my name wasn't good enough for her.

Women who are really adamant about not changing their name . . . don't have their children's best interest at heart.

My first wife didn't take my name. At the time I didn't mind, but in retrospect . . . well, I wonder if that didn't say something about our relationship.

A woman who is really comfortable with her identity and knows she's independent doesn't have to make a big show of it and hit everyone in the face with it.

The man's name should be used by both husband and wife to represent the idea that marriage is a melding of two into one.

It should be treated simply as a matter of preference, not a matter of power or control.

Women:

When men talk about a woman taking a man's name as a sign of "melding," they ignore the fact that the person doing the melding is the woman.

I was proud to *share* the name of a man who believes in me more than I believe in myself.

A name denotes who you are, and now that you have substituted "Mrs." for "Miss" you are a wife.

Instead of promoting a woman's right to keep her *maiden name,* why not just say she chooses to keep *her name.*

I've kept my maiden name. My husband did not seem to care one way or another, but his mother was not real happy about it.

A woman who gives up her name for her husband's has immediately created a power imbalance in the relationship.

When a woman sheds her birth name, she sheds part of herself. I unthinkingly shed that part of myself when I got married but would never do it again.

A man whose feelings are hurt when a woman refuses to give up her own name is not a man at all. He's a little boy who needs to grow up.

I think that keeping your own name is just a simple, natural way to be always yourself.

My blood boils every time I hear a man imply that wives who retain their names are "uncontrollable bitches." Or, that they are simply "not committed."

As for the "melding" one of the male respondents mentioned, there's only one way to meld two into one, and that's to make a new name, an anagram composed of both their surnames, as, in our case, Barkansplaney, Plankeraybans, and Yarbankpansel would be new words—neologisms—produced by combining and mixing Bernays and Kaplan. Several couples have done this: when Skye Kerr married Deane Rynerson (hard to say which is the female and which the male), they created a new name out of old parts for both to bear: Rykerson. In the same vein, when Jennifer Lynn Wilcha married David Alan Smith, they both dropped their surnames and assumed the name Allyn, a telescoping of Lynn and Alan. In a land dedicated to egalitarianism, this practice seems to make ultimate sense, even though the newlyweds' parents may not be all that happy about the disappearance of *their* names. Other less than ideal solutions to the problem of name loss suggest themselves. One is the hyphenated name, with the woman's first. Another is the Spanish way: with y—and—linking his and hers. Yet a third—and, although awkward, much the fairest—is to invent an entirely new name, containing no remnants or suggestions of anything preexisting in either family, for both to take.

When he was an undergraduate at Princeton in 1939, the psychologist Robert Holt turned in an honors thesis on the bond between name and identity, focusing on what, if anything, happens to the personality after a name change. Apparently this was one of the first empirical studies to deal with the maiden name/married name problem. After interviewing thirty subjects, Holt decided that although "severe emotional disturbances" may ensue when a man changes his name, women who don't want to take their husband's name are "usually maladjusted anyway" and are simply "projecting their difficulties." This astonishing conclusion was echoed by writer and social critic Louis Adamic in his 1942 book, *What's Your Name?* The greater part of this hymn to the United States was devoted to reassuring readers with funny foreign names that heterogeneity is the American way. Be proud of your origins, he said, and resist the temptation to become a "fake yankee." But when it comes to females, Adamic wasn't quite so reassuring. He told the story of a "real-life" professional woman who kept her own name after marriage and who, when her husband died, "suddenly realized she had no real existence apart from him. . . . Now it was pointless to retain her maiden name. To regain her identity, her existence, she took his name which had come to represent them both."

Amy and Leon Kass, both on the faculty of the University of Chicago, put the problem in a sociobiological framework, arguing that "the change of the woman's name, from family of origin to family of perpetuation, is the perfect emblem for the desired exogamy of human sexuality and generation." Their argument may sound familiar to readers of Margaret Atwood's novel *The Handmaid's Tale*. The women in Atwood's futuristic dystopia have only one function, to bear the children of the governing order; if they're not fertile, they're labeled Unwomen and shipped off to the colonies as slave labor. Ofglen (that is, Of Glen), Ofwayne, Ofwarren, and so forth are their possessive-form names, which denote the men who own them for breeding purposes. The Kasses seem to endorse a comparable order of society:

The husband who gives his name to his bride in marriage . . . is owning up to what it means to have been given a family and a family name by his father—he is living out his destiny to be a father by saying yes to it in advance. And the wife does not so much surrender her name as she accepts the gift of his, given and received as a pledge of (among other things) loyal and responsible fatherhood for her children. A woman who refuses this gift is, whether she knows it or not, tacitly refusing the promised devotion or, worse, expressing her suspicions about her groom's trustworthiness as a husband and prospective father.

The high nonsense content of arguments against a woman's keeping her name indicates that the antis are willing to exchange atavism for logic, something that happens whenever a social issue twangs a fragile psychic chord. In this case, it is terror of the uppity woman, the dame who thinks for herself, breathes on her own; of the woman who demands a credit card and an equal voice in how money is spent, who thinks she's capable of making administrative decisions, who insists on maintaining her own identity, keeping her own name! If we don't place this Krakatoa under wraps, we may find ourselves kissing civilization good-bye. Poor woman. Blameless, she's blamed almost as often as the Jew when society starts fracturing.

And yet, even as he resists change and choice, the reactionary is uneasily aware of the paradox in his argument that names aren't all that important. If he really means it, why doesn't he encourage his loved one to keep the name she was born with, the name her teachers knew her by, the tag on her high school diploma? Like the tyrant who bans—or burns—books because he's no fool and knows the awful power of the written word, the reactionaries recognize that a name is *not* simply the label they can dismiss as peelable and that it has profound significance for its bearer. Let her wear her own name and God only knows what will happen. When a woman gives up her name at marriage, she's saying: "While I'm willing to relinquish a piece of my identity for the sake of this union, I do not ask the same of you."

In the mid-nineteenth century some women began to open their eyes, stir, and cry out on the matter of names. A few articulate stalwarts, like Lucy Stone and Elizabeth Cady Stanton, challenged the notion that to marry meant to discard your surname as routinely as you do your jacket in the heat. Since Stone and Stanton were radical feminists, the subject of names folded neatly into their omnibus crusade for women's rights—civil, domestic, financial; all its parts made up one grand iconoclastic adventure.

Lucy Stone was born in 1818 to a New England mother who believed that a husband ruled his family by divine right. Rejecting her inferior status as a woman, Lucy earned enough money teaching school to enroll, at the age of twenty-five, at Oberlin College in Ohio. At Oberlin she read somewhere that "women are more sunk by marriage than men," and when she asked a teacher to please explain what this meant, he told her, deliberately oversimplifying the matter, that the reason men are the dominant partners in marriage was that they didn't have to give up their names. His explanation triggered a lifelong mission. Rejecting her mother's domestic credo, Lucy agitated most of her life on behalf of woman suffrage and (for lack of a better phrase) maiden-namism. Married to businessman/abolitionist Henry Browne Blackwell, she kept her own name, although, in an odd curtsey to custom, she signed herself Mrs. Stone.[4] Many years later, in 1921, she became an icon for fifty professional women who founded the Lucy Stone League in order to spread the gospel of maiden-namism. Their credo: "My name is the symbol of my identity and must not be lost." The league was the brainchild of journalist Ruth Hale, married to a fellow journalist, Heywood Broun. Hale kept her name, although this often involved a struggle. These early activists didn't notice the retrograde implications of the word "maiden" in "maiden name," and it wasn't until the late 1980s that feminists decided the offending sexist term should be dropped in favor of "name," "own name," or "birth name."

The founding members of the Lucy Stone League, known as Lucy Stoners, must have realized how unrepresentative a band they were and what they were up against. Fifty as against millions of married women, who not only didn't care a bit about the psychology of identity but viewed their newly acquired names as insignia of respectability and status to be cherished and flaunted like a four-carat, emerald-cut diamond set in platinum. Never mind, Lucy Stoners enjoyed getting together and talking about their crusade, which was more a philosophical, armchair thing anyway—they couldn't really have believed they could persuade more than a handful of women to follow their example. To convert the majority of American women to Lucy Stonism had as much chance of success as getting them to wear their undergarments outside their street clothes.

The Lucy Stone League was reborn in the early 1950s, its membership shrunken, in Manhattan, where a score of professional women met more or less regularly, issued a bulletin, raised money for scholarships, and eventually billed themselves as a "Center for Research and Information on the Status of Women." Their vice president was Miss Doris E. Fleischman, born in 1892 to a stern, humorless lawyer and a sweet, pliant housewife whose connubial beliefs mimicked those of Lucy Stone's mother. Doris Fleischman dutifully passed these on to her own daughter in a somewhat watered-down version: "Remember, Annie, in an argument with your husband, he's always right." This antifeminist, motherly advice (which the daughter eventually buried with a stake through its heart) was typical of Fleischman's uneasy stance; with one leg in the Victorian era, the other in the twentieth century, her Lucy Stoner "Miss" went about as deep as a skin of Saran wrap, because when she married she thought of herself as a "Mrs."

Doris Fleischman graduated from Barnard College in 1913, having excelled at athletics (she was on three varsity teams and played cup-winning tennis). Verbal, a swift, clean writer, she was offered a reporter's job on the *New York Tribune* on the women's page. (A child of her time, she got her father's permission before accepting the job.) Soon promoted to assistant Sunday editor, she was the first woman to cover a prize fight; her father, afraid for her safety, insisted on accompanying her to Madison Square Garden. In 1919 she was hired away from the *Tribune* by publicist Edward Bernays, a longtime friend. She married him in 1922 and worked for and with him for the rest of her life, which ended in 1980.

The Bernays/Fleischman marriage and professional partnership seem nearly ideal, and in many ways they were remarkably harmonious. But Fleischman never resolved the matter of her surname, that one word which signified not only who she was perceived to be but who she believed herself to be. Two strong waves met within one strong person, creating what must have been crisis after crisis, an ongoing condition unacknowledged to those closest to her: her two daughters and her husband, whom she worshiped. Even in late middle age, she was still flip-flopping over the matter of what to call herself. If you don't know your own name, how do you know who you are?

Fleischman had joined the Lucy Stone League chiefly because Bernays urged her to; many years later he said that his wife became "a Lucy Stoner because her husband wanted her to be one." When they married, Fleischman signed the Waldorf-Astoria Hotel's register in her own name—also on her husband's insistence. It was strictly Bernays's idea; he hoped for some ink in next day's newspapers and was not disappointed. Neither of them apparently grasped the irony that these gestures of liberation were male generated.

When the couple went to Europe a few years later, Fleischman managed to obtain a passport under her name, accomplishing this by the following clever note to the Secretary of State: "Will you kindly have issued to me a passport under my own name. There is no law compelling a woman to use any but her own name, and I have never done so. Since it is apparent that the purpose of a passport is to establish identity, I assume you will not wish me to travel under a false name." Fleischman was the first married American woman with a passport in her own name; it made her a pioneer of sorts.[5]

Fleischman's first daughter, also Doris (why not Edwina, after her father?), was born in 1929, and Fleischman's name was entered on the birth certificate along with her husband's. The New York City registrar duly stamped it "illegitimate," and Edward Bernays was obliged to pay someone inside the bureaucracy to issue a cleaned-up certificate.

Bernays went on to become one of the most successful and visible practitioners of the business of public relations. His wife was known as Miss Fleischman, even to her daughters' friends, who on first being introduced, invariably asked, "Isn't your mother married to your father?" A mother who was "Miss" was as disconcerting as a puma pacing the marble foyer. Miss Fleischman had a room upstairs in the three-storey brownstone the Bernays office occupied just off Madison Avenue on Sixty-fourth Street. There she sat every day, composing news releases and speeches for clients whom she rarely met at work as a professional equal, even though she played hostess to them in her house at dinner parties.

According to a monograph by journalism professor Susan Henry, "In the considerable publicity resulting from the firm's activities, Bernays alone usually was credited with the work being described." Professor Henry picked up on yet another contradiction: the firm's letterhead announced "Edward L. Bernays, Counsel on Public Relations," and in smaller type, one line below, "A Partnership of Edward L. Bernays and Doris E. Fleischman." This was pure doublespeak by Bernays, bought into by Fleischman, at what cost one can only speculate. She was a smart woman who didn't need things spelled out for her, and it's hard to see how this paradoxical arrangement didn't do some irreparable damage. She suffered painful and undiagnosable back pains most of her adult life, as well as arthritis, and toward the end, considerable depression.

At the age of fifty-seven, Fleischman published an article entitled "Notes of a Retiring Feminist" in *The American Mercury,* a popular middlebrow magazine. She focused on the problems she had experienced during her twenty-six years as a dues-paying member of the Lucy Stone League and declared that she had had enough: it was much easier to be Mrs. Bernays than Miss Fleischman. She revealed serious ambivalence toward her two identities. "Mrs. stands to the right of me, and Miss stands to the left. Me is a ghost ego somewhere in the middle." She wrote about how difficult it had been to avoid confusing others who didn't know how to address her and ended up chagrined: "In casual social contacts, I am afraid that I have been a nuisance to my friends, an embarrassment to my family (with the exception of my husband), and a hazard to hostesses. . . . By and large, using my own name has been like swimming up through molasses."

Her not terribly convincing anecdotal material served as rationale for abandoning (a harsher word would be "betraying") her own cause, which she did with this odd flourish: "A Lucy Stoner is mistaken in thinking that keeping her father's name is more significant than taking her husband's name. We were guilty of belief in magic. We thought a name itself had power to confer a separate identity." How could Fleischman not have been aware of the difference between bearing a father's name, the one given her at birth, and a husband's, which involves a compound fracture? She must also have recognized that the belief in "magic" she dismissed is far more powerful than she cared to acknowledge. It is precisely the magic in names that makes any change so traumatic and difficult. Names *do* have the "power to confer a separate identity." Why, after twenty-six years of believing it, Fleischman denied it and wanted out is still a mystery.

For the remainder of her days, it was as if Fleischman were playing hide-and-seek with herself. When she started writing her quasi-autobiography, *A Wife Is Many Women,* she signed all her correspondence with her publisher Doris E. Fleischman. Yet on the title page of the book her name is Doris Fleischman Bernays. Susan Henry cited other inconsistencies:

In 1955, for example, as "Doris E. Fleischman" she coauthored . . . a chapter on "Themes and Symbols" in *The Engineering of Consent,* a book on Public Relations edited by Bernays. Yet four years later when she and her husband bought a 16-page advertising supplement in *The New York Times* aimed at improving U.S.-British relations, the couple was identified as "Doris F. and Edward L. Bernays."

Henry quoted the eighty-year-old Fleischman as admitting that "my husband is a feminist and I am a feminist and we get along beautifully because I obey him all of the time." If Doris Fleischman had at last penetrated the doublespeak to collide with the irony of her life as half Mrs. and half Miss, a creature at cross-purposes with itself, it was a little late to do anything about self-identification; nor was she, in her eighties, up to killing off one of her names for good.

The tale of Helen Beatrix Potter has none of these painful nuances. Here was a woman who knew exactly who she was and what she wanted to be called. Potter was born in 1866 to a nonpracticing barrister, who spent the better part of each daylight hour reading and rereading newspapers in his London club when he wasn't attending to his hobby, photography, and to a conventional mother who left her daughter's care largely in the hands of servants. Potter was raised in a household where the daily schedule of meals, walks, prayers, and bedtime was as reliable as *Bradshaw's Monthly Railway Guide.*

Potter's biographer, Margaret Lane, reported that Beatrix "had been born into a period and a class which seems to have had little understanding of children" and "which laid it down that very young girls, except when they were in pinafores, should be booted and dressed as though they were going to church." A less self-sufficient child would no doubt have stifled inside Bolton Gardens, the Potters' grand London house. But not Beatrix, who, blessed with remarkable powers of observation, visual, aural, and intuitive, listened and learned from her physical surroundings and from the people who visited her parents. She made up stories and filled notebooks with a daily record of her life, written in a code she invented.

During the family's holidays in Scotland, Potter got her first taste for nature in the form of flowers, hedgerow animals, lanes flanked with blackberry bushes, bustling farms, and the wide sky, the large and the minute, all of which seemed, when compared with her life in London, far more interesting than the daily lunchtime dessert of rice pudding and the smell of roasting mutton. By the age of nine or ten, Potter was producing adept drawings of flowers, rabbits, and birds, for the most part realistic and detailed but also touched by occasional fantasy: animals wearing clothes, walking on their hind legs, carrying umbrellas. Beatrix Potter, a shy and private person, was an intellectual and creative prodigy.

Although she had produced hundreds of exact drawings of botanical specimens and had discovered and described a species of fungus, she was denied admission to the Royal Botanic Garden's herbarium. Potter said the idea behind this exclusion was that "I should be sent to school before I began to teach other people." But of course the real reason was that she was a woman and thus not formally trained as a botanist or likely to be.

Potter languished for nearly a decade, suffering bouts of depression and also rheumatic fever so severe she had to stay in bed for months (during which time she memorized several Shakespeare plays). Then, in 1893, when she was twenty-seven, she began to write illustrated letters to the bedridden son of an old friend. The first letter began: "I don't know what to write to you, so I shall tell you a story about four little rabbits, whose names were Flopsy, Mopsy, Cottontail, and Peter." Soon, encouraged by H. D. Rawnsley, a clergyman and author of children's books, she copied and enlarged the contents of her letters to make a book, which she submitted as *The Tale of Peter Rabbit* to a publisher, Frederick Warne & Co. They rejected it at first but then reconsidered, probably the wisest editorial decision they ever made.

Potter continued to write extraordinarily popular children's books, in clear, precise, visual, and always unsentimental prose. "The counter," she wrote in *Ginger and Pickles,* "was a convenient height for rabbits. Ginger and Pickles sold red spotty pocket-handkerchiefs at a penny three farthings." As Potter put it herself: "The shorter and plainer the better." Norman Warne, son of the firm's founder, happily published everything she wrote. When she was forty years old, Potter and Warne fell in love and, in spite of her parents' snobbish disapproval of Warne as someone "in trade," planned to marry. But before they could, Warne died of leukemia. Devastated, Potter used her royalties and a small legacy from an aunt to buy Hill Top Farm, near the village of Sawrey in the Lake District. Lane wrote that this purchase "stood for important decisions and delicate choice . . . she was choosing to be a farmer, in however partial and incomplete a way." Still the dutiful daughter, Potter was able to spend time away from her parents only sporadically at Hill Top. During the eight years after buying the farm, she produced thirteen books—among them *The Tailor of Gloucester* and *Squirrel Nutkin*—six of them directly reflective of her life in Sawrey.

Potter met William Heelis, a solicitor who helped her with the purchase of a second farm near Hill Top, when she was forty-three. Four years later they married. She wrote to a friend that "I am *very* happy, and in every way satisfied with Willie." About Potter's marriage and subsequent self-revision, Margaret Lane wrote:

> She was approaching fifty, and all the best of her creative work was done. As Beatrix Potter she already enjoyed a little measure of fame, and was financially independent; but the change from Miss Potter to Mrs. Heelis went far deeper than the name. It was as if, disliking so much about her earlier life that she could hardly bear to be reminded of it, she deliberately buried Miss Potter of Bolton Gardens and became another person. Mrs. Heelis of Sawrey . . . was absorbed in the life which Beatrix Potter had always wanted.

After becoming Mrs. Heelis, Potter published six books, but they weren't as good as her earlier work. Lane said that "from the moment her eyes began to fail and she lost her power of fine drawing, her stories lost their shape, their emotional concentration, and their poetry." Not so strange for creative juices to dry up with advanced years. What was unusual was the serenity with which Potter accepted the inevitable, finding in Willie and farming a more than merely acceptable substitute for writing books. She seems to have taken to her new career as wife and farmer the way a child throws off her shoes and walks barefoot through the mud puddles. Potter stopped being Potter the day she married. She signed herself "Beatrix Heelis" and, Lane said, hated "being addressed as 'Miss Potter' by even the most appreciative of admirers."

"It is rare," Lane wrote, "for old age to be the happiest period of life, but there is no doubt that in middle age and after Beatrix Potter found a satisfaction and contentment that she had never known in youth." As Mrs. Heelis she became famous in the neighborhood as a farmer and breeder of a rare and hardy strain of sheep. Beatrix Potter—Mrs. Heelis—died of bronchitis in 1943 at the age of seventy-seven.

Unlike Doris Fleischman, Beatrix Potter snipped her life neatly in two when she married. Potter's history begs to be read as an inside-out feminist parable, but one can also think of it as a movie reel run backward, with the solitary, problematic artistic life triumphant at its start and domestic bliss at the other end. No doubt, feminists view as repugnant Potter's abandonment both of her writing and her name. But her eagerness to retool when creativity began to go dry suggests that hers was a personality integrated in a way that eludes most writers and artists, a lot of whom keep on struggling even as they know they can never repeat the passion of their early songs. She was *Miss* Beatrix Potter, author. Then she was *Mrs.* William Heelis, farmer. Both were conscious choices, clearly articulated and executed with joy.

Literary and social critic Diana Trilling, widow of critic and Columbia professor Lionel Trilling, published her autobiography, *The Beginning of the Journey,* in 1993, at the age of eighty-eight. In it she recalled that when she wrote her first full-length book review for publication, she was "afraid of signing it. The thought that my name would be in print revived in me, in all its infant force, my father's prohibition against self-display." Her psychoanalyst helped her to realize, however, that this extreme degree of self-effacement meant just the opposite. "What you really want," he told her, "is to see your name all over the magazine." Yet when *The Nation* bought the review in 1941,

the question arose of what name I should use, my maiden
name [Rubin] or my name as Lionel's wife. Socially I was
always known by my married name. We consulted our
friends at *Partisan Review*. They were united in the advice
that I write under my maiden name; they feared I was going
to be an embarrassment to Lionel. But Lionel was adamant
I write as his wife. From the day I first appeared in print there
was never a moment when his confidence in me wavered.

For all her brilliance, independent spirit, and stamina, in the matter of naming Diana Trilling obeyed male directives.

The problem of how a woman identifies herself after marriage
can be solved in any number of ways that, however irrational,
nevertheless appear to satisfy the solver. Writer Susan Ferraro,
née Flynn, claimed that, after she married, "changing my name
meant defining myself as an adult, choosing my own label. Taking
a new name was about growing up. It was about how, much as I
loved him, I stopped being Daddy's little girl." That makes no
sense whatsoever, for hasn't she, by analogy, transformed herself
into her husband's little girl? While her "label" now read Ferraro,
rather than Flynn, she didn't seem to realize that, as the saying
goes, "he only married me; he didn't adopt me."

"Here I am," wrote Carol Ascher soon after her divorce from
writer Philip Lopate, "thirty-six years old, a woman who has
worked all her adult life, who has been in the women's movement
for nearly a decade. Here I am, assertive and competent, and I
can't find a name for myself." Lopate, she said, was "ugly or
embarrassing. . . . I was ashamed of it, humiliated by its reminder
of a discontinued legal tie." For a while she considered going
back to her birth name, Bergman, when a male friend lit into her.
"You just never take yourself seriously," he said. "You belittle
your past, your social presence. You're a writer. If you change
your name to Bergman now, it'll be like starting from scratch.
Nobody will know who you are." In the end, aware that Bergman
wouldn't do, she recognized an analogy Ferraro had missed: "If

one can't let go of a husband, there may well be a father lurking behind." Finally, after months of chewing on the problem, she settled on her mother's family name, Ascher, although taking this name could be considered a capitulation to "Mommy." Nevertheless, Ascher felt much better, knew who she was. She also had acquired, over the drawn-out process of discovering the proper noun to call herself, a heightened awareness about names and identity. She had always assumed that name change was a problem for women only, and "now I saw that it was also a wider one: part of the suffering of so many in any disenfranchised or minority group."

Sometimes it's difficult not to think: *One step forward, two steps backward.* When Hillary Rodham, Wellesley graduate, practicing lawyer, author, started campaigning for her husband Bill's 1982 reelection as governor of Arkansas, she used her married name and agreed to be identified as "Mrs. Clinton" for the first time. Did she do this because her husband's aides in the war room told her, "The gals out there—to say nothing about their husbands—aren't going to buy this maiden name crap! Bake cookies! Stand by your man!"? In spite of Rodham's capitulation (and some say she's the master politician in the family and knows by heart every intricate step of the dance), William Safire, cranky *New York Times* columnist and cultural dinosaur, took her to task in 1992 for not toeing the traditional female line and for opening her mouth on a host of other issues when he would have preferred it to stay demurely zipped. Easy as it is to understand the pragmatic motivation behind such accommodations, someone with Hillary Rodham's grit could have stuck to her precampaign guns instead and taken her chances that the voters of Arkansas, and later the entire country, wouldn't mind that Bill's wife was still Ms. and not Mrs.

Two of the three Bernays/Kaplan married daughters have kept their names, while the third, the oldest, goes back and forth. Elizabeth Taylor didn't take any of her eight husbands' names, starting with Hilton and ending with Fortensky (who, for better or worse, was not able to hang on). Radio satirist Jack Cole found the string of names acquired (but not worn) over the years by the much-married Taylor irresistible. He paid her this tribute:

> *Here she comes, beat the drums, blow the trumpets,*
> *Dressed in white, there's delight in her stride.*
> *She's played queens, she's played virgins, she's played*
>   *strumpets,*
> *Heaven knows she's equipped to play a bride.*
> *First came Nick, then two Mikes, then came Eddie,*
> *Dick came twice, then a senator named John.*
> *What a date, what a mate, what a* Butterfield 8!
> *Here comes Liz Taylor Hilton Wilding Todd Fisher*
> *Burton Burton Warner, with Fortensky hanging on.*[6]

The Lucy Stone League is no more. A similar organization, called Center for a Woman's Own Name, founded in 1973 and dedicated to "eliminating discrimination against women who choose to determine their own names," is now "defunct," according to the Postal Service. And even as some women, prodded by Madonna, *are* wearing their bras and panties outside, they still tend toward Mrs. when it comes to marriage.

9.
Rules of Engagement:
The Etiquette of Names

There are only two kinds of people in America: those who go around calling strangers and other nonintimates by their first names and those who resent it.

William Raspberry, *Boston Globe*

Emily Post (1872–1960) "did what the first American dictionary makers had done a century earlier," the historian Neil Harris wrote: "defined appropriate usage with special bows to colloquial needs." The socially guileless, adept at the chores and obligations of daily life, applied to her for help in placing a grid over social activities that were being conducted informally, ad hoc, and with a certain anxiety. She was far from the first, but probably the most influential American dispenser of advice on how to behave.

The anxiety Post and her predecessors addressed dated from a previous century, when visiting foreigners like Mrs. Frances Trollope (the novelist Anthony's mother) deplored "the domestic manners of the Americans," suggesting that they had none at all, properly speaking. The natives had habits in place of manners: they chewed tobacco, spat on the nearest convenient surface, settled disputes in eye-gouging matches, pawed strangers and slapped them on the back, exhaled fumes of onions, gin, and corn whiskey morning and night, hollered instead of conversed, and gobbled whatever was set before them. They ate "in self defence," Dickens wrote, "as if a famine were expected. . . . Great heaps of indigestible matter melted away as ice before the sun. Dyspeptic individuals bolted their food in wedges; feeding, not themselves, but broods of nightmares." Manners in general "excite their contempt and often their hatred," Alexis de Tocqueville said of the Americans. "As they commonly aspire to none but easy and present gratifications, they rush onwards to the object of their desires, and the slightest delay exasperates them."

First published in 1922 and titled *Etiquette: In Society, in Business, in Politics and at Home,* Post's confident book, redolent of nostalgia for a better time and displaying the moral firmness of an English nanny, placed within reach of her readers every conceivable rule and principle for leading what she called an "impeccably correct" life. "Manners are made up of trivialities of deportment," she reassured the eager postulant, "which can be easily learned if one does not happen to know them." Not incidentally, *Etiquette* was a guide to social climbing: if you read and followed its instructions to the letter you were, presumably, given at least probationary membership in "Best Society," depicted as fearfully exacting and exclusive but also accessible to anyone who had done his or her homework. Moving upward in society with Emily Post as your Virgil (or Margaret Dumont) had the same paradoxic double appeal as the original Loop the Loop at Coney Island, which was advertised as being both desperately dangerous and perfectly safe.

A professional writer and author of two published novels, Post used her practiced narrative and dramatic skills in episodes starring characters named Mr. and Mrs. Toplofty, Mr. and Mrs. John Kindheart, and Mr. Stocksan Bonds, along with Robert "Bobo" Gilding and his wife, the former Lucy Wellborn, who live at Golden Hall, "that odious Hector Newman," Clubwin Doe, the Richan Vulgars, the Brightmeadows, the Gotta Crusts, the Worldlys, the Oldnames, Mr. and Mrs. Worthington Adams, and the Jameson Greatlakes of Chicago. One of Post's young blades, Mr. John Hunter Titherington-Smith, has a name that would probably run off the edge of his visiting card and, in any case, is "far too much of a pen-full for one who signs thousands of letters and documents." Post advised him to "drop a name or two" or use initials, although even this resecting might not get him in the clear with her. "It is the American custom to cling to each and every [name] given in baptism," she said in mild disapproval, while

> Abroad, the higher the rank, the shorter the name. A duke, for instance, signs himself "Marlborough," nothing else, and a queen her first name "Victoria." The social world in Europe, therefore, laughs at us for using our whole names, or worse yet, inserting meaningless initials in our signatures.

The one apparent intellectual in Post's stable was Professor Bugge; the one artist in Best Society also had a derisive name, Frederick Dauber, which suggests that Post's years as a toiler in upper bohemia may have left her with grudges to settle and that her useful guide can also be read as a sort of roman à clef dedicated "to you my friends whose identity in these pages is veiled in fictional disguise."

After defining Best Society as "an unlimited brotherhood which spreads over the entire surface of the globe . . . an association of gentle-folk," Post gets down to work with a chapter on introductions: how to present, by name, one person to another in order to establish an acquaintance—a crucial rite in any society, whether followed by a handshake, a hand kiss, a bow, or nose rubbing.

> The younger person is always presented to the older or more distinguished, but a gentleman is always presented to a lady, even though he is an old gentleman of great distinction and the lady a mere slip of a girl. No lady is ever, except to the President of the United States, a cardinal, or a reigning sovereign, presented to a man.

"How do you do," she wrote, was the only acceptable way to acknowledge an introduction. "Charmed!" or "Pleased to meet you!" were as taboo as saying "Tendered him a banquet," "Partook of liquid refreshment," "Will you accord me permission?" or "It was so good of you to come to my horrid little shanty." (In later editions, she loosened up enough to endorse the less formal "Hello" and "I'm very glad to meet you.")

Members of Best Society dislike being asked, "What is your name?" [1] If you didn't know someone's name, you were advised to execute a lateral arabesque and consult a third party, to whom you put the question "Who was the lady with the gray feather in her hat?" (On next meeting, if you were not careful, you might say with sweet assurance, "How do you do, Mrs. Featherhead.")

Emily Post was remarkably forthright and even snappish in telling you what to say when someone got your name wrong: "If, after being introduced to you, Mr. Jones calls you by a wrong name, you let it pass, at first, but if he persists you may say: 'My name is Simpson, not Simpkin.' " This was the sort of sensible advice that three quarters of a century later Mrs. Post's successors still dispense, although they're not so patient as she was. "Correct the error right away," said the authors of *The Amy Vanderbilt Complete Book of Etiquette.* "I'm sorry to interrupt you, but my name is Geraldine, not Josephine." In case you don't know or have forgotten the name of someone you're talking to, the Vanderbilt avatars advised you either to come right out with it ("I'm sorry, but your name suddenly escapes me") or to bluff your way through, talking so fast and in such a flattering way that the other person won't even realize you don't know who he is. If you've forgotten the name of one of the two people you're introducing to each other, you can always finesse the problem by saying, "Do you know my friend, John Blank?" and hoping neither will catch on.

"Unless you wish to stamp yourself a person who has never been out of 'provincial' society," Mrs. Post warned, "never speak of your husband as 'Mr.' except to an inferior." [2] It may be hard to imagine how eagerly notions like "inferior," "station," and "underbred" were swallowed by middle-class readers in the 1920s, but there it is. Emily Post knew her audience and the fierceness of its determination to remove every trace of under-breeding and provincialism from their demeanor. She made hay out of a snobbism and punctilio now as archaic as the bustle and the running board. On visiting cards, which were no less than an "index of one's character," a woman was *"never* Mrs. Sarah Smith; at least not anywhere in good society," and "no one should ever address an envelope, except from a bank or a lawyer's office, 'Mrs. Sarah Smith.' " A divorced woman didn't go by "Mrs. Alice Green" (her maiden name)—"unless she wishes to give the impression she was the guilty one in the divorce." The innocent and injured party in her own divorce, the author of *Etiquette,* née Price, appeared on her 1922 title page as "Emily Post (Mrs. Price Post)."

Once in a while Post's probe struck something more profound than empty form. "The born gentleman avoids the mention of names exactly as he avoids the mention of what things cost: both are an abomination to his soul." This was fairly strong language with which to rebuke the retailer of gossip. There must have been something more to it than disapproval of a little tattling: a crucial connection between identifying by name and moral transgression. It was not the story that was so bad, it was that the main character in the story was identified. Names were taboo—utter them at your risk. In this particular context naming names is comparable to Peeping Tom-ism or stealing silverware. To name-drop in order to impress another person is even worse. Name-droppers—skillful players at this game know that first names alone carry the most weight—are pariahs by most polite standards, individuals who borrow other people's light in order to ensure their own visibility. In some societies that do quite nicely without visiting cards, you never, over a lifetime, utter the name of a close relative for fear one of you may be struck dead or outlawed.

When speaking to a social equal, Post decreed, a woman may refer to her husband as Dick, but that doesn't give the other person the same privilege.

It is bad form to go about saying "Edith Wordly" or "Ethel Norman" to those who do not call them Edith or Ethel, and to speak thus familiarly of one whom you do not call by her first name is unforgivable. It is also effrontery for a younger person to call an older by her or his first name, without being asked to do so. Only a very underbred, thick-skinned person would attempt it.

Beyond this brief excursion, the by now pandemic practice of first-naming everybody in almost every circumstance appears only as the shadow of a tiny cloud moving over Mrs. Post's serene landscape in 1922. But by the late 1930s, when she produced a new, revised edition of *Etiquette* (subtitled *The Blue Book of Social Usage*), the cloud had grown to a menacing size. Deploring "present-day familiarity in the use of first names," she came up with a sweeping social observation: "The sole reason why so many men and women who work prefer jobs in factories and stores to those of domestic employ is that the latter carries the opprobrium of being addressed by one's first name." Of course, there was another and more compelling reason: unlike domestics, the factory, store, and office workers could at least expect minimum wages. Still, money aside, who would want to be mopping the floor as Fannie when she could be working the cash register as Miss Farmer? (Now, of course, she's everyone's Fannie regardless of what she does.)

Don't know how to refer to a close relative? Simply rely on "the so-called 'name of safety,' " Post advised. This was what "every well-bred man or woman or child does when speaking to a stranger about any member of the family"; in other words, "my wife," "my sister," "or, if necessary 'my sister Alice.' " By 1969, a year that saw turmoil on college campuses, the surging of the counterculture, and new codes of social behavior, Emily Post's successor as author of *Etiquette* had practically thrown in the towel on the issue of "first names, titles of respect, and descriptive phrases for members of the family." It had "become a hodgepodge of informality and confusion," although she conceded that "you will surely be thought stiff and unfriendly" if you don't first-name an equal or contemporary after you've been introduced. Fighting a rearguard action, she declared with italic emphasis, *"It is a flagrant violation of good manners for children to call their natural parents by their first names."* As for stepparents: "A nickname seems to be the best solution, if one can be found that is appropriate and not a derivative of 'Mother' or 'Father.' "

But even after a revolution which upended or turned inside out many conventions, American men and women are still so unsure of how to act and react with other men and women that the business of etiquette books thrives like innuendo in a gossip column. One of Emily Post's several spiritual daughters is Judith Sylvia Martin, née Perlman, aka Miss Manners ("a registered trademark of United Features Syndicate, Inc."), who gently mocked her subject matter by titling her 1982 book *Miss Manners' Guide to Excruciatingly Correct Behavior.* Like Post, Martin enhanced her instructional material by inventing fictional characters, giving them characterizing names—Jonathan Rhinehart Awful, Jr.; Ian Fright; Mrs. Plue Perfect—and positioning them in minidramas that illustrated the difficulties encountered in making one's way through thickets of social practice to the garden of unconscious, reflexive correctness. Martin understood that names, like Jell-O, are fluid until they finally set. "Anyone allowing himself to be announced at roll call in nursery school by the nickname—'Doopsie,' for example—his parents fashioned from his own inability to pronounce his name in infancy will be marked for life." Martin was all for children experimenting and fooling around with their names "provided they clean up the mess when they are finished," and recommended that "parents give their children the proper equipment—middle names, good combinations of initials, nicknames, names that have alternative spellings—to use when the children inevitably decide that they can no longer tolerate their childhood identities."

Although she was mindful of the link between identity and name, Martin wasn't quite so flexible when it came to adults, those "grown-up people who continue to play with their names and then are insulted when their friends can't keep up with the changes." Characteristically looking over her shoulder toward the

past, she viewed the habit of name changing as "getting worse."
Others might see this mutability as inspiriting evidence that
Americans were no longer so class conscious or snobbish as we
once were. People change their names all the time for a host of
reasons, among them marriage, divorce, career, commerce, politics, theater, and what Martin called "ethnic nostalgia." She cited
what she described as "a typical American family of four generations":

> The family's American history began with a man who Amer-
> icanized his surname when he arrived and a woman whose
> last name reflects a misspelling by an immigration officer. In
> the next generation, there is a daughter who married three
> times, changing her name successively to the full name of
> each husband, preceded only by "Mrs."; and a son who is a
> movie star and was issued a completely new name when he
> signed a studio contract. After that there is a daughter who
> has a hyphenated last name, consisting of her maiden name
> and her husband's last name. She is no longer married to
> him and has, in fact, married someone else, but she must
> retain that hyphenated name because she has made her pro-
> fessional reputation with it. Also in this generation is a son
> who has had an attack of ethnic nostalgia and changed his
> name to that of the family name in the old country.

Almost as much as Emily Post, Martin thrived on rules and
regulations and laid down some of her own: from birth to the age
of seventeen, children should be allowed to name themselves
anything they want. When they graduate from high school, they
should choose a first name and stick with it. When they marry or
start a career, they "must pick a permanent last name." And here
Martin stepped away from her typically moderating stance with
this—for her—radical proposal: the last, permanent name ought
to come from the mother's side. "The system of the matriarchal
line worked fairly well in ancient societies, before women made
the mistake of telling men that they had any connection with the

production of children." One wonders how long it would have taken men to figure it out. In any case, Martin didn't expect her proposal that children be given their mother's last name to catch on, even though, she said, "it would be a much better system, and I stick by it."

Martin jumped on the ever more common practice of people calling strangers by their first names, characterizing this trend as "promiscuous," a trade-off of civility (and privacy) for familiarity. Pre-1969, college teachers addressed their students as Miss or Mister, while students called faculty members Professor or Sir. This practice, while somewhat stiff and forbidding, marked certain frontiers—both verbal and behavioral—one dared not cross. Names have a protective as well as an evaluative halo: last names establish the outer perimeter of your private encampment, first names the inner perimeter.

If you're not on a first-name basis with your teacher, you're probably not going to sleep with him—although it does occasionally happen. If he doesn't call you Mary Jane, he's probably not going to fondle your breast, although this, too, happens from time to time. But when Elmer Student first addressed his psychology professor as Bill and Bill invited Elmer to join the Saturday night poker game, it was an invitation to other eversions (Martin would no doubt have referred to them as "liberties"). It's gone about as far as it can go. Students at most colleges are now required to grade their teachers' classroom techniques and performance on elaborate evaluation forms, while teachers pace up and down the hallway, perhaps remembering a time when it would have been inconceivable for the faculty to care what students thought or for students to believe that evaluating their teachers was part of the course work.

Taking a dire view, Amy and Leon Kass, both of them University of Chicago professors, said they regard first-naming as "symptomatic of a general breakdown of the boundaries between public and private life, between formal and familiar, between grown-up and childish, between high and low, refined and vulgar, sacred and profane." Perhaps only voices crying in the wilderness, they address their students as Mr., Miss, Mrs., or Ms. and insist the students address one another similarly. "Our students do not protest," reported Professor Kass and Professor Kass (Professors Kass?); "nearly all acquire the habit, and some have even told us how much they appreciate the contribution such civility makes to the atmosphere of learning." But it's difficult to believe that the Kass system is going to catch on. Like a sea of lava moving over the Sicilian countryside, once the first-name wave got moving, it was impossible to stop.

Martin advised you to play games with the stranger who lacked the "good manners" to call you by your last name. Thus: "No, no, I'm terribly sorry, you must have misunderstood—Geoffrey is my first name. My last name is Perfect." You feel violated when someone you don't know—over the phone, at the registry of motor vehicles, at the welfare office, at the police station, in a hospital emergency room, anywhere, in fact, where they have your name but you don't have theirs—calls you Pete or Wanda. Forget it; there's little you can do except walk out, hang up, or, better, ask them what *their* first name is and use it. Martin recommended another tactic: "Address the offenders by their last names, no matter how many times they urge you not to. If they tell you only a first name or say, 'Call me Sam,' then address that person as 'Mr. Sam.' "

"There are only two kinds of people in America," the columnist William Raspberry wrote in 1994, "those who go around calling strangers and other nonintimates by their first names and those who resent it." (One of the exceptions he cited: an elderly man who likes nurses to first-name him because this makes him feel younger.) Raspberry (his real name) was especially irritated by a broker who, phoning him cold about stock in an Argentine telephone company, called him Bill. When "Bill" objected, the broker said, "Oh, are you more comfortable with William?" "I didn't know whether to laugh or scream," Raspberry said.

Even though it often backfires, first-naming is now one of the defining features of daily life, all the way from your friendly waitperson, who's going to serve you this evening and whose name you don't necessarily want to be told, to President William Jefferson Clinton, known to the public as Bill, who reportedly is in the habit of writing letters to strangers with "Dear Joe" and "Dear Paula" salutations. If someone in authority calls you by your first name, you feel not only violated—he has come into my house, uninvited, and used my bathroom; she has opened my refrigerator and helped herself to my Brie; he has fondled my wife—but also as if you had lost the crucial first round. When a cop stops you, asks to see your license and registration, and says, "Okay, Gertrude, wanna pop open your trunk for me?" you're hardly in a position to protest or claim your rights as "equal" by asking him to tell you *his* first name. Not everyone seems to mind, however. A survey of 604 patients in primary care settings yielded these results: 96 percent liked their doctor to call them by their first names; 40 percent said they liked the reciprocal privilege; but only 14 percent, predominantly men, actually invoked it. "The physician should feel comfortable addressing almost all patients by first name," the researchers concluded. "This choice will usually be the correct one," although one practitioner (in an article titled "Hi, Lucille, This Is Dr. Gold!") protested that this was an affront to the patient's dignity. The flip side is that withholding a first name is often a tool of subtle or outright intimidation: "How do you do, I'm Doctor Friendly." "All rise for Judge Fairly." "Children, this is your new teacher, Ms. Brightman."

Many people are so uncertain of the choreography that they must be taken by the hand and shown, step by tiny step. "My question is," wrote a seeker of advice to Miss Manners, "how do you properly get on a first-name basis with someone you are beginning to know well?" It's as if, while civilization continues on its dazzling technological march, we've lost the ability to make the most basic social decisions and must resort to consulting an expert. Why doesn't this woman know intuitively when to switch from Ms. Butcher to Beulah? How is it she can't sense all by herself when the moment has arrived, since Ms. Butcher, like all of us, is no doubt sending out signals to be picked up and acted upon?

Martin maintained that without standardized guidelines such as existed in the past, a lot of us risk hurting people's feelings or making them angry. According to her, you ought to know rather than guess what to call someone or how to compose their name on an envelope or invitation—it should all be as explicit as a map. Occupying an office in the Department of the Interior is a man who (with his staff) has the final word on who decides what every unnamed geographic feature should be called; he's a sort of czar of United States place-names. But there's no such authority for personal names, unless you count the courts—and they are there chiefly to keep you from naming yourself a number or something equally baffling or incendiary. We have no one to tell women—all of whose forms of address derive, as Martin reminded us, from the word "mistress"—what we should do about our names. This is *so* American. We *do* guess, try different ways, shapes, sounds; we *do* improvise. When we go against the current, we may get splashed in the face, but it's perfectly legal, so leave us alone! Judith Martin would answer that the idea that all forms are up for grabs is "highly unrealistic." The more guidelines and readable codes we have, the easier it is for us to go about more important business.

Dear Miss Manners:
    What do I call my husband?

Gentle Reader:
    Probably "honey." Possibly you are asking what to call him when referring to him in conversations with other people. Use his name, or, if you have trouble remembering names, refer to him as "my husband." What are to be avoided are terms that suggest you know him too little or too well, such as "Mr." or "Lover."

So many thorny name problems. What do you call your fiancée's parents? What do you call your cleaning woman, and what does she call you? How do you address a doctor you have never seen before? How do you refer to your gay son's partner? What's the correct form of address for a divorced woman? a clergy-woman?

"In using a hyphenated middle name," one of Martin's suppli-cants asked, "does one use only the first letter of the first name for an initial, does one use both initials separately, or does one use both initials, but hyphenated?" It's unlikely that Martin com-posed this intricate query herself. The same thousands of people who try fifteen different shades of pink before deciding on Expir-ing Salmon for their bathrooms also care deeply about such re-finements as the hyphen in a middle name and worry themselves sick about what will happen to little Schuyler when and if the admissions person at St. Grottlesex thinks they have got it wrong.

"No one is ever correctly styled 'Mrs. Elizabeth Wellborn,' " Martin said, "come death, divorce, or famine." She's quite sure of this, although probably not one in a hundred Americans is aware of this esoteric edict and probably wouldn't obey it in any case. The notion behind this and other niceties of etiquette is that if we ignore nuances of "correct" behavior we'll become pariahs. Otherwise why are we so afraid of making mistakes?

10.
Literary Names: The Importance of Being Sherlock

*"Yossarian? Is that his name? Yossarian? What the hell
kind of name is Yossarian?"*
Lieutenant Scheisskopf had the facts at his fingertips.
"It's Yossarian's name, sir," he explained.
Joseph Heller, Catch-22

Oscar Wilde's *The Importance of Being Earnest* is a play about
names and a play on names. Plot, theme, comedy, and motivation
all owe their pulse to one heavily freighted homonym, earnest/
Ernest. "I have introduced you to everyone as Ernest," says Jack
Worthing's friend, Algernon Moncrieff. "You answer to the name
of Ernest. You look as if your name was Ernest. You are the most
earnest-looking person I ever saw in my life. It is perfectly absurd
your saying that your name isn't Ernest." Jack's lady love, Gwen-
dolen Fairfax, tells him, "My ideal has always been to love someone of the name of Ernest. There is something in that name that
inspires absolute confidence." Algernon's fiancée, Cecily Car-
dew, confides to him that she would "pity any poor married
woman whose husband is not called Ernest." This draws from
him the defense that Algernon is "not at all a bad name. In fact,
it's rather an aristocratic name. Half of the chaps who get into the
Bankruptcy Court are called Algernon." "I've now realized for

the first time in my life," Jack says to Gwendolyn as the curtain comes down on Wilde's dazzling comedy, "the vital Importance of Being Ernest."

The author himself—aesthete, poseur, wit, and symbol—was his most dazzling creation and made the name Oscar Wilde, he said, "a household word." "I started as Oscar Fingal O'Flahertie Wills Wilde," he said. "All but two of the five names have already been thrown overboard. Soon I shall discard another and be known simply as 'The Wilde' or 'The Oscar.' " When he served a prison sentence for homosexual offenses, the matter of naming was taken out of his hands—in Reading Gaol, Oscar Wilde of the famous velvet suit and fur-collared overcoat was simply convict C.3.3 and wore a convict's uniform stenciled with arrows. Released in 1897, he left for exile in France under the name Sebastian Melmoth: Sebastian for his favorite saint, martyred under the emperor Diocletian and depicted in Christian art stuck with arrows (emblems of Reading as well), and Melmoth for the hero of a popular Gothic novel (by his great-uncle Charles R. Maturin), a solitary wanderer who had sold his soul to the devil. To the very end Wilde remained faithful to the dictum of Lord Henry Wotton in his novel *The Picture of Dorian Gray:* "Names are everything."

Fictional characters like Jack Worthing and Algernon Moncrieff come into their imagined worlds not as helpless infants but as adults equipped with individualities, histories, and riddles. "Call me Ishmael," Herman Melville's narrator says in the first words of *Moby-Dick,* a four-syllable opening as decisive and now as familiar as the first four notes of Beethoven's Fifth Symphony. This is one of the few times in an almost three-hundred-thousand-word novel that we hear the name. Ishmael, moreover, is probably not his "real" name at all but one assumed as a way of characterizing himself. It comes freighted with associations. Ishmael, in Genesis the son of Abraham and the Egyptian servant Hagar, is an outcast, a nomad, a dweller in the wilderness. This is how the narrator sees himself and wishes the reader to see him: Ishmael —a first name, a rhetorical device for establishing narrative intimacy—is the one-word biography of a young sailor-scholar who, feeling November in his soul, signs on for a long voyage.

Compared to naming a character, naming a baby is a breeze. Despite what adoring parents think they can already perceive on its features, their baby is a zero, an unknown. Whatever name baby gets is ultimately random, arbitrary, and neutral despite the semantic or connotative spin parents may put on it. Names of characters, however, convey what their creators may already know and feel about them and how they want their readers to respond. "In a novel names are never neutral," David Lodge wrote, drawing on the language of semiotics. "They always signify, if it is only ordinariness," and arriving at names is an integral part of creating characters. Names "produce an extraordinary illusion," Isaac D'Israeli (father of the Victorian novelist and politician) noted, adding that "the accidental affinity or coincidence of a *name*, connected with ridicule or hatred, with pleasure or disgust, has operated like magic." It's this "magick bias," as Laurence Sterne called it, that the writer of fiction counts on to convince readers that invented characters have a real existence.

No one knows for sure where Shakespeare got the name Shylock. It may come from the Hebrew *shallach,* meaning "cormorant" and, by extension, a greedy, rapacious person; or from the obsolete English dialect word "shullock," expressing contempt; or from some other source as yet unidentified. But the name fused for good with the character. Shylock is as packed with messages as a DNA molecule, as generic as Sherlock, Oedipus, Don Quixote, Romeo, Hamlet, Iago, Uncle Tom, Tartuffe, Robinson Crusoe (and his man Friday), Scrooge, Huckleberry Finn, Caspar Milquetoast, Scarlett O'Hara, Holden Caulfield, and Lolita.[1] By and large, serious fiction writers try to invest their characters with names that are at least not easily forgotten, although there are plenty of weak, unconvincing characters with interesting names as well as strong characters with colorless names: Elizabeth Bennet in Jane Austen's *Pride and Prejudice,* Frederick Henry and Catherine Barkley in Ernest Hemingway's *A Farewell to Arms,* and, carrying this to an extreme, Franz Kafka's K. (*The Castle*) and Joseph K. (*The Trial*). Kafka's method of naming characters was as rational as his fiction is fantastic. "Georg has the same number of letters as Franz," he wrote in his diary apropos the main character of his novella *The Judgment*. "In Bendemann, the 'mann' is there only to strengthen the syllable 'Bende.' . . . But Bende has the same number of letters as Kafka, and the vowel 'e' is repeated in the same position as the vowel 'a' in Kafka." He conducted this self-conscious little exercise in projection through naming because his story, like his identity, "came out of me like a real human birth" and he wanted to "reach the body itself."

It's tempting to try to break such names down into their constituent meanings and associations, and also to speculate how a writer's imagination allows a particular name to fasten itself, like sperm to ova, to a particular character. Literary scholars, especially those who practice the subspecialty of literary onomastics, have devoted a great deal of time, energy, and ink to exploring what one semiotician called the connotative value of names that function as "symbolic, metaphoric, metonymic, or allegorical discourse." The yield from these probes may be piquant but not momentous.

St. Louis–born T. S. Eliot, for example, apparently derived Prufrock ("The Love Song of J. Alfred Prufrock") from a local furniture store, the Prufrock-Littau Company, but this discovery mainly tells us that while you can take the boy out of St. Louis, you can't take St. Louis out of the boy. Part of the overarching irony of Eliot's poem derives from the conjunction of two brawny nouns—"proof," "rock"—and a distinctly precious, fastidious character who measures out his life "with coffee spoons" and has a fancy name, parted in the middle (like J. Pierpont Morgan or F. Scott Fitzgerald), that can be punned as "prude in a frock." One scholar has suggested that the obtrusive but unexplained initial *J* in J. Alfred Prufrock may stand for Jesus, for Jean (Jean Verdenal "may have been Eliot's lover in Paris"), or for some other Christian name that Prufrock wished to hide because it had "feminine or girlish connotations." And so on, into the dark tunnels of speculation.

Charlotte Brontë would be amazed by what she could have learned about her own work if only she had lived into the twentieth century to read Lynn Hamilton's article "Character Names in *Jane Eyre* and the War of Earthly Elements." Hamilton linked Brontë's system of proper naming in *Jane Eyre* to the four constituent elements of classical cosmogony, earth, air, fire, and water:

> The elements suggested by these names are symbolic: air of freedom of spirit and restlessness, water of mobility and beneficence, fire of passion and destruction, and earth of immobility and egoism. Brontë also uses the earthly elements to symbolize moral values. Water and air are life-giving, so characters whose names associate them with the elements tend to rank higher on the moral scale than characters whose names link them with earth.

The overobvious reigns: "The name *Eyre* is perhaps Brontë's masterpiece of naming. It is not only a name but a pun. One of its meanings links the heroine to air, the most ethereal and ungraspable of the elements." Eyre can also be read as a pun on Aire, a river near Brontë's home base at Haworth, Yorkshire. When we first meet Jane, she is a young orphan living with a family named Reed, which brings to mind "immobility and dryness, forming a contrast to Jane's restlessness, purpose, and beneficence." Later, with Helen Burns, Jane's fellow orphan at Lowood Institution, Brontë "introduces the strain of fire imagery into the system of naming in *Jane Eyre*. The name in association with the character conveys the purity of a flame." Hamilton explored the abuse and eventual martyrdom Helen suffers at the hands of the evil Miss Scatcherd, a Lowood history and grammar teacher. "The suggestion of 'scratch' and 'sherd' in *Scatcherd* corresponds not only to the abrasiveness of her character, but also links her to the earthly element."

Helen's death is prefigured in her first name, related here to the Greek *helios*, meaning "sun": "Helen's fervor and brightness are self-immolating," Hamilton wrote. "The difficulty she faces is

suggested by alternating readings of her name both as a verb—
her spirit *burns* brightly—and noun (Helen's life is marked by
brutal *burns*)." Helen's first name, Hamilton added as a sort of
lagniappe, may also "be meant to suggest destruction by fire, *i.e.,*
the razing of Troy." By this point in the analysis, one shouldn't
blame any reader for not wanting to submit even to cursory expli-
cations of the names of Miss Temple (uniting "the earthly with
the spiritual") ; Edward Rochester (suggesting place, land, *earth*);
Grace Poole (water again), the custodian of Rochester's attic-
bound wife; and the Rivers family, Jane's cousins. "Rochester
needs Jane to temper his sensuality and self-interest," Hamilton
concluded, "but Jane's etherealness also needs a balancing element." Brontë said it in four words: "Reader, I married him."

The characters in allegorical or didactic works like *Everyman*
(Fellowship, Good Deeds, Worldly Goods) and *The Pilgrim's
Progress* (Christian and his wife, Christiana; Faithful; Mr.
Worldly   Wiseman;   Great-heart)   have   uninflected,   one-
dimensional names that tell you what to expect, and require no
interpretation. Shakespeare relied on this simple but effective
device for minor characters like Shallow, Silence, Fang, Snare,
Feeble, Bullcalf, and Doll Tearsheet (*Henry IV, Part 2*) and Bottom, Flute, Snout, Snug, and Starveling (*A Midsummer Night's
Dream*). Sir Amorous La Foole appears in Ben Jonson's *Epicene;*
Subtle, Sir Epicure Mammon, and Tribulation Wholesome in *The
Alchemist*. Restoration and eighteenth-century comedies introduced Mr. Horner, Mr. Pinchwife, Sir Jasper Fidget, Mrs. Squea-
mish, Sir Fopling Flutter, Mr. Smirk, Sir Benjamin Backbite, and
two characters whose names have since passed into common
usage—Lady Bountiful and Mrs. Malaprop. Lieutenant Scheisskopf, Captain Aardvark, and Major Major Major Major in Joseph
Heller's *Catch-22* and Hammer and Nailles in John Cheever's
Bullet Park are recent examples.
     Many writers, asked how they know when they have tagged a
character correctly, are apt to answer, "It feels right," meaning
the name has a satisfying sound, heft, and rhythm, along with

something subliminal and associative that releases a powerful, reflective emotion, the way a scent or musical phrase does. For Marcel Proust, the magical name Guermantes evoked a duchess, a dynasty, a history, a place, and his first childhood recognitions. It was "like one of those little balloons which have been filled with oxygen or some other gas; when I come to prick it, to extract its contents from it, I breathe the air of the Combray of that year, of that day, mingled with a fragrance of hawthorn blossom." The two syllables of Guermantes were like the famous morsel of madeleine soaked in warm tea that transported Marcel out of the present to revisit a "vast structure of recollection." His great book, *Remembrance of Things Past*, is in part an extended meditation on the language and talismanic power of names.

"What you want in a name," John Updike said, "is something odd enough without being grotesque . . . something with a little electricity." Electricity (loosely understood) may have been "dimly" on his mind, Updike conceded, when he surnamed the hero of his *Rabbit* tetralology Angstrom, recalling the Swedish physicist who mapped the solar spectrum (light waves are measured in angstroms). But the word "angst" was also "out there, begging to be noticed," Updike said, a vestige of his preoccupation with Søren Kierkegaard, the Danish philosopher and religious thinker, author of *Fear and Trembling*. For Kierkegaard, as Updike once wrote, "to be human is *inherently* to be a problem," and this is true of Rabbit running, at rest, and all the time between. Nicknamed Rabbit because he has a broad white face, pale blue irises, "and a nervous flutter under his brief nose," Updike's hero marries Janice Springer, her family name suggesting—prophetically, as their story develops—upward mobility, entrapment (springes snare small game like rabbits), and a natural foe of rabbits, the springer spaniel. Updike said he sometimes uses phone books as a source for his names, especially ethnic ones, again looking for something odd but not odd enough to be grotesque. As for nonethnic names: Richard Maple—"leafy, innocent, young, and WASP-y"—took Updike a while to find, but when he did he jumped on it.

At the opposite end of the process is a writer like novelist William Gaddis, who claims to pick up names for his characters from the tags worn by highway toll collectors. But even Gaddis would have to admit that a choice made in this apparently random way is not so random after all. Even a name glimpsed at a toll booth has to have at least some faint, as-yet-unacknowledged link or sympathetic vibration to the character on whom the author decides to pin it. The novelist-narrator in Lydia Davis's *The End of the Story* gives this account of her difficulties in finding this link.

> [The editor] said the names were wrong. She did not want the hero to be named Hank. She thought no one could fall in love with someone named Hank. She said it made her think of "handkerchief." Of course it isn't true that no one can fall in love with someone named Hank. But she meant I could choose any name I like for my hero, while men named Hank, and the men and women who fall in love with them, are not free to choose. . . . A friend of mine who has written several novels told me a few months ago that in one novel she went ahead so fast . . . that the name of one character changed twelve times in the course of the book.

The same accidental but also fated process that Gaddis counts on applied to Boris Pasternak's Zhivago (seen on a manhole cover —the manufacturer's name) and J. D. Salinger's Holden Caulfield (telescoping the last names of a friend and the movie actress Joan Caulfield).

Jonathan Swift coined the name Vanessa (as in Vanessa Redgrave). It was a reversal and telescoping of Esther Vanhomrigh, the name of a pupil he believed was in love with him. Fiona, coined by the eighteenth-century Scottish poet James Macpherson, was taken over by the romancer William Sharp for his pen name, Fiona Macleod, and became as popular as Vanessa and Wendy (in J. M. Barrie's *Peter Pan*). Writers who would rather borrow than invent can always call up a computer program described by Holy Cross professor emeritus John H. Dorenkamp as follows:

> All it is is a list—or rather three lists of names: surnames, men's first names, and women's first names. The creator of the list says there are 4000 names. You can add to the lists (or delete, if you like) and modify already existing names. Most of the surnames appear to be Anglo-Saxon, although there are others which are more diverse. It is not a multicultural list. The first names have a certain blonde quality as well, but they are more diverse. Many of the first names sound like last names, e.g., Dacey, Trahern, and Knox. There is also Chen, Inger, Haldan, and Yule. Women's first names are more exotic, including Abibi, Alula, Binga, Faline, Sachiko, Thora, and Wenche.

A bonus feature of this program allows our imaginatively strapped author to shuffle first and last names. Among the weird couplings that emerge from the grab bag: Waldemar Hathaway, Wilton Cardozo, Emmanuel Froebel, Arne Liszt, Reuben Crusoe, Kenneth Ludendorff, and Roper Woolworth for males; for females, Eustacia Flotow, Ginger Immelman, Janet Mercator, Whitney Descartes, Aditi Sargent, and Yoshiko Repplier. "I don't know about you," Dorenkamp said, "but I wouldn't trust anyone named Whitney Descartes or Arne Liszt."

What the designer of this computer monster doesn't realize is the trouble an author can get into by giving a disagreeable character a last name that belongs to only a handful of real people— Dorenkamp, for instance. When the paperback edition of Bernays's first novel, *Short Pleasures,* was published in 1963, she was sued for a million dollars by a man who had the same unusual surname as one of her characters, a predatory, bisexual summer-theater director. The plaintiff was someone she had never met or heard of.

She discovered, too late, that there were only five people in the

Manhattan telephone directory with that name, and they were all related to one another. It cost her thousands simply to defend the suit, which was eventually settled out of court. She had been advised that in similar cases juries generally find for the plaintiff, figuring that writers are rich, unethical, and exploitative. As a final shot, her lawyer told her that in the future she should avoid giving characters anything but common names. John Updike was luckier; he furnished an unsavory character in *Couples* with the name of a man he knew, but this man merely frowned at him after the book came out. As for users of Dorenkamp's computer program, be wary of the Emmanuel Froebels and Yoshika Reppliers who may be waiting in ambush.

Sherlock Holmes and Dr. Watson: for us the names are as fixed as the tides and the rising of the sun. Any other names for Arthur Conan Doyle's two main characters would be unthinkable (except as parodies, like Stately Homes and Picklock Holes, Potson and Watsis). And yet in 1886, when Doyle began writing the detective story that first made him famous, *A Study in Scarlet* (originally titled *A Tangled Skein*), he was still scrambling for a name for his hero. "What should I call the fellow?" he recalled asking himself. "One rebelled against the elementary art which gives some inkling of character in the name and creates Mr. Sharps or Mr. Ferrets." He decided on Holmes, in honor of one of his favorite authors, Dr. Oliver Wendell Holmes, whose visit to England that spring was widely reported in the newspapers. "Never have I so known and loved a man whom I had never seen," Doyle said. But the right first name to go with Holmes eluded him. First it was Sherringford (or Sherrinford, as Doyle set it down in a notebook), but this wasn't quite right—too soft, too liquid—for a man with a profile as sharp as a carving knife and a mind wound as tightly as a watch spring. "It had no clean crack of the bat," as one of Doyle's biographers, the mystery writer John Dickson Carr, put it. "He studied it, toyed with it, and then—entirely at random—he hit on the Irish name of Sherlock. Sherlock Holmes! This time it had the click of an opening key."

Watson, Holmes's indispensable confidant and chronicler, a medical doctor like Doyle himself, shows up in an early draft of *A Study in Scarlet* as Ormond Sacker. This yokes suggestions of the dandy (Ormond) and the tradesman (Sacker, a maker of sacks or bags), which, both singly and together, simply don't fit a retired British army surgeon, a bit on his uppers, compelled to economize by sharing digs with a distinctly peculiar roommate: a self-described consulting detective, "the only one in the world," who appeared "to know every detail of every horror perpetrated in the century." Ormond Sacker eventually bowed out in favor of plain, sturdy, reliable, true-blue John H. Watson, M.D.—"Good old Watson!"—surnamed in honor, and by permission, of Doyle's friend and medical colleague James E. Watson, M.D., of Southsea, Hampshire.

Charles Dickens's Book of Memoranda, a compilation begun in 1855 when he was forty-two, contained almost two hundred name entries, among them Laughley, Minnitt, Snosswell, Froser, Tuzzen, Squab, and Sugg. For boys, he had Joey Stick, Henry Ghost, George Muzzle, Zephaniah Fury, Robert Gospel; for girls, Sarah Goldsacks, Catherine Two, Miriam Denial, Alice Thorneywork, Birdie Nash. Some were genuine neologisms; others, names Dickens had spotted on signposts or death notices. Apparently he couldn't get down to the work of writing a novel until he had baptized his principal characters; he didn't know who they were or where they were going until they were safely inside the skin of their rightful names, just as Oliver Twist's story, like Rumpelstiltskin's in the German folk tale, cannot be resolved until his true surname (Leeford) reveals itself. Dickens's brilliant roster of invented character names, some of which have passed into common speech, reads like an incantation: Ebenezer Scrooge, Uriah Heep, Seth Pecksniff, Sairey Gamp, Wilkins Micawber, Sir Mulberry Hawk, Wackford Squeers, Ned and Charles Cheeryble, Thomas Gradgrind, Josiah Bounderby.

For the author, finding names like these is a complicated process involving sound, emotion, and association as well as an awareness of social and political choreography. Sometimes it's accomplished in a flash, sometimes it involves several stages. Writing *A Christmas Carol,* Dickens tried out Little Larry, then Small Sam and Puny Pete before he was satisfied with the equally alliterative (and now universally recognizable) Tiny Tim. Before Martin Chuzzlewit's surname was firmly in place, he was Chuzzletoe, Chuzzlebog, and Chuzzlewig, the "chuzzle" echoing the word "chouse," an innocent, a dupe, as Martin turned out to be when he came to America only to be swindled by the fraudulent Eden Land Corporation. Bully Stryver, Charles Darnay's defense counsel in *A Tale of Two Cities,* carries a clear enough message (you'd want him on your side if you were in the dock for treason). Sydney Carton, a wastrel who in his single redeeming moment takes Darnay's place on the guillotine, seems deliberately flat and colorless, but it's worth recalling that the French phrase *un homme de carton* means an idler, a flaneur, a nullity.

Occasionally Dickens put reverse spin on a name. Steerforth in *David Copperfield* perfectly suits the sterling, forthright, generous, and loyal fellow we see at first. In giving a name that inspires trust to a character who turns out to be devious and treacherous, Dickens covertly warned the reader to beware: Steerforth promises something too good to be true. Like Oliver Twist, David Copperfield undergoes a crucial change of name. His aunt Betsy Trotwood bestows her surname on him in place of David after he escapes from his brutal stepfather, Edward Murdstone. "Thus I began my new life," reports young Trotwood Copperfield, as he is to be known from then on, "in a new name, and with everything new about me. Now that the state of doubt was over, I felt, for many days, like one in a dream." A witness to this scene is Betsy Trotwood's boarder, Mr. Dick, who by his own choice had undergone a comparably decisive transformation. "Babley—Mr. Richard Babley—that's the gentleman's true name," Betsy Trotwood warns her nephew.

But don't you call him by it, whatever you do. He can't bear his name. That's a peculiarity of his. Though I don't know it's much of a peculiarity, either; for he has been ill-used enough, by some that bear it, to have a mortal antipathy for it, Heaven knows. Mr. Dick is his name here, and everywhere else, now—if he ever went anywhere else, which he don't. So take care, child, you don't call him anything *but* Mr. Dick.

It's David's stepfather, Edward Murdstone, who should not have been able to "bear his name," loaded as it is with dark and menacing associations. The "stone" in Murdstone, some scholars claim, calls up the slabs under which David's father lies and David's mother will soon lie as well. "Murd," as in "murder," again suggests the two deaths as well as being a homonym of the French *merde.* Couple these constituents with Dickens's extratextual memories of early abandonment and bereavement, and you get a name rich in both fictional and autobiographical protein. Murdstone comes off as a man so supremely cold and brutal that anyone meeting him on the printed page will never be able to put him out of mind. Basil Rathbone, who played him in the 1935 production of *David Copperfield,* became so identified with this villain in the eyes of the moviegoing public that it was a while before he could land a sympathetic role—or so the Hollywood legend goes.

Biographer Leon Edel wrote that Henry James's "passion for finding the right names for his fictional characters stemmed from a sense that wrong names had been bestowed within his family's experience. It was difficult to be an individual if one's name were a family tag pinned to the cradles of helpless babes." James was a colorless enough surname to begin with, but for several generations the males in the family had been christened either William or Henry. Younger brother of the philosopher William James, the novelist Henry, named for their father, loathed being a Junior. He lopped it off as soon as Henry Senior died but remained sensitive about juniorship to the end of his days. In a fifteen-hundred-word letter to his nephew William, who in 1913 was about to name his newborn infant William as well, Henry begged him—unavailingly—to reconsider:

> Of course, it is happy and delightful that your father's first grandson should be a William again—but I can't but feel sorry that you are embarking afresh on the unfortunate mere *Junior.* I have a right to speak of that appendage—I carried it about for forty years. . . . Apparently, however, you don't dislike it in your own case, or you wouldn't so serenely reduce your helpless child to it. Let me nevertheless plead against it!

James vented a compensatory passion for right and individual naming in his fiction. The notebooks he kept between 1878 and 1915, the year before he died, contain about forty separate lists, raw material for his stories and novels, that add up to more than a thousand names. A sample entry: "Mrs. Parlour—Mrs. Sturdy—Silverlock—Dexter Frere—Dovedale." Some are distinctly Dickensian or caricaturing: Tagus Shout, Cridge, Noad, Squirl, Trig, Pinching, Sugg, Cushion, Arrow, Popkiss. (When it came to servants, James often gave them the back of his hand by dismissing them with monosyllables: Banks, Bates, Gotch, Hack, Steel.) Along with Loinsworth and Coxon, the modulating sequence of "Ledward—Bedward—Dedward—Deadward" in notes made in 1893 has suggested to at least one biographer that the celibate James was working out his anxieties about sex, but we'll let that speculation stand as it is.

"One of the great mysteries of literary history," David Lodge said, "is what exactly the supremely respectable Henry James means by calling one of his characters Fanny Assingham," a portmanteau of three words relating to hindparts.[2] Some names—Hyacinth Robinson, Maggie Verver, Nanda Brookenham, and Fleda and Anastasius Vetch—sound contrived or downright weird, but most are brilliantly on target. Lambert Strether (of *The Ambassadors*) combines two surnames, in the established manner of upper-class Americans.³ Miss Birdseye (*The Bostonians*) is a "ticklish spinster," a tireless worker for lost causes, who, like Dickens's Miss Havisham, doesn't need a first name; Caspar Goodwood, "the son of a proprietor of well-known cotton mills in Massachusetts," is Isabel Archer's energetic but unsuccessful suitor (*Portrait of a Lady*); Daisy Miller came to stand for a type —the American girl, audacious and innocent, in an encounter with Europe. ("That ain't her real name; that ain't her name on her cards," her little brother Randolph volunteers. "Her real name's Annie P. Miller," of Schenectady, New York). The names Jeffrey Aspern and Miss Bordereau (*The Aspern Papers*) decode the plot of this short novel: Aspern was where Napoleon met his first military defeat; Bordereau is French for "memorandum" or "note," suggesting the papers the narrator will never get to see. Playing games with names in James is like drilling for oil in the Persian Gulf—there's always more.

Some writers—James Joyce, Eliot, Fitzgerald—play with and assemble names for their own sake, for their poetry, music, and associative richness, and out of them create litanies and Homeric catalogues that have an undeniable incantatory force. In the Cyclops section of *Ulysses,* set in Barney Tiernan's pothouse, Joyce recites a hundred names and nicknames, mythological, historical, and fanciful, from "Cuchulin, Conn of hundred battles, Niall of Nine Hostages" to "Peg Woffington, the Village Blacksmith, Captain Moonlight, Captain Boycott, Dante Alighieri, Christopher Columbus, Boss Croker, Herodotus, Jack the Giantkiller, Gautama Buddha, Lady Godiva, the Lily of Kilarney," and more. Each is the equivalent of a dab of color in a pointillist painting. Eliot played with exotic names in "Gerontion": Mr. Silvero, Hakagawa, Madame de Tornquist, Fraulein von Kulp.

"Once," says Nick Carraway, the narrator of *The Great Gatsby,* "I wrote down on the empty spaces of a timetable the names of those who came to Gatsby's house that summer." Either the timetable was unusually empty or Carraway's handwriting unusually small—the list fills two printed pages. Some of the names are comic and suggestive—S. B. Whitebait, James B. ("Rot-

Gut") Ferret, George Duckweed, S. W. Belcher, Miss Haag, Miss Claudia Hip. Others come equipped with minimalist histories: "Doctor Webster Civet who was drowned last summer up in Maine," "Newton Orchid who controlled Films Par Excellence," "Henry L. Palmetto who killed himself by jumping in front of a subway train in Times Square," "young Brewer who had his nose shot off in the war," "Mr. P. Jewett, once head of the American Legion."

Among these twentieth-century connoisseurs and *feinschmeckers* of names, the Brillat-Savarin is Vladimir Nabokov, who wrote under many pseudonyms, including Vladimir Sirin, V. Cantaboff, and the anagrams Dorian Vivalcomb, Vivian Calmbrood, and Vivian Darkbloom. As character or narrator he also appears in his work as Blavdak Vimori, Mr. Vivian Badlook, Baron von Librikov, and a few other contrivances. *"Lolita* is famous, not I," he said. "I am an obscure, doubly obscure, novelist with an unpronounceable name." Responding to an interviewer's question about "colored hearing," he examined his initials: "V is a kind of pale, transparent pink: I think it's called, technically, quartz pink. This is one of the closest colors that I can connect with the V. And the N, on the other hand, is a grayish-yellowish oatmeal color." For this author, names not only had color and perfume but mobility and hypnotic power, as in the opening passage of his "famous" book:

Lolita, light of my life, fire of my loins. My sin, my soul. Lo-lee-ta: the tip of the tongue taking a trip of three steps down the palate to tap, at three, on the teeth. Lo. Lee. Ta. She was Lo, plain Lo, in the morning, standing four feet ten in one sock. She was Lola in slacks. She was Dolly at school. She was Dolores on the dotted line. But in my arms she was always Lolita.

The novel's plot, as vagrant as a dream, follows the emphatically named Humbert Humbert in his fatal passion for Lolita. When he finds his nymphet's name among forty on a Ramsdale school mimeographed class list, he responds with a "spine-thrill of delight" to the "tender anonymity" of "Dolores Haze," the first name and surname together "like a pair of new pale gloves." In its repetitions, ethnic variety, humor, and counterbalancing flatness, Nabokov's remarkable list seems real and invented at the same time, a triumph of artifice. Out of some of the names on the list he constructs imagined portraits: "Grace and her ripe pimples; Ginny and her lagging leg; Gordon, the haggard masturbator . . . Ralph, who bullies and steals; Irving, for whom I am sorry." The mimeographed list of names "is a poem I know already by heart," Humbert says. "A poem, a poem, forsooth!"

11.
New Names,
New Identities

*And when she said, "But my name, Auntie—my name's
Regina Dallas," I said: "It was Beaufort when he covered
you with jewels, and it's got to stay Beaufort now that he's
covered you with shame."*

Edith Wharton, *The Age of Innocence*

Every American citizen, and every applicant for citizenship under
the immigration laws, has a common-law, free-speech, and pursuit-
of-happiness right to take and use a new name so long as it isn't
offensive, confusing, inciting to violence and racial hatred, or
taken for some unlawful purpose such as fraud, flight from the law,
evasion of debt or bankruptcy, or the commission of a crime. So
long as it isn't also a number, a hieroglyph, or a visual symbol, the
new name becomes as legal as if it had been given at birth. Americans don't need formal permission of the court to rename themselves, but many nevertheless submit a petition. They want to assert
continuity of identity and property rights, make the change a matter
of public record, and dispel any lingering qualms they feel about
sailing under false colors. "If you change your name with or without legal recourse," *The Amy Vanderbilt Complete Book of Etiquette* counseled, "you may send out an announcement card to
friends and relatives." And Emily Post told you how to word it:
"Mr. and Mrs. John Original-Name announce that . . . they and
their children have taken the family name of Miller."

The formal requirements, procedures, and waiting periods vary from state to state, especially in the case of married or divorced women who want to go back to using their original names. The reasons applicants give for taking a new name range from habitual usage, marital breakup, embarrassing mispronunciation, religious conversion (frequently to Islam), and ethnic pride to aesthetic and idiosyncratic considerations and just plain convenience (as in the case of the Michigan man who in 1935 took the name Pappas in place of the original thirty-seven-letter Pappatheodorokomoundoronicolucopoulos). Apparently, assuming good faith on the part of the petitioner, almost any reason is as good as any other, and few petitions for name changes are denied. Each year for the past decade or so, about three hundred people in New York City have filed an application to the Civil Court, supplied a birth certificate, paid a $50 filing fee, and sat tight for eight weeks after publishing formal notice of the intended change in a newspaper. "I am an incest survivor," one woman wrote in her application. "I never want my father to find me." Another beneficiary of the Civil Court is the former Hassan Romieh, a publisher and twice self-nominated presidential candidate. He's now known as George Washington America. This may not get him elected and his wife may never be First Lady, but, he says, at least she can "be called Mrs. America without having to go to Atlantic City."

Ophthalmologist and tennis star Richard Raskin underwent a sex change operation and began a new life as Renee Richards—"Richard reborn"—author of an aptly titled memoir, *Second Serve.* "I had at least twenty-five separate changes to make," he said, "ranging in importance from my medical degrees to my gasoline credit cards. Passport, voter registration, driver's license, United States Tennis Association membership—the list kept getting longer and longer, and I began to realize how much paper people are involved with in this society."

When an ordinary taxpayer and working person who is neither a celebrity nor a prisoner decides for complex personal reasons that he or she wishes to be known *only* by a number, the resulting debate shows how volatile naming is as a social and legal issue. It also shows how fundamentally undecided we are, after almost twenty-five centuries of philosophic debate, starting with Plato, about just what a name is in the first place: whether it acquires real meaning in and through the person who owns it, the way clothes take on the shape and scent of the wearer (and even "make the man"), or is just an arbitrary, intrinsically meaningless sign. (See Chapter 12.)

All of these issues and more, either directly or indirectly, emerged in public discussion and court record from 1975 to 1980, when a Fargo, North Dakota, high school teacher, Michael Herbert Dengler, petitioned the state district court for permission to change his name to 1069. 1069 expressed his individuality and personal philosophy, he explained, each of its four digits, respectively, standing for his relationship with nature, time and movement, the universe, and "essence." He claimed to have been helped in arriving at 1069 by his reading of *Symbolic Logic* by the mathematician and literary fantasist Charles Lutwidge Dodgson (who renamed himself Lewis Carroll for public consumption). "Any single Thing, which we can name so as to distinguish it from all other Things," Carroll wrote, "may be regarded as a one-Member Class," and that name defines it. A unique individual, as Dengler regarded himself, is "a one-Member Class."

Dengler's supervisor, concerned with Social Security payments, tax reporting, and other such administrative matters, urged him to petition for a name change. He thereby launched Dengler on a five-year legal odyssey that took his case to the District Court in Fargo, the North Dakota Supreme Court, and, from there, after Dengler moved out of state, to a District Court in Minnesota, the Minnesota Supreme Court, and finally the United States Supreme Court in Washington, D.C.

At his court appearances, Dengler signed in with numerals and said that although he wanted his name pronounced "one-zero-six-nine," some people called him "Ten-sixty-nine," "Niner," and "Zero." Playful judges asked if he would accept Juan in place of 1 or be addressed as "Dr. 9" if he went on to earn his Ph.D. In response to prodding from the bench as to "the aberrant sex connotations of the expression 69," he said that neither he nor his girlfriend found it embarrassing or bizarre. All the same, the North Dakota District Court judge denied Dengler's petition, and the state Supreme Court subsequently upheld his ruling:

> Symbols, signs, figures, marks, characters, designs, diagrams, emblems and insignia are simply not suited for use as names. If the Court indulges the present request of a philosophy enthusiast to use numerical symbols as a legal name, it could hardly deny use of other symbols to subsequent petitioners. A musician, for example, might seek an inimitable grouping of eighth notes as his name. A mathematician might want a particular equation, a financier the dollar sign, an astrologer the symbol for Sagittarius. It is easy to visualize the confusions and complexities such a system of personal identification would breed.

Dengler had no better luck in Minnesota, a district judge there ruling that a number name like 1069 not only went against practicality and common sense but was "offensive to human dignity," "inherently totalitarian in nature," and provided "additional nourishment upon which the illness of dehumanization is able to feed and grow to the point where it is totally incurable." In the end, after the Minnesota Supreme Court denied his appeal and the United States Supreme Court declined to hear the case "for lack of a substantial federal question," Dengler was left in a confusing and contradictory situation that the courts were unable to resolve: he had every common-law right to use 1069 as his official name, but the gas company and the motor vehicles bureau were equally justified in refusing to recognize it. They insisted a name wasn't a name if it didn't have two parts, a first and a last, a common law definition that had been in force ever since the Norman Conquest.[1] Dengler might have done as well if he had disregarded numbers, symbolic logic, and "one-Member

Classes" and instead followed the example of Odysseus, who tricked the Cyclops Polyphemus by calling himself Nobody. Or, like the enigmatic hero of Jules Verne's *Twenty Thousand Leagues Under the Sea,* he could have taken the name Nemo, meaning the same thing.

"Name-changing is as American as a basketball hoop over a garage door, as green money, as sliced bread, as competitive overeating," Ted Morgan, formerly Sanche de Gramont, wrote in an engaging personal chronicle, *On Becoming American.* "It's one of the overlooked freedoms," "part of the culture." This has been true ever since the first adventurers came to the colonies to start from scratch and the colonies decided to call themselves the United States of America. For new citizens, Morgan said, requesting a name change on their certificate of naturalization can be as casual an act as telling your waitperson "how you want your eggs done." Scion of a ducal French family, from whom he inherited the title of count, he decided in his mid-forties to shed his European past and its social aura and start a second life as an ordinary United States citizen. To do this he needed a new "name that conformed with the language and cultural norms of American society, a name that telephone operators and desk clerks could hear without flinching." Unlike most new citizens, in changing his name he traded down rather than up on the normal status scale.

The way he went about effecting this transformation acknowledged the magical or occult nature of the name he was born with and was not altogether willing to shed.

I decided that my new name should be an Americanized rearrangement of the letters in my old name. The ingredients were the same, but the product was new and improved. I did not want to pick a name out of thin air, but to operate within precise boundaries, the letters of my last name. My commonplace American name would have a hidden link with my old name. I would recycle the old name.

From the nine letters of de Gramont he derived nineteen anagrams that made some sort of phonetic sense, among them Red Montag, O. D. Garment, Monte Drag, Gert Monad, Rod Magnet, Mo Dragnet, and Mr. de Tango.[2] He settled conservatively on Ted Morgan, which was "forthright and practical, incisive and balanced," and suggested a character type: someone trustworthy and understanding who got along well with women, children, dogs, and editors.

As Sanche de Gramont, reporter for the *New York Herald-Tribune,* he had been the only French citizen to win the Pulitzer Prize; as Ted Morgan, naturalized citizen of the United States, he went on to a notable career as biographer of Winston Churchill, FDR, and Somerset Maugham and historian of early American settlement. With the exception of its happy resolution, his life story parallels that of an earlier French émigré and writer, Michel-Guillaume-Jean de Crèvecoeur ("Mr. Heartbreak," as John Berryman rendered the name in *The Dream Songs,* "the New Man, / Come to farm a crazy land"). In 1769, after ten years of touring the American colonies, Crèvecoeur settled in Orange County, New York. Taking the English name J. Hector St. John, he recounted his impressions of the generic "American, this new man," who had stripped himself of "ancient prejudices and manners" and would "one day cause great changes in the world." His book, *Letters from an American Farmer,* made him a literary celebrity and remains a classic text about life in the emerging young nation. During the Revolutionary War, "Mr. Heartbreak" lost his wife to disease, his children to strangers, and his house and farm to a marauding band of Loyalists and Indians.

For Sanche de Gramont, taking the name Ted Morgan had been the decisive event in becoming "this new man." Warning against the move, his brother, a psychoanalyst, argued, "Your name is like a part of your body; it is bound up with the development of your psyche. It is an abbreviated way of stating your relationship to your family and your society. To tamper with that could be dangerous. . . . Psychoanalysts' offices are full of name-changers." Morgan answered, "They're also full of people who haven't changed their name." He said that whatever anxieties he may have felt about the "dissociation," "identity diffusion," hazard to established "ego defense patterns," and symbolic parenticide connected with his name changing were put to rest by the example of Erik H. Erikson, guru of the celebrated identity crisis. By the second half of the twentieth century, identity crisis had become a rite of passage as well as a mantra for Americans coming of age.

In *Young Man Luther,* a psychobiographical study, Erikson defined this crisis as coming at a time when "each youth must forge for himself some central perspective and direction, some working unity out of the effective remnants of his childhood and the hopes of his anticipated adulthood." The child of a Danish mother and her Danish lover (whose name Erikson never knew), he had been reared in Germany by a Jewish stepfather, Dr. Theodor Homburger, a pediatrician whose last name he took. Blond and blue eyed, Erikson recalled, "I acquired the nickname 'goy' in my stepfather's temple; while to my schoolmates, I was a 'Jew.' " He became a "German superpatriot" in order to live down his Danish origins, but then found that "my Jewishness was too much for the patriots, and their anti-Semitism too much for me." "Driven to be original," he rebelled against everything his bourgeois family stood for, set out as a wandering artist ("a sort of transitional beatnik"), became instead a member of Sigmund Freud's circle in Vienna, and published his first psychoanalytic paper as Erik Homburger. Eventually he rejected the "negative identity" that came with being both a bastard and a stepson and renamed himself Erik Erikson, literally Erik son of Erik, making himself both parent and child of the same psychosocial entity. But he kept the *H* of Homburger as his middle initial, "out of gratitude," he said, "but also to avoid the semblance of evasion." "I felt a sense of kinship with Erikson," Morgan wrote. "He had understood that America had a particular identity. It was a country where immigrants merged their ancestral identities into the common one of the self-made man."

• • •

Apart from the name given him at birth, "there's really very little that a man can change at will," Saul Bellow wrote in his novella *Seize the Day.* By taking a new name, as his protagonist Tommy Wilhelm (born Wilhelm Adler) does, an unfinished person may hope to enter into more satisfactory transactions both with the world outside and with his or her "true soul," the naked self. Such changes are organic, transformative, more than merely nominal, as Bellow must already have known when, at the age of twenty-one, he petitioned the court for permission to call himself Saul instead of Solomon. Inscribed Sigismund Schlomo in the family Bible, Sigmund Freud dropped the Schlomo as soon as he could and replaced Sigismund (a name that often figured in anti-Semitic jokes) with Sigmund. But he continued to have what he would have called a "problem" in this department, especially when his professional enemies in Vienna played on the contrast between psychopathology, which was his turf, and "joy," the literal meaning of Freud (*Simcha* in Hebrew). In London at the end of his life, he was about to sign the Charter Book of the British Royal Society simply Freud when he was told that the privilege of using this preemptive shorthand form was reserved for royalty and nobility and had been denied even to Isaac Newton and Charles Darwin.

Like most people impatient with surface reality, Freud viewed names as screens in front of something with more curves. In most families, naming the children is a joint enterprise; when only one parent bestows a name, it is usually the mother. In this complete autocrat's family, he named his six children without consulting his wife, Martha; he also got to ride first class in the train while she and the kids sat on wooden benches in third. Historian and biographer Peter Gay examined both Freud's conscious and unconscious motives for giving his three sons and three daughters —all born within eight years—the names he did. The first child, a daughter, Freud named Mathilde, after the wife of his mentor, the Viennese internist Joseph Breuer. The next was a boy whom Freud called Jean Martin, thereafter known as Martin; he too had been given the name of a Freud mentor, the French neuropathologist Jean-Martin Charcot. These namings paid off, so to speak, some of Freud's most significant intellectual debts. Next came son number three, Oliver, named for Oliver Cromwell, one of Freud's heroes. ("I had resolved to use this very name if it should be a son," Freud wrote, "and I greeted the newborn with it, highly *satisfied.*") He called his third son Ernst after yet another mentor, the physiologist Ernst Brücke. The last two children, both girls, were named Sophie and Anna, each as a bow to the niece and daughter of Freud's religion teacher, Samuel Hammerschlag.

So far, this was fairly straighforward: the father consciously names his children after people he is grateful to. Digging deeper, Gay found another layer of ore:

> If the names of Freud's six children generate rich associa-
> tions to his social habits, religious stance, and scientific com-
> mitments, they also supply important evidence for his
> unconscious life. I submit that ultimately all his children's
> names lead back to one figure, and to Freud's long-standing
> struggle with it: his father, Jacob.

Not everyone will be willing to follow Professor Gay to this point, although he made a plausible case for Freud's unresolved conflicts about Jacob. What Gay failed to make convincing is the double-sidedness of naming someone after a father figure. In what way is this evidence of unresolved conflict? You could just as easily read it as evidence of a conflict resolved, another debt paid off. "The names Freud gave his six children," Gay concluded, "record his heroic and historic bid for inner freedom, a freedom that was the essential condition for his discoveries."

For reasons of psychic as well as aural euphony, David Henry Thoreau altered the order of his names to Henry David Thoreau. At the insistence of her husband, who discerned her future to be that of "a *literary woman,*" Mrs. H. E. Beecher Stowe began to sign herself, as he said, "only and always *Harriet Beecher Stowe,* which is a name euphonious, flowing, and full of meaning."

Nathaniel Hawthorne revised the spelling of the family name, adding the *w;* William Faulkner added the *u* to the family Falkner, explaining years later that he had not wanted "to ride on grandfather's coat-tails" and was glad to have "such an easy way to strike out for myself." Virginia-born and Nebraska-raised novelist Willa Cather found her way from the baptismal Wilella through Willa Love Cather, Willa Lova Cather, and a transsexual identity (cropped hair, masculine clothing), William Cather, M.D. (or William Cather, Jr.) to the final Willa Sibert Cather, as she signed her will. She had taken the Sibert from an uncle on her mother's side who was killed fighting for the Confederacy, and became his "namesake," she wrote in 1902, ten years before she published her first novel. The evolution of her name was an intimate part of her evolving vocation and sexual identity. Pearl Grey of Zanesville, Ohio, had been resigned to following the career of his father, a country tooth puller, until he took a trip to Arizona and began publishing as Zane Grey, author of *Riders of the Purple Sage* and other horse operas.

The future author of *Miss Lonelyhearts* and *The Day of the Locust,* Nathan Weinstein, born in New York City in 1903, entered Brown University by appropriating the academic credentials of another student named Nathan Weinstein; he managed to maintain the deception until he graduated. Dandy, esthete, decadent, and mystic, he also passed through a Schilleresque phase as Nathaniel von Wallenstein Weinstein before settling on Nathanael West.[3] The catalyst for this final change, he said, had been "Go west, young man," and go west he did in a literal sense as well, to California, where he wrote for the movies and died in an auto accident. The new name expressed "the new identity he had invented," wrote his biographer—West, too, like Ted Morgan, had become "a new man by an act of his own will." More recently, Allen Stewart Konigsberg, born in 1935, has made Woody Allen his legal name since the 1960s, synonymous with two separate and interchangeable personas, a schlemiel and a purposeful filmmaker–comedy writer. "While the character has almost no control over what happens to him," wrote Allen's biographer Eric Lax, "the man has almost complete control over what he does." He enjoys the same degree of autonomy and instant recognition as Charlie Chaplin.

Thomas Lanier Williams III fled from his family in Missouri, attended three universities, and traveled the United States and Mexico before renaming and redefining himself as Tennessee Williams in honor of his father's Tennessee forebears; he now had a purpose (a friend nicknamed him Tennacity) and a vocation in the theater. At the age of thirty-four, he achieved his first major success with *The Glass Menagerie*. Truman Streckfus Persons became Truman Garcia Capote when his mother remarried. He coldly rebuked his father for calling him by the old name. "I would appreciate it if in the future you would address me as Truman Capote, as everyone knows me by that name." Conversely, John Berryman ("a good name for a poet") had been born John Smith ("ludicrously unpoetic"), but felt he had betrayed his dead father by making the change. "This act of disloyalty I will never, never be able to repair," he told his wife, Eileen Simpson. "To 'make a name' for myself. . . . Can you see how ambivalent my feelings are about this ambition?"

In 1863, at the age of twenty-seven, Samuel L. Clemens, an itinerant journalist writing to his paper from Carson City, capital of the Nevada Territory, began a travel letter with "I feel very much as if I had just awakened out of a long sleep." He signed off with "Yours, dreamily, Mark Twain." Taking this new name was as decisive for this writer as the later transformation of the Polish mariner Józef Teodor Konrad Korzeniowski into the English novelist Joseph Conrad. The first known appearance in print of the most famous pseudonym in American literature signaled a great personal discovery—the end of a moratorium—that Sam described in a letter to his brother Orion: "I have had a 'call' to literature, of a low order—*i.e.*, humorous. It is nothing to be proud of, but it is my strongest suit." He was going to turn his talents "to seriously scribbling to excite the *laughter* of God's creatures." "You had better shove this in the stove," he said in a remarkably prophetic postscript. "I don't want any absurd 'literary remains' and 'unpublished letters of Mark Twain' published after I am planted," which, of course, is precisely what has happened. No major American writer generated so large an archive of personal papers (including literary remains and about ten thousand letters) or a career—leading from village and mining camp to mansion, domestic bliss, wealth, and world fame—that has so much in common with fairy tales.

Pen names were nothing new to Samuel Clemens when he adopted Mark Twain. He had already published under W. Apaminondas Adrastus Blab, Sergeant Fathom, Thomas Jefferson Snodgrass, Quintus Curtius Snodgrass, and several other inventions. For many American humorists of his day—among them David Ross Locke (Petroleum V. Nasby), Robert Henry Newell (Orpheus C. Kerr), and Charles Farrar Browne (Artemus Ward)—a pen name, the droller the better, was both a familiar literary convention and a professional necessity, its primary function being to brand-name a public personality and its distinctive product. American humorists looked to the spectacular example of their contemporary Charles Dickens, who at the age of twenty-five had made his debut in 1836–1837 as Boz, author of a popular collection of *Sketches* and the even more popular *Pickwick Papers*. Ten years later Dickens explained that Boz was "the nickname of a pet child, a younger brother, whom I had dubbed Moses, in honor of the Vicar of Wakefield; which being facetiously pronounced through the nose, became Boses, and being shortened, became Boz. 'Boz' was a very familiar household word to me, long before I was an author, and so I came to adopt it."

For Charles Dickens, Boz represented only an early stage in his development—he put it aside in favor of his real name when he published *Oliver Twist* and *Nicholas Nickleby* shortly after. It would have been too constricting an identity for the great novelist Charles Dickens. For Samuel Clemens, however, Mark Twain was a permanency for the rest of his life and even posthumously, as a registered trademark (a fortuitous pun on the first name) by which his executors and publishers hoped to extend his copyrights beyond their statutory limit.

His friend's life read like an *Arabian Nights* story, the novelist and critic William Dean Howells said. In this seemingly inexhaustible saga of a thousand and one adventures and vicissitudes, Mark Twain, a created public and professional identity, served as the genie who led Aladdin to riches, a palace, and the hand of the sultan's daughter. But for the private Samuel Clemens, husband, father, and householder, Mark Twain was also the Old Man of the Sea, the inescapable nemesis who held Sindbad the Sailor captive.

Like Dickens, Clemens offered an official, or canonical, "history of the *nom de plume* I bear." Mark Twain was "an old river term," he said, "a leads-man's call, signifying two fathoms—twelve feet [of depth]. It has a richness about it; it was always a pleasant sound for a pilot to hear on a dark night; it meant safe water." But it could mean just the opposite, a warning that the steamboat had shoaled through Mark Three into dangerous water. Clemens said he took the name from an old Mississippi River pilot, Captain Isaiah Sellers, "who used to write river news over it for the *New Orleans Picayune*. He died in 1863 and as he could no longer need that signature, I laid violent hands upon it without asking the permission of the proprietor's remains." No one has ever been able to confirm that account or to remove the powerful suspicion that the entire story, Captain Sellers and his nom de plume included, was an invention. Even the derivation of Mark Twain from the river term for two fathoms has been disputed. Maybe, as one scholar suggested, the name originated not on the Mississippi River but on dry land in Nevada and referred to the practice of tolerant saloon keepers of chalking up two drinks on credit.

Aside from derivation and literal meaning, the name raises a number of questions. Is Mark a first name and Twain a last, or is Mark Twain indivisible like Yankee Doodle or Postal Service? If you want to look him up in an index, which do you turn to first—Clemens, Samuel; Mark Twain; or Twain, Mark?[4] This shouldn't be surprising, since at the beginning of his career even the author, source of this confusion, didn't quite know what to call himself. He signed some early letters to family members Mark. But because they may have objected to this as putting on airs, he soon reverted to Sam. William Dean Howells called him Clemens "instead of Mark Twain, which seemed always somehow to mask him from my personal sense." On the other hand, George Bernard Shaw, an equally practiced professional in manipulating public identities, addressed him in a letter as "My dear Mark Twain—not to say Dr. Clemens (although I have always regarded Clemens as mere raw material—might have been your brother or your uncle)." (Before arriving at the magisterial Shaw, an identity known for short as GBS, Shaw himself—in his youth called Sonny in Dublin and George in London—wrote under Corno di Bassetto and about a dozen other pseudonyms, including Horatia Ribbonson, Julius Floenmochser, George Bunnard, Redbarn Wash, and the Rev. C. W. Stiggins, Jr.)

Samuel Clemens was Sam to his family and people from Hannibal, Mark to old newspaper and lecture circuit friends, Twain to others, and Mr. Clemens to most. On at least a hundred occasions in his public life, he must have come close to murderous exasperation when Scripture-spouting wags quoted the Sermon on the Mount: "Whosoever shall compel thee to go a mile, go with him twain." (Hardly anyone is able to tolerate jokes and quips about his or her name. When put to the test, names are sacred.) His wife, Olivia, balked at the vernacular Sam and the baptismal Samuel and called him Youth, which was "her name for him among their friends," Howells said. (In Vienna in the late 1890s, *"der Jude Mark Twain"* was the target of anti-Semites, who assumed Samuel was a Jewish first name.) His favorite daughter, Susy, believed he was a great man, but sometimes expressed her aspirations for him in open resentment of that deliberate and brilliant literary creation Mark Twain. "How I hate that name! I should like never to hear it again! My father should not be satisfied with it! He should show himself the great writer that he is, not merely a funny man! Funny? That's all the people see in him —a maker of funny speeches!" She wanted him to be a moral philosopher and the author, not of *Huckleberry Finn,* which she disliked for its coarse realism and low characters, but of *The Prince and the Pauper* and other genteel fictions.

Despite all the confusion, several things are reasonably clear. In all likelihood Samuel Clemens simply invented the name Mark Twain. It is associated with the river, timeless symbol of the creative unconscious; he invested it with magical or occult significance; and, looking down long vistas of predestination that stretched all the way back to Adam's disobedience, he said that the name with which he signed his Carson City letter "was the cause of my presently dropping out of journalism and into literature." He once signed a hotel register "S. L. Clemens. Profession: Mark Twain." Sometimes he obliged autograph hunters with "Yrs Truly—Samuel L. Clemens / Mark Twain." His pseudonym put a liberating distance between the humorist, novelist, and satirist, a public figure, and Samuel L. Clemens, householder, family man, and intensely private citizen. But at the same time it is the edgy traffic between the two identities—their opposing pulls and obligations, their "twainship" and twinship—that makes him a rich subject for biography and the psychology of naming. Mark Twain simply *sounds* right, like Tom Sawyer, which was an "ordinary" name, the author told an interviewer. It "seemed to fit the boy, some way, by its sound," in the same way that

> there was something about the name "Finn" that suited, and "Huck Finn" was all that was needed to somehow describe another kind of boy than "Tom Sawyer," a boy of lower extraction or degree. Now, "Arthur Van de Vanter Montague" would have sounded ridiculous applied to characters like either "Tom Sawyer" or "Huck Finn." . . . One doesn't name his characters haphazard.

Nor himself.

A few weeks before his thirty-sixth birthday, Walter Whitman, former printer, schoolteacher, house builder, and newspaper editor, now the author, proprietor, and publisher of a literary work in press, registered a copyright with the clerk of the United States District Court for the Southern District of New York. When it went on sale in July 1855, the book was as arresting in format and detail as its contents: the most brilliant and original poetry yet written on the continent, at once the fulfillment of American literary romanticism and the beginnings of American literary modernism. The reader's eye was caught first by the frontispiece portrait of an unidentified bearded man wearing the broad-brimmed hat, open-necked shirt, and rough trousers of a laborer or common seaman. There was no author listed on the title page, which bore only the words *Leaves of Grass,* a small decorative rule, and the legend "Brooklyn, New York: 1855." The copyright page was more informative but not conclusive, for the Walter Whitman named in the statutory boilerplate was conceivably the author's publisher or assignee or even, as some readers might have concluded, a conservator appointed in cases of mental insta-bility or incompetence. Ten pages of double-column prose eccen-trically punctuated with strings of periods were followed by eighty-three pages of verse, at first glance clusters of prose sen-tences printed like Bible verses; the twelve poems were untitled except for the insistent head caption for each, "Leaves of Grass." Only in a passage on page 29 did the reader discover the connec-tion between the bearded layabout of the frontispiece, the anony-mous author, and the copyright holder:

> *Walt Whitman, an American, one of the roughs, a kosmos,*
> *Disorderly, fleshy and sensual . . . eating, drinking and*
>   *breeding,*
> *No sentimentalist . . . no stander above men or women or*
>   *apart from them . . . no more modest than immodest.*

In an age of triple-barreled literary eminences who thundered their names in Jovian trochees and dactyls—William Cullen Bryant, John Greenleaf Whittier, Ralph Waldo Emerson, Henry Wadsworth Longfellow, James Russell Lowell—the author of *Leaves of Grass* followed the populist examples of Andy Jackson,

Kit Carson, and Davy Crockett. Along with Walter, for purposes of public discussion he rejected the cooly formal Whitman. "I like best to have the *full name* always," he was to say. The official name Walt Whitman became as close to being indivisible as Mark Twain. "Give both words," he said, "and don't be afraid of the tautology." Just as Samuel Clemens awoke from "a long sleep" to sign himself Mark Twain, Walt Whitman awoke from the first half of his life and was dazzled by the "happiness" he saw:

> *I cannot be awake, for nothing looks to me as it did before,*
> *Or else I am awake for the first time, and all before has*
> *been a mean sleep.*

To this day no one is altogether certain of the identity of the mysterious B. Traven, known best as the author of *The Treasure of the Sierra Madre*. He may have been Berick Traven Torsvan, born in the United States in 1890, or Ret Marut, born in Germany in 1882 and possibly the bastard son of Kaiser Wilhelm II. He remains as much of a riddle as the French George Psalmanazar, who claimed to be a native of Formosa; the English Junius, author of letters pillorying King George III; and the American Deep Throat, supposed key informant in the Watergate scandal, but who may not have existed at all.

These are names taken in order to hide rather than advertise, and in this respect there's the same sort of difference between a pseudonym (literally, "false name") and an alias (the short form of *alias dictus*—"otherwise called" or "aka") as there is between half full and half empty. It depends on the result you're looking for, the direction you're running in. At the far end of the scale, if you want to disappear altogether, are generic anonyms like John Doe, Jane Doe, and Fnu Lnu, the last sometimes mistaken for an Asian name although it's police-report shorthand for "first name unknown / last name unknown."

Meyer Zeligs, a psychoanalyst who studied Whittaker Chambers, confessed courier and espionage agent for the Soviet Union, traced him from his birth in 1901 as Jay Vivian Chambers through so long a string of name changes and aliases that it was no wonder that in testifying against Alger Hiss it was easy for Chambers at least to pretend he had forgotten some of them: Charles Adams (when he ran away from home), Charles Whittaker, John Kelly, George Crosley (and also Carl, when he met Alger Hiss), Lloyd Cantwell, David Breen (when he obtained a passport), Jay Chambers, Jay V. David Chambers, David Chambers, Whittaker Chambers (when he went to work for *Time* magazine), John Land, J. Dwyer, Vivian Dwyer, David Dwyer, David Whittaker Dwyer. This "endangered young man," as Zeligs called him, was struggling to achieve "a new identity," but he had also pledged himself to a Dostoevskian or Victor Hugoesque underground existence in a world of subterfuge and disguise.

"Men and women may work together in the underground for years," Chambers himself recalled, "may become close friends without ever knowing (or asking) one another's real names." Didier Lazard, a French Jew who for several years during World War II lived under a false name in order to evade arrest by the Germans and the Vichy government, left a remarkably introspective and sensitive account of his experience. A member of a distinguished upper-middle-class family of bankers, doctors, and intellectuals, he acquired, during his time of hiding, a taste for adventure and secrecy along with "a sort of joy in living outside the law" and a recognition of previously undeveloped psychic riches and reserves. At first, naively, he chose to call himself Gilbert Olivier, because he liked the name. He quickly realized that it was a monstrous blunder for someone in danger of being arrested and killed to list himself on a forged identity card with a name that did not agree with the initials on his shirts and handkerchiefs. Finally, in order to preserve those initials along with the familial continuity they represented, he reversed their order and settled on Lucien Didier, developed a new personal history and social matrix, and began to observe in himself, and record, "the psychological twists involved in living under a pseudonym":

The process of constructing a second personality was a very slow one for me. I do not like to disguise myself. I have never taken part in theatricals. In brief, I do not have the habit of *playing* a role. But events forced me to it. . . . Nevertheless, when I got a false identity card, then a visiting card, and a little bit later a false diploma in the field of law, my self-assurance began to grow. I eliminated from my real past certain elements; I conserved certain others. I tried to simplify to a maximum all of the elements of my past life in order to diminish the number of questions which one could ask me. . . . When I knew the Germans were making spot checks, I went over all the fabricated details of my new life like a student going over his lesson. . . . My personality began to develop a certain consistency. Each day that passed, each happening that I lived through, worked to differentiate it from my former self.

Even in his dreams he managed to keep his fraudulent existence separate from the true one: whether he was sleeping or awake, "there was always the fear of being discovered." It was months after the liberation of France before he was able to sign his real name with any ease and spontaneity, but by then the impostor Lucien Didier had established himself in a position of authority over the authentic Didier Lazard. Lucien now saw as faults in Didier certain personality traits that Didier had once thought of as "marks of quality."

Didier Lazard's mirror image is a man from the other side in the war, an eminent literary scholar, Professor Hans Schwerte. In 1995—at the age of eighty-six—he was unmasked as Hans-Ernst Schneider, former Nazi party member, senior S.S. official (*Hauptsturmführer*), and member of Heinrich Himmler's personal staff. Among his other activities, Schneider confiscated Jewish libraries and supplied equipment for medical experiments on prisoners at Dachau. At war's end he managed to get hold of documents that allowed him to pass himself off as Hans Schwerte, a common soldier, remarry his wife (who claimed her first husband, Hans-

Ernst Schneider, had died in the battle for Berlin), adopt their own daughter, repeat his studies at the University of Erlangen, and win academic eminence, recognition, and honors as a cultural historian and rector of Aachen, a major German university. He had become an outspoken critic of nationalism, a left-liberal political figure, and altogether an apparently committed foe of the Nazi past. He was postwar Germany's "ray of hope," as one of his colleagues put it. His new personality, like Didier Lazard's, had developed "a certain consistency." Until his unmasking, Schwerte aka Schneider had succeeded in contriving a new identity that rejected—or at least was understood to reject—the totalitarian loyalties and war-criminal past of the old one. "Some see his life," *The New York Times* reported, "as a parable of modern Germany, turning its back on the past to build a new society," a Saul turned Paul. Others see him as a fugitive from the law who managed to hide long enough for the statute of limitations to run out. Which was his "real" name? Which was the "real" person? "I didn't hide my identity," Schwerte explained. "I turned it in for a new one."

As a theme or fantasy, at any rate, taking to the open road to start a new life is as American as name changing. Huck Finn, who had passed himself off as Sarah Williams and George Jackson, lighted out for "the Territory" because Aunt Sally was going to "sivilize" him. The boy who had been Mark Twain's model for Huck supposedly ended up as "justice of the peace in a remote village in Montana and was a good citizen and greatly respected." A nineteenth-century California miners' song speaks for many others who also lighted out, but these were fugitives from justice listed as aka on "wanted" posters:

Oh, what was your name in the states?
Was it Thompson or Johnson or Bates?
Did you murder your wife
And fly for your life?
Say, what was your name in the States?

Whitman's "Song of the Open Road" and Jack Kerouac's *On the Road* offer the same prospect William Least Heat Moon (born William Lewis Trogdon) celebrated in his book *Blue Highways* —"a beckoning, a strangeness, a place where a man can lose himself." "I've changed my name," says a character in Sam Shepard's play *Simpatico*. "I've moved all over the place. I was in Texas for a while . . . Arizona. Nothing came from any of it. I've just got—further and further—removed."

It's still possible in America to take a new identity, disappear, and stay underground. Rosemary Leary, once married to psychedelic apostle Timothy Leary, managed to live under a false identity for twenty-three years "with my passport under my pillow, my shoes by the bed, planning escape routes." Even though her jail sentence for marijuana possession has finally been dismissed, she still uses a pseudonym but won't divulge it—she's afraid of losing her job as manager of a country inn.

Unless you're in the custody of the Federal Witness Protection and Relocation Program, but even if you're not a fugitive from the law, going underground is a difficult proposition, especially now that numbers and databases rather than names have become the chief instruments of governmental control. You would probably have to start off by acquiring an authentic-looking birth certificate that shows the new name you've chosen: you can either order the birth certificate of a dead person who was born about the same time you were, or you can start fresh by creating one and aging it in your toaster oven to give it an authentic look. This then becomes your breeder document for a Social Security card (easily forged), driver's license, credit card, passport, and other supportive proofs of identity. There are books that claim to be able to show you how to go about this, among them *Scram: Relocating Under a New Identity* by James S. Martin. Another, signed Doug Richmond, has an even better title: *How to Disappear Completely and Never Be Found.*

Over the past twenty-five years, according to Robert Sabbag, reporting in *The New York Times Magazine* in 1996, more than fifteen thousand people have found refuge under the Federal Wit-

ness Protection and Relocation Program, their new names and
new places of abode so layered in security that these are known
only to three or four officials in the U.S. Marshals Service. Sabbag followed the reidentification and relocation experience of a
felon named Jess Brewer, who had a history in organized crime
that made him a likely target for revenge. It took Brewer and his
female companion, Remedios Devera, a day to come up with a
new family name, which had to be ethnically compatible but not
traceable even to distant antecedents on either side.

Brewer and Devera also took new first names for themselves,
an index of their "personal paranoia" (as one official put it), but
they drew back from renaming their three children, on the
grounds that the children already had enough of a problem learning to live with the new surname. After their paper trail was
officially backstopped and they were issued new identity documents, Brewer and his family not only ceased to exist as far as
their old identities were concerned but apparently had never existed at all:

> "What was really uncomfortable," Brewer says, "was
> when they started calling us by our new names." Before
> leaving the orientation center, Devera and Brewer spent a lot
> of time practicing what she refers to as "our second name"
> —writing it, teaching the children to spell it—creating and
> rehearsing signatures. "When we left that place," Brewer
> says, "I felt like a new person."

12.
The Language of Names

The master's right of giving names goes so far that it is permissible to look upon language itself as the expression of the power of the masters.
Friedrich Nietzsche, *On the Genealogy of Morals*

Cratylus, Plato's fourth-century B.C. dialogue about the origins of language and naming, takes up what appears to be a simple question: why should Hermogenes, who is a penniless and luckless fellow, have a name that means "son of Hermes"? Since Hermes was the god of good luck, wealth, and clever dealing, all of them strangers to this putative son, Hermogenes must be a walking oxymoron, a two-headed creature like Dr. Dolittle's Push-me-pull-you. Hermogenes doesn't see it this way, however, because he believes names are purely arbitrary: "Any name, which you give," he says, "is the right one, and if you change that and give another, the new name is as correct as the old. We frequently change the names of our slaves, and the newly imposed name is as good as the old: for there is no name given to anything by nature; all is convention and habit of the users." Regardless of its literal meaning and derivation, Hermogenes, he says, is the right name for him, because that's what he answers to. What a person is called is not only who he is but what a name is.

His friend Cratylus takes the opposite position, that names are "natural and not conventional" and should have a certain "truth or correctness in them." Mediating between the two, Socrates concludes that names, being the product of a rational process—

language—are based on nature but also modified by convention and usage. This split-down-the-middle and rather opaque conclusion appears to satisfy both parties, but further discussion through the ages has continued to take the form of a debate between those like Cratylus, who say names are natural and real, and those like Hermogenes, who say they're conventional, arbitrary, and in one sense merely nominal. For almost twenty-five centuries philosophers, linguists, logicians, and psychologists have been trying to define the nature and function of names. They've arrived at surprisingly little agreement, even though, like everyone else, they all answer to names and speak a language of names.

By Cratylus's standards, Adam would have to have been a founding naturalist. The creator gave him dominion over "every living thing that moveth upon the earth"—including great whales, cattle, fowl of the air, and beasts of the field—and charged him with the task of naming them. According to extrabiblical legend, the first man invented language and named himself Adam, because he had been formed out of *adamah,* dust of the earth. His descendants likewise were to bear names that said something quintessential, all the way from Abraham (meaning "father of a multitude") in Genesis to the rich sheep owner in 1 Samuel, Nabal (meaning "fool"): "As his name is, so is he," his wife tells King David; "Nabal is his name, and folly is with him."

Barely one hour old when God put him to the task of naming all of creation, the legendary Adam proved to be better at it than the angels themselves, even better than Satan, the greatest of the angels, who became envious and plotted Adam's undoing. "O Lord of the world," Adam said as he named each creature according to his understanding of its distinctive personality and appearance, "the proper name for this animal is ox, for this one horse, for this one lion, for this one camel." He named the ox ox because it was slow, strong, and stubborn like an ox; the lion lion because it had a lionlike mane and roared like a lion (and the chicken chicken, presumably because it was chicken). To name was to create, know, possess, and master. We could call Adam the first poet; he named things after their appearance or essence and, as Emerson wrote, gave "to every one its own name and not another's. . . . Each word was at first a stroke of genius, because for the moment it symbolized the world to the first speaker."

This sort of nominal realism, as the Swiss developmental psychologist Jean Piaget called it, is what Humpty-Dumpty had in mind in his answer to Alice's plaintive question *"Must* a name mean something?" "Of course, it must," he said. *"My* name means the shape I am—and a good handsome shape it is, too. With a name like yours, you might be any shape, almost." Even before this fantasticating colloquy, Alice had known he was Humpty-Dumpty; all she had to do was to look at this large human-looking egg that had eyes and a nose and mouth. "It can't be anybody else! . . . I'm as certain of it, as if his name were written all over his face!"

Earlier, Alice had asked, "Why do things have names at all?" Insects, for example, have names, but they don't answer to them. A gnat "about the size of a chicken" tells Alice she would be better off if she managed to "lose" her name. Your governess won't be able to summon you to lessons, the gnat argues, "because there wouldn't be any name for her to call, and of course you wouldn't have to go, you know." Carroll teased the reader with these and other questions that go back to the crux of Plato's dialogue. What *is* a name? Is it a conventional marker, a social construction, a mere handle? Or does it *mean something* in itself and either stand for some quality within the person who bears it or have the power to shape that person by acting as a sort of destiny or matrix.

A child of five and a half knows his own name, Piaget noted, yet cannot define the word "name" beyond describing its function, "to call something by." When asked how he knows that the sun is the sun, he answers, "Because it shines." For young children, as well as primitive peoples, the dominant characteristic of the sun—its shine—and its name are inextricably linked, and neither the child nor the primitive can conceive of one as existing without the other. "The name is . . . in the object," Piaget said, "not as a label attached to it but as an invisible quality of the object. To be accurate we should not therefore say that the name 'sun' implies a yellow ball, etc., but that the yellow ball which is the sun really implies and contains the name 'sun.' " Piaget claimed that between the ages of five and ten children pass from a nominal-realism stage, in which they believe names belong to things and emanate from them, through a second stage (names were invented by God or the first men), to a final recognition of names as conventional and authorless and of things as having existed even before they had names.

Words are not the things they name, according to Ferdinand de Saussure, the founder of the modern science of linguistics, but are arbitrarily associated with these things and take their distinctive meaning only in the context of other words. Still, most of us, at least on some subliminal level, are in bondage to nominal realism and regard names as if they were sacred. Names aren't fate, in the sense that they make us who we are, but we've got to live with them all the same. Solomon, again in extrabiblical legend, was able to command demons, specters, and spirits of the night because he knew their names. In a similar fashion, William James wrote, "the universe has always appeared to the natural mind as a kind of enigma, of which the key must be sought in the shape of some illuminating or power-bringing word or name."

John Stuart Mill, the nineteenth-century British philosopher, was probably the most decisive expositor of the Hermogenes position, that names are conventional and arbitrary; what a man is called, to put it simply, is what a name is and no more than that. "When we name a child by the name of Paul, or a dog by the name of Caesar," Mill wrote,

these names are simply marks used to enable those individuals to be made subjects of discourse. It may be said, indeed, that we must have had some reason for giving them those names rather than any others; and this is true; but the name once given is independent of the reason. . . . A proper name is but an unmeaning mark which we connect in our minds with the idea of the object, in order that whenever the mark meets our eyes or occurs to our thoughts, we may think of that individual object.

According to this line of reasoning, when you introduce someone by name, the only information you're conveying is the name itself, a linking of phonemes (units of sound) rather than morphemes (units of meaning). Miller and Baker, for example, may once have denoted occupations, but now we would call them "just names." They're dead metaphors like the "arms" or "legs" of a chair. We don't expect sociologist Mike Miller and his wife, psychoanalyst Jean Baker-Miller, to have flour on their hands and clothing. On the other hand, there are semantically meaningful names, established by tradition, usage, and association, that communicate specific information about ethnicity, gender, and species. Fido and Rover, for example, are clearly dogs and not cats or children, but when they become strays and are taken off to the pound, their names vanish. The famous "Boy Named Sue" was the victim of a malicious wrench of established meaning.

Reasoning that names are just arbitrary markers, Mill used an example from the *Arabian Nights* tale of Ali Baba and the Forty Thieves. In order to identify the house where Ali Baba has hidden his sacks of gold, the scout for a band of robbers marks the front door with a piece of chalk. Morgiana, Ali Baba's clever and faithful slave, notices the chalk mark and decides that someone has designs on her master's treasure. She makes a similar chalk mark on the front doors of several other houses on each side of Ali Baba's. The scout leads the robber captain to Ali Baba's street but now isn't able to tell which house holds the treasure. "The chalk was still there," Mill wrote, "but it no longer served the purpose of a distinctive mark." (Morgiana eventually disposes of the forty thieves by boiling them in oil, but that goes beyond the point Mill is making here.)

If everyone in a group is named Smith, considered as the verbal equivalent of a chalk mark, what's the practical value of a name? But this is precisely why people are *not* all named alike and why the Smiths of this world have different first names and initials, just as one chalk mark can be distinguished from another by color and shape. Moreover, chalk marks and doors do not interact with each other, while people and their names do. Bill Smith and Margaret Smith are not common nouns but proper names that may even have a certain connotative aura, as in "He doesn't dress like a Bill," "She doesn't behave like a Margaret."

"The most obvious rejoinder to Mill's theory of the meaninglessness of names would be this," the linguist and philologist Ernst Pulgram wrote in his monograph *Theory of Names* (1954). "If proper names are meaningless, why and how do they exist?" Words that no longer have any dictionary meaning simply disappear from the language, but names endure. They are "onomastically meaningful" even though they may have no lexical value or "literal" meaning; Hardy may be feeble and Brunette may have blond hair, but they're known as Hardy and Brunette all the same. Pulgram cited the Danish philologist Otto Jespersen, who argued that, contrary to Mill, proper names are the most meaningful of nouns, their "contextual value" being much greater than their "dictionary value." "The name of a man is like his shadow," said Pulgram:

It is not of his substance and not of his soul, but it lives with him and by him. Its presence is not vital, nor its absence fatal. If a man were to move in perennial darkness, he would have no shadow, and if he were content to dwell in solitude, he would need no name.

Arrived at through nearly fifty densely reasoned pages, Pulgram's scrupulously articulated definition of this shadowlike entity illustrates just how thorny the problem is when approached on a high level of abstraction:

A proper name is a noun used . . . in a non-universal function, with or without current lexical value, of which the potential meaning coincides with and never exceeds its actual meaning, and which is attached as a label to one animate being or one inanimate object . . . for the purpose of specific distinction from a number of like or in some respects similar beings or objects.

Bertrand Russell, the British philosopher and mathematician, argued that proper names are simply "ghosts of substances," not names at all but abbreviated descriptions. But this approach, as William James might say, only takes us up a metaphysical road and away from a useful answer to the question What is a name? James's pragmatic method looked toward concreteness, facts, action, power, application: in this case the "practical cash-value" of ideas about names when derived from or applied to experience.

Onomastics is an ungainly word, with irrelevant echoes of mastectomy, mastication, masturbation, and the paving material called mastic. But it's useful nonetheless, even indispensable in some contexts, especially because there's no other single word for the study of proper names. Under the subject heading "onomastics," a world library catalogue database will show over four hundred entries, including periodicals like *Onomastica Canadiana* consisting of many volumes. Geographically they range from Asia, Balkan Peninsula, and Bulgaria to Ukraine, Wales, and Yugoslavia (now known as "former Yugoslavia"). In the field of scholarly publications, worldwide there are at least two dozen journals of onomastics, while many others run related articles.

The major professional focus for this field of study in the United States is the quarterly journal *Names.* It's published by the American Name Society, organized in 1951 and dedicated to the systematic study of the etymology, origin, meaning, and application of all categories of names, geographical, scientific, and commercial as well as personal. The society's stated goal is not only to study names and disseminate the results of such study but "to make the American people conscious of the interest and importance of names in all fields of human endeavor and in all subjects taught in our schools and colleges." Despite this laudable program, you would still be inviting trouble if you ask the person standing next to you in your neighborhood saloon how he or she feels about onomastics.

The American Name Society claims about nine hundred members, not much in comparison to the Modern Language Association's thirty thousand but a toehold in the world of scholarship nonetheless. It sees the study of names as supremely interdisciplinary, ramifying into practically every field of knowledge, including history and prehistory, sociology, folklore, cultural anthropology, psycholinguistics, and literary criticism. Leaving personal names aside for the moment, onomastics takes in a welter of categories and subcategories: toponyms, place-names; odonyms, street names; anemonyms, names of winds and storms. (Agnes, Bob, Diana, Hugo, and other names assigned by the National Hurricane Center have to be "easy to pronounce and politically and culturally sensitive.") Eponyms are people, places, or things after which other people, places, or things are named— the Heimlich maneuver, for example, is better known than the man who developed it, Dr. Henry Heimlich of Cincinnati; and the same principle applies to Halley's comet (Edmund Halley) and Murphy's Law (Edward Murphy). Acronyms—words formed from the initial letters of other words—and other new coinages are distinctive, indispensable features of twentieth-century speech: CD-ROM, SNAFU (and FUBAR), WASP, Gestapo, radar, sonar, quasar, and laser, for example; witty Velcro combines two French words, *velours* and *croché* (hooked); humvee, the U.S. Army's all-purpose people hauler, is easier to say than "high-mobility multipurpose wheeled vehicle."

Onomastics also takes in the names people give to planets, stars, galaxies, and constellations and, on a more local level, to their sweethearts, boats, dogs, cats, horses, birds, cars, sexual organs, and houses (Bedside Manor and Dunroamin, for example). A host of invented product names have passed into common usage, many of them—Band-Aid, Kitty Litter, Kleenex, Scotch tape, Tabasco, Vaseline, Walkman, Xerox (and Velcro)—becoming generic even though proprietors fight a rearguard action by insisting these words be capitalized, treated syntactically as proper nouns or adjectives, and protected by the familiar typographical bug, a superscript R within a circle, meaning "Registered Trademark." All of the above, and much more, is meat for the study of names as both philological artifacts and indicators of social, technological, and commercial history.

In 1988 Harvard awarded tenure to a sociologist, Stanley Lieberson, whose scholarly specialty was the study of first names. "I'm just gathering all sorts of data," he said, claiming that first names were a "very unusual topic for sociologists" and that he had no clear idea of the questions he wanted to address or the conclusions he expected to reach. But with the exception of Lieberson and a few other investigators, the study of names, whether in itself, or as a subdiscipline, or as an application, doesn't have much standing in academia. It even appears to be something of a stigma where hiring and promotion are concerned.

As to why this is, in the March 1994 issue of *Names* Thomas E. Murray, an English professor at Kansas State University, offered several explanations, one of them being the conviction in academic circles that names are a trivial subject for serious scholarly work. He quoted one senior professor as saying, "Next we'll have someone claiming credit for an article on stamp collecting or astrology." A second added, "Searching through telephone books for names of one ethnicity or another is hardly an academic endeavor. My grandmother used to do that, and she had only an eighth-grade education!" Murray cited another contributing factor: the news media love stories about names and deal with them in a soft-news, filler, or playful way that by implication and extension trivializes the entire subject. "Rose by any other name wouldn't be as feminine" is how the San Diego *Union-Tribune,* falling back on an inescapable Shakespearean tag, headlined its account of the forty-second annual meeting (1994) of the American Name Society. The story went on to cite the titles of several presentations described as having caused "quite a buzz" at that meeting: "Commercial Aircraft Names: Brief History and Current Patterns," "School Team Names in Washington State," and "Street Names in Senlis, the Oldest Inhabited Town in France."

Without seeming quite to acknowledge the irony of the problem, Professor Murray put his finger on yet another crux:

> I would ask you to consider which of the following commands more respect: *Names* or *Onomastica Canadiana? American Name Society* or *International Congress of Onomastic Sciences?* Given that businesses spend millions of dollars trying to discover the "right" names for their products and that prospective parents often spend months trying to find the "right" names for their babies, perhaps the time has come for the American Name Society to begin searching for names that will lend a greater sense of authority and seriousness to who we are and what we do.

This may be the time to call in the professionals at NameLab and Whatchamacallit.

But Professor Murray might be willing to admit that it's not a name alone that's needed to lend a legitimizing "sense of authority and seriousness" to onomastics in this country but a higher, more rigorous and sophisticated level of work as well. There's a great deal of Mickey Mouse research, string collecting, computer-aided statistical analysis gone wild. Here are a few sample article titles and abstracts:

> Herbert Barry III. "Parental Namesakes in the Families of the Presidents of the United States" (*Names,* 1983). "Among the 39 Presidents of the United States, including Reagan, the fathers of 33 (85%) each had a son (the President or a brother) given the same first name."

> Frank Nuessel. "Objectionable Sport Team Designations" (*Names,* 1994). Applying strict standards of political correctness, the author compiled a list of names (and logos), includ-

ing Warrior, "now considered racist, especially those that refer to Native Americans."

James S. Kus. "Changing Names on Peruvian Trucks" (*Names*, 1994). Abstract: "Peruvian trucks often carry a distinctive name, usually painted on the front of the vehicle. These names show distinctive regional patterns, particularly between more 'conservative' (rural and Andean) and more 'progressive' (urban) parts of the country."

Grant W. Smith. "The Sound and Sense of Othello" (ANS paper, December 1994). "This paper links the sound of Othello's name to its meaning. Shakespeare would have pronounced the 'th' as a simple /t/. Thus, the name requests the free and open expression of the truth: 'O-Tell-O.' "

Angela G. Ray. "Calling the Dog: The Sources of AKC Breed Names" (*Names*, 1995). Abstract: "The official names of the 136 dog breeds currently recognized by the American Kennel Club reflect the role of the canine in human civilization. Some names are exotic, but most are practical."

Rudi Hartmann. "Dinosaur Place Names in Colorado" (ANS Annual Meeting, December 1995).

Ellen Johnson. "Hidden Meaning of Names of Rock Bands in Athens, Georgia" (ANS Annual Meeting, December 1995). Examines "the esoteric meaning and/or flashes of illumination that produced such monikers as the *BBQ Killers, Icky Wail,* and *Porno for Pyros.* "

It's hard to say what this sort of work adds up to, but then again there's something to be said not only for pure scholarship (and the collecting itch) but for any line of speculation and inquiry that yields amusing and piquant results. The psychological study of personal names, although inconclusive statistically, at least reveals how irresistible the subject is.

Wayne E. Hensley and Barbara A. Spencer. "The Effect of First Names on Perceptions of Female Attractiveness" (*Sex Roles* XII, 1985). "The results indicated that the impact of a desirable or undesirable first name on attractiveness is minimal."

Richard E. Kopelman and Dorothy Lang. "Alliteration in Mate Selection: Does Barbara Marry Barry?" (*Psychological Reports* LVI, 1985). "Tests the assortative mating hypothesis in terms of a variable not previously examined: alliteration, partners whose two first names begin with the same letter."

Kenneth M. Steele and Laura E. Smithwick. "First Names and First Impressions: A Fragile Relationship" (*Sex Roles* XXI, 1989). "Overall, the results argue against too much emphasis on the possible deleterious effects of a particular first name."

Often the empirical research into the linkage of names, identity, self-acceptance, self-esteem, and social recognition arrives at predictable conclusions through intricate methods. It's a bit like pulling teeth through the armpit. One such study by a pair of personality psychologists asked a large core group of college students and a smaller comparison group of somewhat older non-students to supply three answers to the question Who are you? Most of the people gave their names as their first answer, and this held true regardless of gender or career stage. A second pair of investigators subsequently ran a series of somewhat similar studies, changing the question Who are you? to Who am I? on the assumption that respondents, who were sure to know their own names, would move on to a different first answer. The results were not dramatically different, nor were they in other such studies, including some conducted on children, and they led only to familiar conclusions that could be summed up as follows: names are a "central aspect of the self- concept" and serve as "identity pegs" and "essential anchorage points" of personal identity.

An experiment in which sleeping people were hooked up to EEG machines made "a convincing case," Kenneth Dion, a University of Toronto psychologist, reported, "that mention of one's name by others has considerable power to elicit the individual's attention, presumably because of its special significance to the bearer of the name." This shouldn't surprise parents, schoolteachers, and children, or people in noisy situations like cocktail parties and business meetings who claim they can tell, from across a crowded room, when they're being talked about.

On the plus side of onomastics, one can cite two first-rate and eminently readable reference books edited by Patrick Hanks and Flavia Hodges, *A Dictionary of First Names* and *A Dictionary of Surnames*. Another useful compilation, Leslie Dunkling's *The Guinness Book of Names,* covers the subject from babies to locomotives. As his title suggests, Noah Jacobs's *Naming Day in Eden,* goes back to the origins of language. Leonard R. N. Ashley's *What's in a Name?* is diverting and informative, while Linda Rosenkrantz and Pamela Redmond Satran's *Beyond Jennifer and Jason* (discussed in an earlier chapter) claims to have "revolutionized baby naming." Anthropologists like Lucien Lévy-Bruhl and Claude Lévi-Strauss have stimulated an entire literature about the function of names and naming practices in other than advanced Western societies. "The newborn child is at last transformed into a definite human being," Lévy-Bruhl wrote in *The "Soul" of the Primitive.*

> Ceremonies, differing according to the tribes, play their part in this event. As a rule, the most important of these consists in giving the infant a name or, as they often put it, in "discovering" what its name is—that is, which member of the family is reincarnated in him. Thus we can understand that the name is not . . . merely a label, but a constituent and individuating element of the personality.

Hopi personal names, according to one study, are totemic and ritualistic, reflect social structure and continuity, and have an

independent expressive function as well. Some of these names—
Yellow Fox Putting Up the Yellow Dawn Light," for example—
are "tiny imagist poems," "individually authored poetic compo-
sitions that comprise a literary genre." Two by now classic books
by George R. Stewart, *Names on the Land* and *American Place-
Names,* combine a magisterial command of geography, linguistics, folklore, and history with an engaging prose style. From
Sublime (Oregon) to Peculiar (Missouri), from Rich (Oklahoma)
to Poorman's Bottom (Nebraska), from Pilares (Texas) to Post
Office Cave (California), Stewart explored place-names as self-
contained narratives, showing how they grew "out of the life, and
the life-blood, of all those who had gone before."

Studied in a comparably broad context, other sorts of names
also serve as a means of unpacking the past and informing the
present. Kilroy, as in "Kilroy was here," the most popular piece
of graffiti ever, can be read as a capsule history of the United
States during the World War II era. Born in the merchant marine
or U.S. Navy in 1939, "Kilroy was here" soon began to appear
on practically any and every conceivably inscribable surface
wherever American soldiers and sailors passed through. For a
while it was practically the national motto. Kilroy had an image
as well as a name and a motto—the upper face and the fingers of
a bald-headed man seeming to peer at the world from the other
side of a wall—but whether he was laughing, playing peekaboo,
escaping, or about to climb over, it's impossible to say. No one
knows who the original Kilroy was, if indeed he was a real
person, or who created him, or what his name means, and the
range of speculation and derivation is considerable. One sociologist deconstructed Kilroy as "Kill the king (*roi*)," but though this
may sound plausible, as a punning expression of GI antiauthori-
tarianism it's improbably allusive—this version would have been
more appropriate to the war against George III. Whatever his
antecedents, Kilroy was the emblem, John Hancock, and recognition signal of Americans far from home, lonely, bemused, and
mischievous, perhaps the lineal descendants of tourists Mark
Twain had satirized a century earlier for scribbling their names

on monuments in Greece and Egypt instead of outhouse walls at home.

"Kilroy was a name that proved a community could be geographically far-flung," Don Nilsen of Arizona State University reported at the 1994 annual meeting of the American Name Society. "The sheer matter of repetition, of seeing how many different places they could find the message or put the message, became a reassuring joke giving G.I.'s something to smile about in a world gone mad." Eventually, as he receded into history, Kilroy took on the meaning, now obsolete as well, of a nonentity, a sad sack. Jeep and GI; Bill Mauldin's cartoon soldiers, Willie and Joe; and Dear John (kiss-off letter: "I don't want to hurt you, but . . .") are similar verbal artifacts of the Kilroy era, evidence that names that "become household words . . . not only identify a community, but bind it together."

Notes

Chapter 1. Masters of the Good Name

1. "As everybody knows," Clodd wrote, "the words 'disaster' [referring to stars], 'lunatic' [moon], and 'consideration' [stars again] embalm the old belief in the influence of the heavenly bodies on man's fate."
2. "The Gypsies have been called the Romany people since they left India. Now, the 'new-old' Government of Romania feels that Romany is too close to its name and has decreed that from now on the Gypsies in Romania cannot call themselves Romany, but should refer to themselves as Tzigane. That is why there is the saying in the Balkans, 'You never know what the past will bring!' " Bela Liptak, letter to the editor, *The New York Times,* May 19, 1995.
3. On a less oceanic level, the novelist W. Somerset Maugham said that on days when he couldn't think of anything to write, he jump-started his creative mill by writing his name "over and over and over again until something comes."
4. In the case of Robert L. Rooke, an investment broker who died in 1994 at the age of 103, this commemorative practice neared a saturation point. "Over the years he helped build the Rooke Chapel, named in honor of his parents, as well as Bucknell's Freas-Rooke Swimming Pool and Freas-Rooke Computer Center. In honor of his 100th birthday, Merrill Lynch dedicated a new Rooke Management Case-Studies Room in Bucknell's Rooke Chemistry Building." Obituary in *The New York Times,* July 1, 1994.
5. In 1967, "an Inuit named Moses, appropriately enough, was sent forth to visit all of his flock, some 15,000 souls dispersed over a frozen territory larger than Britain, France, and Germany combined, to invite each one to choose a surname." Mordecai Richler, "The Style and Substance of Pierre Trudeau," *Times Literary Supplement,*

April 8, 1994. Richler said he was subsequently solicited by an Inuit woman who introduced herself as Sophie Football.

Chapter 2. American Adam

1. Ten of the thirteen—76 percent—permanent elected officers of the Harvard Class of 1945 were suffixed "Junior," as opposed to 21 percent for the class as a whole and about 3 percent for the general population. On the other hand, in the same area of purely anecdotal information, a 1971 study found there were three times as many "juniors" in psychiatric treatment as in the general population.
2. Other early New Englanders were named Seaborn, Experience, Wait-still, Preserved, Hopestill, Wait, Thanks, Desire, Unite, and Supply. Comparably, "The first three babies born . . . on the first day of South Africa's post-apartheid era were boys named Freedom and Happiness and a girl named Thankful." *The New York Times,* April 28, 1994.
3. By overriding congressional fiat a peak in Idaho bears the last name of the late Charles Donaldson, a justice of the Idaho Supreme Court, even though, as the chairman of the Idaho Geographic Names Advisory Council protested, "there is no connection to the site by the person commemorated, except that it has been said that his law clerk was on top of the named mountain at the time Donaldson died of a heart attack in the YMCA swimming pool." Steven Lagerfeld, "Name That Dune," *Atlantic,* September 1990.
4. "The name was transmitted through the Spanish, who spelled it in Spanish fashion, and partly changed it by folk etymology. Americans further transformed the pronunciation, apparently assuming it was of French origin. Current pronunciation is approximately *d'shay.* A museum-piece of a name!" George R. Stewart, *American Place-Names* (New York, 1970).
5. It's only a runner-up, however, to the New Zealand place-name Taumatawhakatangihangakoauauotamateapokaiwhenuakitanatahu (fifty-seven letters) and the Welsh town of Llanfairpwllgwyngyllgogery-ychwyrndrobwllllantysiliogogogoch (fifty-eight), the latter, in part, the invention of a local bard in the nineteenth century.

Chapter 3. Names in the Melting Pot

1. Daniel Defoe's *Robinson Crusoe* shows this process at work in seventeenth-century England. The hero's father was a German immigrant named Kreutznaer, "but by the usual corruption of words in England we are now called, nay, we call ourselves, and write our name, 'Crusoe.' " Son of a London butcher, James Foe, Defoe himself had fancied up the family name by adding the "De," just as Claus von Bülow added the "Von" to his.

2. In a later case reported by Robert Rennick, "a Michael Kabotchnick (no kin to the other Kabotchnik, but in this case an immigrant from Vilna, Lithuania who came to Boston in the mid-Eighties and established himself in the clothing business in that city) changed his name to Cabot without recourse to a court of law. The illustrious Cabot family this time was successful in abrogating the change. . . . Kabotchnick moved to Brockton, Mass., changed his name to Kabot and later to Kabat and then dropped out of history."

Chapter 4. Black Naming: "An Old and Controversial Issue"

1. *The Official Scrabble Players Dictionary,* 1978 edition, defines "jew" as "to bargain with—an offensive term." In 1994, someone at B'nai Brith got around to reading the Scrabble Bible, as it is known in tournament circles, and persuaded the Merriam-Webster editors to remove "jew" as a verb.

2. A crucial alteration in texture resulted when Thorough Good Marshall changed his name to Thurgood Marshall. This was the grandfather of the late Supreme Court justice.

3. When *Roots* was published in 1976, a mob smashed the windows of a Detroit bookstore in order to grab and make off with copies of the book. By the time of Haley's death sixteen years later, this 587-page book had sold over 6 million copies and had been translated into thirty languages.

4. The commonest black surname in the United States, Johnson is second only to Smith in frequency.

Chapter 5. City of Names

1. As adjective or noun, "Mickey Mouse" carries a broad range of meanings: sentimental and insincere; showy or meretricious; shoddy, inferior; simple, elementary, easy; petty, inconsequential; a screw-up; a stupid person. See Robert L. Chapman, ed., *New Dictionary of American Slang* (New York, 1986).
2. Copyright 1973 Dick James Music Limited (London) and Dick James Music, Inc. (New York). Used by permission. All rights reserved.
3. Christened Billings Learned Hand and called Bunny by the women in his family, he felt he had been burdened with a "sissy" name, started signing himself "B. Learned Hand," and was relieved when college and law-school classmates took the initial B. to stand for the masculine "Buck." Even after he adopted the shortened form of Learned Hand and became one of the preeminent jurists of his century, he remained vulnerable to the suggestion that Learned was an adjective. See Gerald Gunther, *Learned Hand* (New York, 1994).

Chapter 6. "A Strange Kind of Magick Bias"

1. "To avoid evoking cultural associations which may prove negative," Namelab said, "words which are obviously constructed for international function (*Sony, Kodak, Acura*) are often superior to natural words suggestively based in a particular language." The marketing experts at Chevrolet clearly didn't realize that in Latin America "Nova" may mean "It doesn't go" (*No va*). The principle at work here is that one man's gift may be another's poison (the meaning of the German word *Gift*).
2. The name "Hitler," as it turns out, was not at all a rarity among Galician-Jewish families since the mid-nineteenth century, according to Robert N. Rennick, a circumstance that "never ceased to infuriate" the Führer. Rennick has traced the history of a number of Jewish "Hitlers," including a rabbinical candidate, Israel Hitler, who opted for Harrison, Hiller, or Hilton in its stead. ("Hitler and Others . . . ," *Names*, 17 [1969], 199–207).

Chapter 7. A Boy Named Sue and Others

1. © Copyright 1969 Evil Eye Music, Inc., Daytona Beach, Florida. Used by permission.

Chapter 8. Maiden Names

1. From "Maiden Name" by Philip Larkin. Reprinted from *The Less Deceived* by permission of The Marvell Press, England and Australia.
2. *The New York Times* reported in 1995 that its "society news department has noted a slight drop in the percentage of women keeping their surnames. A decade ago, nearly half of the women kept their names. Today it divides equally among those who are keeping their names, those who are taking their husband's name, and those who say they don't know what they'll do. Even those who keep their surnames frequently say they'll change as the children arrive."
3. Allowing for special cases, of course. One of Ann Landers's readers, signing herself "A Blusher," reported she was going out with "a wonderful fellow who has an odd last name"—let's assume it was Fuchs—often mispronounced to sound like "a dirty, four-letter word. Should I ask him to change it?" Landers's advice to "Blusher": "I see nothing wrong in asking him to change the spelling of his name because it will be your name too."
4. Lucy had allied herself to a remarkable family. Blackwell's two sisters were among the first women medical school graduates; his sister-in-law was the first American woman to be ordained a minister.
5. Thirty years later, when her married daughter Anne tried to get a passport under *her* name, she was informed it was impossible: if you're married your passport bears your husband's name. So much for progress.
6. By permission of Jack Cole. Larry Fortensky is no longer holding on.

Chapter 9. Rules of Engagement: The Etiquette of Names

1. The word "etiquette" comes from the Old French *estiquet,* meaning a "label." That's what a name is, in part.

2. Vladimir Nabokov's Humbert Humbert notes this "provincial" man-
   nerism in his new wife (Lolita's mother). "Oh, she was very genteel:
   she said 'excuse me' whenever a slight burp interrupted her flowing
   speech, called an envelope an ahnvelope, and when talking to her
   lady-friends referred to me as Mr. Humbert."

Chapter 10. Literary Names: The Importance of Being Sherlock

1. A few invented place-names that likewise are now generic: Utopia
   (Thomas More), Lilliput (Jonathan Swift), Erewhon (Samuel Butler),
   Never-Never Land (James Barrie), Shangri-la (James Hilton).
2. Epifania FitzAssenden, a character in George Bernard Shaw's *The
   Millionairess* (1936), must be Fanny's first cousin. Shaw's earliest
   commercial stage success (1911) was titled *Fanny's First Play.*
   Cleishbotham, a country schoolmaster in Sir Walter Scott's *Old Mor-
   tality* (1816), combines the Scottish dialect *cleish,* meaning "to
   whip," with a common variant of "bottom." The three character
   names are fundamentally the same.
3. A current Cincinnati social register yields dozens of such surname
   combinations. They're like formal dinners consisting only of two
   desserts. Some examples: Powell Crosley, Odell Bernius, Foster
   Gamble, Hobart Fullerton, Booth Shepard, and Starbuck Smith.
   "Turn them around, and they sound just as good," said Joan Fox,
   writer and hostess extraordinaire of Cincinnati and Truro, Massachusetts. "It's really elite naming because we poor Jews could never do
   this. Moskowitz Katz sounds just as bad as Katz Moskowitz."

Chapter 11. New Names, New Identities

1. A few years later a man in California unsuccessfully petitioned the
   court for permission to rename himself III, as in the Roman numeral.
   The court rejected III because it was not a name, within the common
   law definition of a name, and suggested that such numbers or symbols would only lead to confusion.
2. In a comparable anagrammatizing move, Canadian-born Arnold
   Isaacs reversed the letters of his last name and became Italian-
   sounding Scaasi, prominent American fashion designer.

3. West would probably have sold his soul to the devil to acquire the richly associative full name of his prolific contemporary Frederick Schiller Faust (1892–1944), "King of the Pulps." As Max Brand, David Manning, and other pseudonyms, Faust wrote or dictated Westerns (among them *Destry Rides Again* and *Singing Guns*), Dr. Kildare medical adventures, and detective novels—altogether about 25 million words.

4. For librarians, Mark Twain/Samuel Clemens has long been a problem in authority control, the primary name used in catalogues. "In the late seventies," Nicholson Baker wrote, "the second version of the Anglo-American cataloguing rules created a convulsion of despair in libraries when it demanded that Samuel Clemens be officially called Mark Twain, just because more of his books appeared under his primary pseudonym than under his real name." "Discards," *The New Yorker,* April 4, 1994.

Books and Articles Consulted

Louis Adamic. *What's Your Name?* New York, 1942.

"Afro-American or Black: What's in a Name?" *Ebony,* July 1989.

Richard D. Alford. *Naming and Identity: A Cross-Cultural Study of Personal Naming Practices.* New Haven, 1987.

John Algeo. *On Defining the Proper Name.* University of Florida Humanities Monograph Number 42. Gainesville, Fla., 1973.

Christopher P. Andersen. *The Baby Boomer's Name Game.* New York, 1987.

Karen Armstrong. *A History of God.* New York, 1993.

Matthew Arnold. *Civilization in the United States.* Boston, 1888.

Leonard R. N. Ashley. "Flicks, Flacks, and Flux: The Omnomasticon of the Moving Picture Industry." *Names* 23 (1975).

———. *What's in a Name?* Baltimore, Md., 1996.

Ronald L. Baker, ed. *The Study of Place Names.* Terra Haute, Ind. 1991.

Howard F. Barker. "Surnames in the United States." *The American Mercury* XXVI, no. 102 (June 1932).

Ross W. Beales, Jr. "Naming Patterns in Westborough, Massachusetts, 1710–1849." Unpublished paper.

J. Bergman et al. "How Patients and Physicians Address Each Other in the Office." *Journal of Family Practice* 27, no. 4 (October 1988).

"Black Names." *Newsweek,* July 29, 1968.

Edward Gaylord Bourne. "The Naming of America." *American Historical Review* X, no. 1 (October 1904).

Roger Brown. "How Shall a Thing Be Called?" *Psychological Review* 65 (1958).

Margaret M. Bryant. "Names in Everyday Speech." *Names* 6 (1957).

John Sibley Butler. "Multiple Identities." *Society,* May/June 1990.

Dale Carnegie. *How to Win Friends and Influence People.* New York, 1936.

Lewis Carroll. *Alice's Adventures in Wonderland.* London, 1865.
————. *Through the Looking-Glass.* London, 1871.
————. *Symbolic Logic.* London, 1896.
Lucile Hoerr Charles. "Drama in First-Naming Ceremonies." *Journal of American Folklore* 64 (1951).
Edward Clodd. *Magic in Names and in Other Things.* London, 1920.
Collectio Rituum: The 1964 English Ritual. Collegeville, Minn., 1964.
Thomas Crook with Christine Allison. "The Art of Remembering Names." *Reader's Digest,* July 1992.
Everette E. Dennis. "Racial Naming." *Media Studies Journal,* Summer 1994.
Joey Lee Dillard. *Black Names.* The Hague, 1976.
Kenneth L. Dion. "Names, Identity, and Self." *Names* 31 (1983).
Isaac D'Israeli. *Curiosities of Literature.* London, 1791–1834.
Leslie Dunkling. *The Guinness Book of Names.* Enfield, Middlesex, U.K., 1993.
Erik H. Erikson. "Autobiographic Notes on the Identity Crisis." *Daedelus,* Fall 1970.
Avner Falk. "Identity and Name Changes." *Psychoanalytic Review* 62 (1975–76).
Zoltan J. Farkas. "The Challenge of the Name *America.*" *Names* 13 (1965).
Doris E. Fleischman [Bernays]. "Notes of a Retiring Feminist." *The American Mercury,* February 1949.
Robert F. Fleissner. "Caliban's Name and the 'Brave New World.' " *Names* 40 (1992).
John Forster. *The Life of Charles Dickens.* New York, 1928.
James George Frazer. *The Golden Bough: A Study in Magic and Religion.* New York, 1922.
Sigmund Freud. *The Psychopathology of Everyday Life.* London, 1901.
————. *Totem and Taboo.* London, 1913–14.
Wilbur G. Gaffney. "Tell Me Your Name and Your Business..." *Names* 19 (1971).
Herb Gardner. *A Thousand Clowns.* New York, 1962.
Henry Louis Gates, Jr. *Colored People.* New York, 1994.
Peter Gay. *Freud: A Life for Our Time.* New York, 1988.
————. *Reading Freud.* New Haven, Conn., 1990.
Louis Ginzberg. *Legends of the Bible.* New York, 1956.
Andrew Greeley. "Religion Around the World." *Origins,* June 10, 1993.

John Gross. *Shylock: A Legend and Its Legacy.* New York, 1994.

Alex Haley. *Roots: The Saga of an American Family.* Garden City, N.Y., 1976.

Wayland D. Hand. "Onomastic Magic in the Health, Sickness, and Death of Man." *Names* 32 (1984).

Patrick Hanks and Flavia Hodges. *A Dictionary of Surnames.* New York, 1988.

———. *A Dictionary of First Names.* New York, 1990.

Kelsie B. Harder. "Charles Dickens Names His Characters." *Names* 7 (1959).

———. "Dickens and His Lists of Names." *Names* 30 (1982).

Peter S. Hawkins. "Naming Names: The Art of Memory and the NAMES Project AIDS Quilt." *Critical Inquiry* 19 (Summer 1993).

———. "Stitches in Time." *The Yale Review,* July 1995.

Wayne E. Helmsley and Barbara A. Spencer. "The Effect of First Names on Perceptions of Female Attractiveness." *Sex Roles* 12 (April 1985).

Susan Henry. "In Her Own Name: Public Relations Pioneer Doris Fleischman Bernays." Paper presented to the Committee on the Status of Women Research Session, Association for Education in Journalism and Mass Communication, 71st Annual Convention. Portland, Ore., July 1988.

Joseph E. Illick. "Child-Rearing in Seventeenth-Century England and America." In *The History of Childhood,* edited by Lloyd deMause. New York, 1975.

Harold R. Isaacs. *Idols of the Tribe.* Cambridge, Mass., 1975.

Noah Jonathan Jacobs. *Naming Day in Eden: The Creation and Recreation of Language.* New York, 1959.

Henry James. *The Complete Notebooks.* Edited by Leon Edel and Lyall H. Powers. New York, 1987.

William James. *Pragmatism.* New York, 1907.

Charles E. Joubert. "Factors Related to Individuals' Attitudes Toward Their Names." *Psychological Reports,* December 1985.

Journal of the Anthropological Society of Oxford. Special Issue on Names. 1988.

Fred Kaplan, ed. *Charles Dickens' Book of Memoranda.* New York, 1981.

Amy A. Kass and Leon R. Kass. "What's Your Name?" *First Things,* November 1995.

Richard E. Koppelman and Dorothy Lang. "Alliteration in Mate Selection: Does Barbara Marry Barry?" *Psychological Reports* 56 (June 1985).

Steven Lagerfeld. "Name That Dune: The Power of the Board on Geographic Names Reaches Everywhere." *Atlantic Monthly,* September 1990.

Robert M. Landau. "Names or Number—Which Shall It Be?" *Names* 15 (1967).

Edwin D. Lawson. "Personal Names: 100 Years of Social Science Contributions." *Names* 32 (1984).

Kate Lawson. "Madness and Grace: Grace Poole's Name and Her Role in *Jane Eyre.*" *English Language Notes* 30 (September 1992).

Didier Lazard. "Two Years Under False Names." *Journal of Abnormal and Social Psychology* 41 (1946).

Paul L. Leslie and James K. Skipper, Jr. "Toward a Theory of Nicknames . . ." *Names* 38 (1990).

P. Margot Levi. "K., an Exploration of the Names of Kafka's Central Characters." *Names* 14 (1966).

Claude Lévi-Strauss. *The Savage Mind.* London, 1966.

Lucien Lévy-Bruhl. *How Natives Think.* New York, 1979.

―――. *The "Soul" of the Primitive.* New York, 1966.

―――. *Primitive Mentality.* New York, 1978.

Stanley Lieberson and Eleanor Bell. "Children's First Names: An Empirical Study of Social Taste." *American Journal of Sociology* 93 (November 1992).

Thomas M. Lockney and Karl Ames. "Is *1069* a Name?" *Names* 29 (1981).

David Lodge. *The Art of Fiction.* New York, 1992.

Kathleen McKinney. "The Influence of Choice of Last Name and Career Status on Perceptions of a Woman and Her Spouse." *Free Inquiry in Creative Sociology* 19 (May 1991).

E. Wallace McMullen, ed. *Names New and Old: Papers of the Names Institute.* N.p., 1993.

Mary G. Marcus. "The Power of a Name." *Psychology Today,* October 1976.

Megan Marshall. "The Name Game." *New Age Journal,* October 1984.

Ben L. Martin. "From Negro to Black to African-American: The Power of Names and Naming." *Political Science Quarterly,* Spring 1991.

James S. Martin. *Scram: Relocating Under a New Identity.* Port Townsend, Wash., 1993.

Judith Martin. *Miss Manners' Guide to Excruciatingly Correct Behavior.* New York, 1982.

Albert Mehrabian and Marlena Piercy. "Positive or Negative Connotations of Unconventionally and Conventionally Spelled Names." *Journal of Social Psychology* 133 (August 1993).

H. L. Mencken. *The American Language.* New York, 1936.

————. *The American Language: Supplement Two.* New York, 1948.

John Stuart Mill. *A System of Logic.* London, 1843.

Ted Morgan. *On Becoming American.* Boston, 1978.

Samuel Eliot Morison. *The European Discovery of America: The Southern Voyages, 1492–1616.* New York, 1974.

Toni Morrison. *Song of Solomon.* New York, 1977.

Cullen Murphy. "A.K.A." *Atlantic Monthly,* May 1994.

Alleen Pace Nilsen. "American Indians—Taking Back Their Names." Names Institute paper. 1994.

Don Nilsen. "From Kilroy to Whitewatergate: What Makes Names Memorable." Names Institute paper. 1994.

C. P. Oberndorf. "Reaction to Personal Names." *Psychoanalytic Review* V (January 1918).

P. Robert Paustian. "The Evolution of Personal Naming Practices among American Blacks." *Names* 26 (1978).

Pauline C. Pharr. "Onomastic Divergence: A Study of Given-Name Trends Among African Americans." *American Speech* 68 (Winter 1993).

Jean Piaget. *The Child's Conception of the World.* New York, 1965.

Robert Plank. "The Use of 'Jr.' in Relation to Psychiatric Treatment." *Names* 19 (1971).

Emily Post. *Etiquette.* New York, 1922 (and subsequent editions).

Stephen Potter. *The Complete Upmanship.* London, 1970.

Newbell Niles Puckett. *Black Names in America.* Boston, 1975.

Ernest Pulgram. *Theory of Names.* Potsdam, N.Y., 1954.

Paul Radin. *Primitive Religion.* New York, 1937.

Allen Walker Read. "Is the Name *United States* Singular or Plural?" *Names* 22 (1974).

————. "The Numerical Naming of People." *The Fourth Lacus Forum, 1977.* Columbia, S.C., 1978.

Janine W. Reed. "The Process of Name-giving . . ." *Dissertation Abstracts International* 53 (July 1992).

Robert M. Rennick. "Judicial Procedures for a Change-of-Name in the United States." *Names* 13 (1965).

————. "Hitler and Others Who Changed Their Names and a Few Who Did Not." *Names* 17 (1969).

————. "The Nazi Name Decrees of the Nineteen Thirties." *Names* 18 (1970).

————. "The Alleged 'Hogg Sisters.' " *Names* 30 (1982).

————. "The Inadvertent Changing of Non-English Names by Newcomers to America: A Brief Historical Survey and Popular Presentation of Cases." *New York Folklore Quarterly* 26 (1970).

Renee Richards with John Ames. *Second Serve*. New York, 1983.

Edward G. Robinson. *All My Yesterdays: An Autobiography*. New York, 1973.

Linda Rosenkrantz and Pamela Redmond Satran. *Beyond Jennifer and Jason*. New York, 1994.

Alice S. Rossi. "Naming Children in Middle-Class Families." *American Sociological Review* XXX (1965).

"The 'Rumpelstiltskin Effect.' " *Harvard Magazine,* November/December 1995.

Oliver Sacks. *An Anthropologist on Mars*. New York, 1995.

Arthur Scherr. "Change-of-Name Petitions of the New York Courts." *Names* 34 (1986).

Leila Obier Schroeder. "A Rose by Any Other Name: Post-Marital Right to Use Maiden Name: 1934–1982." *Sociology and Social Research* 70 (July 1986).

Mary V. Seeman. "The Unconscious Meaning of Personal Names." *Names* 31 (1983).

Alex Shoumatoff. *The Mountain of Names*. New York, 1985.

James K. Skipper, Jr. "Public Nicknames of Famous Football Players and Coaches: A Socio-Historical Analysis and Comparison." *Sociological Spectrum* 9 (Spring 1989).

Richard Slotkin. *Gunfighter Nation: The Myth of the Frontier in Twentieth-Century America*. New York, 1992.

Ralph Slovenko. "The Destiny of a Name." *Journal of Psychiatry and Law,* Summer 1983.

David Scott Smith. "Child-Naming Practices, Kinship Ties, and

Changes in Family Attitudes in Hingham, Massachusetts, 1641–1880." *Journal of Social History* 18 (1985).

Una Stannard. "Manners Make Laws: Married Women's Names in the United States." *Names* 32 (1984).

Kenneth M. Steele. "First Names and First Impressions: A Fragile Relationship." *Sex Roles: A Journal of Research* 21 (1989).

Laurence Sterne. *Tristram Shandy.* London, 1759–67.

George R. Stewart. *Names on the Land: A Historical Account of Place-naming in the United States.* New York, 1945.

———. *American Place-Names.* New York, 1970.

Harry Stone. "What's in a Name: Fantasy and Calculation in Dickens." *Dickens Studies Annual* XIV (1985).

John Sumser. "Not Just Any Tom, Dick or Harry: The Grammar of Names in Television Drama." *Media Culture & Society* 24 (1992).

Isaac Taylor. *Words and Places.* London, 1873.

John Thornton. "Central African Names and African-American Naming Patterns." *The William and Mary Quarterly,* October 1993.

Elizabeth Tooker, ed. "Naming Systems." *Proceedings of the American Ethnological Society,* 1980.

Nancy Tuckerman and Nancy Dunnan, eds. *The Amy Vanderbilt Complete Book of Etiquette.* New York, 1995.

Booker T. Washington. *Up from Slavery.* New York, 1901.

Mary C. Waters. "The Everyday Use of Surnames to Determine Ethnic Ancestry." *Qualitative Sociology* 12 (1992).

Peter Whitely. *"Hopitutungwni:* 'Hopi Names' As Literature." In *On the Translation of Native American Literatures,* edited by Brian Swann. Washington, D.C., 1992.

Walt Whitman. *An American Primer.* Philadelphia, 1904.

Doris Wilkinson. "Americans of African Identity." *Society,* May/June 1990.

Shelley Winters. *Shelley: Also Known as Shirley.* New York, 1980.

Helen P. Wulbern. "The How and Why of Name-Changing." *The American Mercury* 64 (June 1947).

Robert K. Young et al. "The Effects of Names on Perception of Intelligence, Popularity, and Competence." *Journal of Applied Social Psychology* 23 (1993).

Meyer A. Zeligs. *Friendship and Fratricide: An Analysis of Whittaker Chambers and Alger Hiss.* New York, 1967.

Wilbur Zelinsky. "Classical Town Names in the United States: The Historical Geography of an American Idea." *The Geographical Review* LVII (1967).

Richard Zweigenhaft. "Unusual First Names: A Positive Outlook." *Names* 31 (1983).

Acknowledgments

We'd like to thank the following men, women, and one child for the invaluable help they gave us via interviews, information, suggestions, and useful material:

Robert Atwan, Ronald L. Baker, Cameron Beck, Mimi Berlin, Sissela Bok, Edward Chalfant, Heather Cole, John Dorenkamp, Seth Effron, Wayne H. Finke, Joan Fox, Henry Louis Gates, Jr., Maggie Giles, Sig Gissler, Richard M. Held, Scott Heller, Gordon Hyatt, Fred Kaplan, Hester Kaplan, Alex Kotlowitz, David Lemos, Elaine Marshall, Megan Marshall, Judith Martin (Miss Manners), Robert K. Merton, Herbert Mitgang, Ted Morgan, Alleen Nilsen, Don Nilsen, Roger L. Payne, Jane Rabb, Allen Walker Read, Patricia Shepherd, Ralph Slovenko, Michael D. Stein, Tobias Stein, Gladys Topkis, John Updike, Palmer Williams.

We also want to acknowledge the contributions made by the members of our 1993 Faculty Seminar on Names and Naming at the College of the Holy Cross: Ross W. Beales, Jr., Richard Carson, Deirdre Haskell, Mary Lee S. Ledbetter, Mark Lincicome, Royce A. Singleton, Jr., Susan Elizabeth Sweeney, Edward H. Thompson, Jr., J. Ann Tickner, and Margaret Wong.

Finally, our grateful thanks to our agents, Sterling Lord and Gina Maccoby, for their labors on our behalf and to our editor, Frederic W. Hills, for his confidence in this project.

Index

254 *Index*

About the Authors

Justin Kaplan's first full-length book, *Mr. Clemens and Mark Twain*, has achieved the status of a modern classic of biography. It won both the Pulitzer Prize for Biography and the National Book Award in Arts and Letters. Among the many other books he has written or edited are biographies of the poet Walt Whitman (for which he won a second National Book Award as well as a National Book Critics Circle nomination) and of Lincoln Steffens, the father of investigative reporting and muckraking journalism. He is General Editor of the 16th edition (1992) of *Bartlett's Familiar Quotations.*

Born in Manhattan, Kaplan did his undergraduate and graduate studies at Harvard. He worked for several years in a New York publishing house before becoming a writer. He was elected to the American Academy of Arts and Letters in 1985.

Anne Bernays is the author of eight novels, among them the award-winning *Growing Up Rich* and *Professor Romeo,* cited as a "Notable Book of the Year" by *The New York Times Book Review.* She has published short stories, poems, essays, travel pieces, and reviews in numerous national magazines and newspapers, among them *The Nation, Sports Illustrated, New Woman, American Heritage,* and *The New York Times.*

Bernays has been a teacher of fiction writing since 1975. From 1992 to 1995 she held the Jenks Chair in Contemporary Letters at the College of the Holy Cross. She has also taught at the Harvard Extension School, the University of Massachusetts, Boston College, Emerson College, and other institutions. She is cofounder of PEN/New England and a member of the Advisory Board of the National Writers Union.

Married since 1954, Justin Kaplan and Anne Bernays live in Cambridge and Truro, Massachusetts. They have three daughters and five grandsons.

9 780684 838670